SO-DFV-450

WITHDRAWN
UTSA LIBRARIES

THE REUNIFICATION
OF
CHINA

THE REUNIFICATION OF CHINA

PRC-Taiwan Relations in Flux

LAI TO LEE

New York
Westport, Connecticut
London

Library of Congress Cataloging-in-Publication Data

Lee, Lai To.
    The reunification of China : PRC–Taiwan relations in flux /
Lai To Lee.
      p. cm.
    Includes bibliographical references and index.
    ISBN 0–275–93772–0
    1. China—Politics and government—1976–   2. Taiwan—Politics and
government—1975–   3. Chinese reunification question, 1949–
I. Title.
DS779.26.L43   1991
951.05—dc20   90–44388

British Library Cataloguing in Publication Data is available.

Copyright © 1991 by Lai To Lee

All rights reserved. No portion of this book may be
reproduced, by any process or technique, without the
express written consent of the publisher.

Library of Congress Catalog Card Number: 90–44388
ISBN: 0–275–93772–0

First published in 1991

Praeger Publishers, One Madison Avenue, New York, NY 10010
An imprint of Greenwood Publishing Group, Inc.

Printed in the United States of America

The paper used in this book complies with the
Permanent Paper Standard issued by the National
Information Standards Organization (Z39.48–1984).

10 9 8 7 6 5 4 3 2 1

Library
University of Texas
at San Antonio

To my wife,
Yin Ling,
and children,
Zhanyu and Yiying

Contents

Preface

Although I have been watching the developments in China ever since my days as a graduate student, my professional interest in the reunification of China started in earnest when I was invited by the Atlantic Council to present a paper for its conference on "Taiwan in the Next Decade: Western Interests and Options," held in March 1985 at Airlie House, Virginia. The paper was subsequently published as an article entitled "Taiwan and Southeast Asia: Realpolitik par Excellence?" in *Contemporary Southeast Asia*, Vol. 7, No. 3 (December 1985). I must add that the Atlantic Council conference also jolted me into thinking more about the views presented in the meeting, particularly those of Li Shenzhi, Zi Zhongyun, Yu-ming Shaw, Alexander Lu, Huan Guocang, and others. As a result, when I was approached to write another paper on the People's Republic of China (PRC)–Taiwan relations by the Second Quadrilateral Conference on "Economic Policies, Political Trends, and Regional and Global Security Issues in the Pacific-Asian Region," sponsored jointly by the Institute of East Asian Studies, University of California, Berkeley; the Asia Pacific Association of Japan, Tokyo; the Centre for Strategic and International Studies, Jakarta; and the Asiatic Research Center, Korea University, Seoul, I accepted the invitation and wrote a paper on "The PRC and Taiwan—Moving toward a More Realistic Relationship." The paper was discussed in two rounds of discussion, one held in Yogyakarta, Indonesia, in August 1987 and another held in Berkeley, California, in January 1988 and benefited from the comments of the participants in the conference. I would especially like to thank Robert A. Scalapino, Seizaburo Sato, and Nobuo Miyamoto for their suggestions in this regard. The revised paper was eventually published in a book called *Asian Security Issues: Regional and Global*, edited by Robert Scalapino and others in 1988.

Having done some work on the conflicts between Beijing and Taipei, I was most delighted to write another article on the subject for a special "China at Forty" issue of *The Pacific Review*, at the invitation by David Goodman, one of the editors of the journal. The article, entitled "Taiwan and the Reunification of China," was published in the journal in Vol. 2, No. 2 (1989).

As I accumulated more research materials and knowledge on the events in the Taiwan Strait, I decided to write a book on the subject while I was taking my sabbatical leave from 1988 to 1989. In this regard, I would like to acknowledge the National University of Singapore with thanks for the leave and for the financial help given to me. In addition, my gratitude also goes to all those who helped me in one way or another in the conduct of my research during my sabbatical leave. These included John Wong of the Department of History, University of Sydney; Zhao Baoxu, Wang Jisi, Zhang Hanqing, and Gong Wenxiang of the Department of International Politics, Peking University; Ji Xiaolin of the Chinese Educational Association for International Exchanges of the PRC; Li Shenzhi, He Di, Yan Jiaqi, You Chunmei, Zhao Chen, and Guo Xiangzhi of the various institutes of the Chinese Academy of Social Sciences; Chen Qimao, Yang Jiemian, and Ji Guoxing of the Shanghai Institute for International Studies; Wang Muheng, Liao Shaolian, Han Qinghai, and Zhu Tianshun of Xiamen University; S. C. Fan, Edward Chen, Ming K. Chan, and Coonoor Kripalani-Thadani of Hong Kong University; Chang King-yuh, David S. Chou, and Chen Hurng Yu of the Institute of International Relations in Taiwan; and finally James W. Morley, Gerald L. Curtis, and Anne Muldowney of the East Asian Institute of Columbia University.

In addition to the original research that I put in to produce this book, I should point out that I also tapped freely the research findings of my previous works, particularly the three articles on the PRC and Taiwan in parts of this study, and I would like to thank the publishers and people involved for allowing me to do this.

When I was about to finish the preliminary draft of this study, the momentous Tiananmen Square incident of June 1989 took place. As the incident will have wide implications and repercussions, including an effect on the reunification issue, I was interested in examining the related developments after the crackdown to make the study more complete and up-to-date. Consequently, a postscript covering events of the last months of the 1980s, from April to December 1989, was added to the manuscript.

Let me close by emphasizing that while all those who have helped me may take the credit for any thoughtful comments this book may offer, I, as usual, am alone responsible for any errors, omissions, or misinterpretations in this study.

Introduction

Ever since the departure of the Kuomintang (KMT) from mainland China to Taiwan in 1949, the question of the reunification of China has been haunting both sides of the Taiwan Straits. In the case of the People's Republic of China (PRC), established by the Chinese Communist Party (CCP) in 1949 on the mainland, the CCP was initially keen to "liberate" Taiwan. However, by the late 1970s, the CCP, began to change its antagonistic attitude toward Taiwan, at least on the surface. Clear signs and concrete proposals to reunify the country were issued by the CCP mainly in the 1980s. In fact, Deng Xiaoping himself had emphasized at the 12th Party Congress in September 1982 that one of the three major tasks for China in the 1980s would be "to strive for the inclusion of Taiwan in the actualization of the reunification of the motherland."[1] Likewise, the KMT has gradually retreated from its desire to "recover" the mainland in view of the changing domestic and international environment in the 1980s. Instead, it has been ritualistically highlighting the significance of reunifying China under the "three principles of the people." More important, this has been supplemented by various moves to ease links between the mainland and Taiwan in order to launch, inter alia, a political offensive against the PRC. With the advent of the 1990s, it is timely to take stock of the ups and downs in PRC–Taiwan relations so far.

What this study proposes to do is, first, to scrutinize the policy of the CCP toward the KMT and vice versa on the reunification issue in the 1980s. From the policy statements, decisions, and actions taken by both sides of the Taiwan Strait, the study intends to find out the consequences,

intended or unintended, on CCP-KMT relations. While the early part of
this study as presented in Chapters 1 and 2 may look into the policy
demands, debates, and conflicts of each side, it concentrates primarily on
the dominant policy on reunification of the CCP and of the KMT. It follows
that this part is more concerned with the preferences of the policy-makers
in Beijing and Taipei. Such an elitist approach, reflecting primarily the
values of the governing leaders, has more utility for the analysis and
explanation of policies in a communist system—the PRC and a developing
political entity—Taiwan.[2] Nonetheless, it should not be mistaken that the
societies on both sides of the Taiwan Strait are each a monolithic political
entity. To the contrary, both may have an elaborate and even conflict-ridden policy-making process that is not always susceptible to the scrutiny
of an outsider. As such, the early part of this study on the reunification of
China is oftentimes concerned more with the final product of the decision-
making process than with the process itself. It remains to be noted that
both sides of the Taiwan Strait, of course, have special agencies and
personnel to handle the issue in the 1980s.

In the case of the CCP, it is known that the United Front Work
Department of the Central Committee has a Taiwan Affairs Office. More
important, within the party center, a Taiwan Affairs Office (Dui Tai
Bangongshi) was established around 1980.[3] While the office actually has
a director for day-to-day administration, it is under the supervision of a
leading member of the CCP. It is known that the leading member was Deng
Yingchao, and possibly Liao Chengzhi at the very beginning; the job was
passed over to Yang Shangkun later on. Toward the end of the 1980s, it is
possible that Wu Xueqian, another Politburo member, took over the bulk
of the work in view of Yang's advanced age and many responsibilities.[4]
The leading member of the party is, from all indications, especially
delegated by the Politburo to supervise Taiwan affairs. As always, final
decisions on Taiwan affairs—or, for that matter, all important functional
areas—are made by the Politburo, the Standing Committee of the Politburo, or by the kingpin of Chinese politics, Deng Xiaoping.

With increasing contact with Taiwan, and the significance of work on
Taiwan affairs, a leading group on Taiwan affairs in the party center was
established at the end of 1987.[5] The group, headed by Yang Shangkun,
and possibly by Wu Xueqian later on, has about ten members and its
membership includes the director of the party's Taiwan Affairs Office, the
head of the United Front Work Department of the Central Committee, the
director of the Overseas Chinese Affairs Office in the State Council, and
leading members from the economic, military, foreign affairs, cultural, and

propaganda apparatus. Quite obviously, this leading group is the most powerful party organization coordinating work on Taiwan affairs.

Apart from the party apparatus, the State Council also has units dealing specifically with Taiwan. Notably, within the State Council, the Overseas Chinese Affairs Office, the Ministry of Foreign Economic Relations and Trade, and last but not least, the Ministry of Foreign Affairs, have offices dealing with Taiwan affairs.[6] With increasing emphasis on separating the party from state affairs, and the possible need to use governmental and not party organizations in dealing with Taiwan, a separate Taiwan Affairs Office was known to have been established in the State Council in September 1988. The new director was Ding Guangen, an alternate member of the Politburo and concurrently appointed as vice-minister of the State Planning Commission.[7] As work on Taiwan begins to increase in importance, it is quite natural that similar offices will be established in other central party and state organizations in the PRC. Provincial and local offices of these central offices will also be set up if necessary.

Besides the party and state apparatus, other institutions are also called upon to support the CCP's effort to woo Taiwan. These include the Chinese People's Political Consultative Conference; democratic parties including the Revolutionary Committee of the Chinese Kuomintang and Taiwan Democratic Self-Government League; mass organizations such as the All-China Federation of Taiwan Compatriots, Taiwan Fellow-Students Association, and the newly established Association for the Promotion of Peaceful Reunification of China, established in 1988; and research institutes, notably the Institute of Taiwan Studies of the Chinese Academy of Social Sciences, Taiwan Research Institute of Xiamen University, and the Taiwan Research Association established in August 1988 in Beijing.

As for the KMT in the 1980s, it is certain that the Central Standing Committee, dominated by President Chiang Ching-kuo until the end of 1987, was the most important organ dealing with policy toward the mainland. Within the KMT center, however, there is a Department of Mainland Operations. The department, together with the intelligence activities of the Ministry of Defense of the Taipei government, provides the leading members of the KMT with the latest developments on the mainland. Chiang's demise in January 1988 produced a period of uncertainty. However, with the rise of Lee Teng-hui as president of the government and chairman of the KMT after the latter's 13th party congress, it was revealed that a more elaborate apparatus was established to deal with the mainland. According to Lee, the KMT had formed a nine-member group, the Committee for Guidance on Mainland China Affairs, to formulate Taiwan's policy toward mainland China.[8] The group, headed by Mah Soo-lay, former secretary-general of the KMT, was answerable to the KMT's 31-member Central Standing Committee. All proposals from the group must be submitted for approval to the Central Standing Committee. As in Chiang Ching-kuo's time, the chairman of the KMT could submit his own proposals to the KMT apart from the nine-member group. And there are reasons to suggest that, judging from the analysis of later chapters of this study, the president and some other powerful figures of the KMT could bypass the Committee for Guidance on Mainland China Affairs in formulating policies toward the other side of the Taiwan Strait.

Once the policy has been approved by the KMT, it would then be implemented by the Executive Yuan, as before. Within the Executive Yuan, it was known that there was a consultative group by the name of Lixing Small Group, which helped formulate the economic strategy against the mainland. This group, as explained by Premier Yu Kuo-hwa in early 1988, was appointed by the Executive Yuan. Its membership included leading figures from major governmental organizations. As a consultative group, it had no power of its own, and whatever suggestions and proposals it made had to be approved by the Executive Yuan.[9] The group was, however, dissolved when a cabinet-level Mainland Affairs Task Force was established in August 1988.[10] Headed by Vice-Premier Shih Chi-yang with Ma Yin-jiou, chairman of the Research, Development, and Evaluation Commission, as executive secretary, the newly formed task force was established to coordinate the execution of policies from the KMT. The task force holds meetings frequently to examine the problems of implementing policies toward the mainland, and recommends to the Executive Yuan as regards the propriety and feasibility of easing links with the mainland.

On top of the state apparatus, support for the KMT's policy toward the mainland comes from various research institutes and civic organizations. These include, notably, the National Chengchi University's Institute of International Relations, the National Red Cross Society in Taiwan, Grand Alliance for Reunification of China under the Three Principles of the People, and others. With demands for visits to the mainland and more approval for certain categories of mainland Chinese to come to Taiwan, the KMT has to rely on, or sometimes create, less politically oriented civic organizations to coordinate activities between the two sides so as to tone down the official nature of these contacts.

To many, the conflict between the CCP and the KMT is primarily a domestic issue. In fact, the CCP has always emphasized that reunification must be tackled without outside interference. However, it is obvious that the civil war in China was internationalized and that international politics did and does play a part in setting the environment in which the issue can be solved. As a result, it is appropriate to look at the policies of other countries toward reunification. This study concentrates on the policies of the major powers, which by definition can wield more influence than other countries and can add or ease pressure on the PRC or Taiwan. Our focus will be on the United States. For historical reasons, and from the point of view of realpolitik and economic development on both sides of the Taiwan Strait, the United States could play a role—maybe a critical role—in the war and peace of China if it wants to. Even if it does not outwardly show any interest in reunification, it will have certain influence in resolving the problem, as demonstrated in Chapter 3.

By the end of the 1980s, it was clear from the policy study of Beijing and Taipei with regard to reunification that the resolution was by no means close at hand. It begs the question of whether there is an alternative solution. Will the CCP use force? Is it likely that Taiwan will become independent? To be sure, there have been various proposals from nonofficial sources, primarily Chinese and foreign individuals who have shown a keen interest in contributing their views on reunification. The big question is, To what extent has Beijing or Taipei been receptive to these suggestions? Thus, Chapter 4 looks at some of these proposals to see if they are realistic. Such an examination can also broaden our views and demonstrate plausible ways by which the road to reunification can be mapped out.

While there may be an impasse on how to reunify the country, it is obvious that social and economic contacts between the PRC and Taiwan via third countries have become commonplace. Peace in the Taiwan Strait has also been maintained so far. As a result, Chapter 5 examines the interactions and trends in the Taiwan Strait, and sees to what extent they will help in the reunification of China. Specifically, the chapter looks into the visitation program sanctioned by Taipei and the cultural exchanges and economic discourse between Beijing and Taipei. With these analyses, the study casts an eye on the future of reunification in the concluding chapter.

NOTES

1. Deng Xiaoping, *Jianshe You Zhongguo Tese De Shehui Zhuyi* (Building Socialism with Special Chinese Characteristics), revised ed. (Hong Kong: Joint Publishing, 1987), p. 3.

2. Even in a pluralistic democracy such as the United States, it has been argued that public policy reflects the prevailing values of the elites primarily. See, for example,

Thomas R. Dye and L. Harmon Zeigler, *The Irony of Democracy* (Belmont, Calif.: Wadsworth, 1970).

   3. Li Da, ed., *Taiwan Yu Santung* (Taiwan and the Three Exchanges) (Hong Kong: Wide Angle Press, 1988), p. 6. See also *China Directory 1981* (Tokyo: Radiopress, 1980), p. 23.

   4. *China Times* (Taipei), 16 June 1988.

   5. Li, *Taiwan Yu Santung*, p. 1.

   6. *United Daily News* (Taipei), 29 May 1986.

   7. *Straits Times* (Singapore), 12 September 1988. See also *Free China Journal* (Taipei), 19 September 1988.

   8. *Free China Journal*, 29 August 1988. *The Nineties*, January 1989, p. 45.

   9. *United Daily News*, 26 March 1988.

   10. *Central Daily News* (Taipei), 24 August 1988.

1
Beijing's Initiatives

THE SETTING

To understand Beijing's policy toward Taipei in the 1980s, it is important to note the backdrop and circumstances under which it was mapped out. A succinct and concise analysis of the genesis of Beijing's reunification policy will be presented here, so as to detect the continuities or changes in that strategy. For analytical purposes, it is useful if Beijing's policy is divided into three main types of strategy: (1) the military offensive, (2) the diplomatic offensive, and (3) the "peaceful" offensive. While the meaning of these three offensives is to a large extent self-explanatory and will be dealt with subsequently, it should be emphasized at the beginning that these are not mutually exclusive. In fact, a mixture of these strategies was oftentimes actually practiced by Beijing. In addition, one strategy seems to be more dominant than the others at one time or another, as demonstrated later on.

The Military Offensive

In its search for a way to reunify the country, the CCP was no doubt ready to use force to "liberate" Taiwan. In fact, as early as 1950 it was ready to launch an amphibious operation against the KMT in Taiwan. This was, however, frustrated by Taiwan's preventive action and the necessity to move northward many of the People's Liberation Army (PLA) troops in the south because of the outbreak of the Korean war.[1] More important, the complete reversal of the U.S. "hands-off" policy to exclude Taiwan in

its defense perimeter to that of using the Seventh Fleet to prevent any attack
on Taipei, as announced by President Truman on June 27, 1950, had
effectively forestalled Beijing and Taipei from using the military option
thereafter.[2] Notably, in the three major Taiwan Strait crises, the U.S.
presence was instrumental in stopping a major CCP-KMT armed conflict.[3]
In the first such crisis, the United States helped Taipei evacuate its forces
from the Tachen Islands in early 1955. More important, the signing of the
Mutual Defense Treaty in December 1954, between Washington and
Taipei, demonstrated clearly the U.S. determination to protect Taiwan and
the Pescadores, forcing the CCP to drop its "liberation" of Taiwan and its
shelling of Matsu and Quemoy. In the second crisis of 1958, heavy
exchange of artillery fire between the two sides broadened the U.S.
commitment to include the defense of Matsu and Quemoy. The unequivocal support given to Taiwan by the United States to resist the CCP's
military action ended in restoring an "even-day" cease-fire in the Taiwan
Strait. While peace was restored and more bloodshed was avoided, the
U.S. intervention in the civil war no doubt was regarded as most unfor-
givable by the CCP. However, the United States ironically also "saved"
the CCP in the third Taiwan Strait crisis when Chiang Kai-shek was
contemplating invading the mainland after the disastrous Great Leap
Forward. President Kennedy made it clear in 1962 that the United States
would not support the invasion, reconfirming the defensive character of
Washington's commitment to Taipei. Consequently, another major military confrontation between the CCP and KMT was averted, and the Taiwan
Strait remained relatively peaceful.

The Diplomatic Offensive

With the foreclosure of the military option by the United States, the CCP
tried some other measures to reunify China. As with the KMT, these
included the CCP's use of propaganda broadcasts, infiltration of agents,
and mobilization of support from the overseas Chinese against the other
side. More important, perhaps, the CCP held talks with the United States
in Geneva, and later in Warsaw, asking for withdrawal of U.S. military
from Taiwan and nonintervention in Chinese domestic affairs. The PRC
also fought hard against Taiwan for international recognition as the sole
and legitimate government of China. However, as far as the reunification
of China was concerned, the CCP did not seem to gain much headway.
And when it was engulfed in the Cultural Revolution, it was too concerned
with its domestic turmoil in the mainland.

When China began to ease out of the tumultuous phase of the Cultural Revolution, it began to reap some successes for international recognition of the regime and dilution of U.S. support to the KMT. This is demonstrated vividly in the fight for the seat in the United Nations. As is well known, the U.N. seat was occupied by Taiwan until 1971, because of U.S. support for the KMT. In fact, Chinese participation in the Korean War not only gave the U.S. a chance to push through a General Assembly resolution condemning the PRC as an aggressor, but it also allowed it to obtain a sizable majority for its resolution not to consider any change in China's representation. The moratorium on debating the issue was renewed annually until 1961. With decreasing support given to the moratorium, the United States, however, devised a new strategy to exclude the PRC, starting in 1961. On the U.S. initiative, the well-known "important question" resolution was passed by the General Assembly. This required a two-thirds majority to reach a decision on the representation of China. Apparently this worked until 1965, when there was a draw between those forces supporting and those against Beijing. However, the PRC's admission was still delayed by the isolating effect of the Cultural Revolution. It was not until 1970 that Beijing had, for the first time, gained the support of a simple majority in the United Nations though the two-thirds majority required still blocked its passage. When Richard Nixon was elected president of the United States, his administration began to take steps to improve relations with the PRC. Notably, it withdrew the Seventh Fleet from the Taiwan Strait. Certain trade and travel restrictions on the part of the United States were also removed. Most important, the United States announced its desire to improve relations with the PRC, and stated that it would no longer oppose admission of the PRC to the United Nations if Taiwan was also seated. Following the so-called Ping-Pong diplomacy by Beijing, and in view of the changing U.S. mood and the greater scope it offered for diplomatic flexibility, Nixon announced in July 1971 that he had agreed with Beijing to visit China the following year. Sensing that Nixon might abandon Taipei, many other states also began to shift their recognition to the PRC. When the United Nations debated the Chinese representation question in October 1971, Henry Kissinger was in China, arranging Nixon's visit to the PRC. Many states apparently interpreted this as a lack of U.S. interest in preserving Taipei's seat. As a result, the favorable 1971 vote for Beijing—76 for, 35 against, 12 abstentions, and 3 absent—in the U.N. General Assembly was not unexpected. In fact, the General Assembly earlier had rejected the resolution requiring a two-thirds majority. Beijing's diplomatic breakthrough to membership, and the ousting of Taiwan in the United Nations, became the most spectacular achievement in the contest for international recognition. No doubt Beijing was able to have some success earlier in establishing diplomatic ties with France in 1964 and with Canada in 1970. But its success was marred by its diplomatic isolation during the Cultural Revolution. Moreover, the diplomatic support given to Taipei by the United States until the Nixon administration certainly restrained other states from recognizing the PRC. However, with the U.N. seat settled in Beijing's favor and the dawning of a Sino–U.S. détente, the floodgate of diplomatic ties with Beijing was opened. Taiwan's support from the United States also suffered a major blow when Nixon visited China and the Shanghai communiqué was signed in February 1972. Beijing claimed in the communiqué that the PRC was the sole legal government of China, a point which was not challenged by the United States. While acknowledging that all Chinese on either side of the Taiwan Strait maintained there was but one China, and that Taiwan was part of that China, the United States also stated its interest "in a peaceful settlement of the Taiwan question by the Chinese themselves".[4] Although a few pending issues, such as the establishment of diplomatic relations between the United States and PRC and U.S. ties with Taiwan, were not settled, Beijing's marked improvement in relations with Washington was obvious. Taking advantage of the disappointment and anxiety of Taipei with the Sino–U.S. détente, Beijing began to issue more "peaceful" gestures and proposals for reunification.

The "Peaceful" Offensive

It should be noted that isolated instances of "peaceful" offensives against Taipei existed as early as the 1950s. In 1955, Zhou Enlai proposed in Bandung that there were two possible methods to "liberate" Taiwan—the military way and the peaceful way—and China was willing to take the peaceful option to "liberate" Taiwan, if possible.[5] Under the influence of the Bandung spirit, Zhou again mentioned this in a plenary session of the first National People's Congress in June 1956, adding that when the time was suitable, it was hoped that Taiwan would send its representatives to negotiate with China on the conditions and stages for the "peaceful liberation" of Taiwan.[6] Shortly thereafter, Zhou openly suggested that there could be a third alliance between the CCP and KMT. These "peaceful" offensives were repeated to a certain extent in the Eighth Party Congress and by Mao himself when he mentioned China's interest in a third CCP-KMT alliance in April 1957.[7]

However, the KMT did not lend its ear to these "peaceful" gestures. The sincerity of the CCP was all the more doubted as a result of the military adventure of the CCP in 1958 in the second Taiwan Strait crisis, the frenzied pace of the Great Leap Forward, and the subsequent Cultural Revolution. Zhou Enlai, Peng Dehuai, and others did harp on these themes occasionally. But these isolated statements did not seem to prove much impact, and it is doubtful they were the dominant line pursued by the CCP after 1958.

As China rejoined the family of nations after the chaotic phase of the Cultural Revolution, as demonstrated by its takeover of the seat in the United Nations and Nixon's historical visit to Beijing, the "peaceful" offensive began to reemerge. Although using diplomatic pressure to isolate Taiwan in the international community, the CCP seemed at the same time to be interested in gaining the goodwill of its counterpart in Taiwan. Evidence includes statements by Liao Chengzhi, one of China's spokesmen on the Taiwan issue, and Fu Zuoyi, former commander of the KMT forces in North China, appealing to the KMT to take steps to negotiate on reunification, shortly after the announcement of the agreement between Beijing and Washington in 1973 to establish liaison offices in each other's capital. Beijing also released over 500 KMT prisoners in 1975. More important, the CCP seemed to have retreated from its antagonistic position on the Taiwan question starting in mid-1978.[8] However, the gestures by the CCP did not pick up much momentum, especially when it was engulfed in its internal power struggles. The deaths of Zhou Enlai, Zhu De, and Mao Zedong did not give China much breathing space or time to map out a design toward Taiwan. It was only after the arrest of the Gang of Four, and especially the rehabilitation of Deng Xiaoping and others, that the CCP could rethink its policy toward Taiwan and reassess the situation. This rethinking and reassessment, however, must be examined with a much broader perspective. It is proposed here that at least three major events paved the way for the resurgence and articulation of a new "peaceful" offensive against Taiwan in the 1980s. They were the decision of the CCP to concentrate on the Four Modernizations; the international environment, notably the establishment of diplomatic relations between Beijing and Washington; and the signing of the Sino-Japanese Peace and Friendship Treaty.

All Chinese sources emphasize that the third plenary session of the 11th Central Committee of the CCP, held in December 1978, heralded a new chapter in the history of China. It was decided that the focus of the work of the party henceforth would be on "socialist modernization," with agriculture as the center of attention. It was apparent that, in order to concentrate on this task, a period of peace and stability would be necessary. And it could be deduced that the creation of tension in the Taiwan Strait by reunifying China via military means would be counterproductive, even if one put aside the question of whether the CCP had the ability to do so. However, the communiqué did not have much to say about Taiwan. It only noted that

> The plenary session holds that the normalization of relations between China and the United States further places before us the prospect of the return of our sacred territory Taiwan to the embrace of our motherland and the accomplishment of the great cause of *reunification*. The plenary session expresses welcome to Taiwan compatriots, compatriots in Hongkong and Macao and overseas Chinese, as patriots belonging to one family, to continue making joint and positive contributions to the *reunification* and construction of their motherland.[9]

The statement did not really tell much about the future strategy of the CCP toward Taiwan, although the tone of the two sentences was rather mild and "peaceful." However, Deng himself had, on the eve of the plenary session in November 1978, mentioned to a foreign correspondent that, "after a *peaceful reunification* of the country is achieved, Taiwan may still retain non-socialist economic and social systems."[10] It shows that Deng already had some ideas of a "peaceful" offensive against Taiwan, and this strategy was reconfirmed in the plenary session. Quite clearly, the term "liberation of Taiwan" was not to be used, also confirmed by Deng later on in his U.S. trip in late January 1979.[11] More revealing was the official cessation of the bombing of Quemoy and Matsu on January 1, 1979, and the issuance of "A Message to Compatriots in Taiwan" by the Standing Committee of the National People's Congress of the PRC, when China and the United States established diplomatic relations. The message called for the establishment of postal, trade, and transportation links between Beijing and Taipei. It promised that the wishes and interests of the people of Taiwan would be respected in reunification talks.[12] Obviously, a new "peaceful" offensive against Taiwan was in the offing.

As indicated in the communiqué of the third plenary session of the 11th Central Committee of the CCP, the establishment of official ties between Washington and Beijing provided new opportunities for the CCP's reunification policy. By the time the plenary session was held, negotiations for the normalization of relations between China and the United States had been completed.[13] Leaders in Beijing knew very well that they had been successful in asking the United States to cut off diplomatic relations with Taiwan and to recognize the PRC as the sole legal government of China, terminate its Mutual Defense Treaty with Taiwan and withdrawing its remaining military personnel from the island. Although the United States had by no means severed all its ties with the KMT government, as demonstrated by later events and lingering conflicts between the PRC and the United States on U.S.–Taiwan ties, the CCP apparently felt that it had finally managed to at least dilute U.S. support for Taiwan.[14] Its enhanced confidence that international feeling was on its side should have boosted its desire to make new moves against Taiwan.

Mention must be made about concurrent progress in Sino-Japanese relations, as evidenced by the signing of the Peace and Friendship Treaty between Tokyo and Beijing in August 1978. Earlier, in 1972, China had successfully asked Japan to recognize the government of the PRC as the sole legal government of China. In addition, Japan stated in the joint statement of September 1972 that it fully understood and respected China's stand that Taiwan was an inalienable part of the PRC, and that Japan would comply with Article 8 of the Potsdam Proclamation. The article stipulated the implementation of the terms of the Cairo Declaration, including restoration of Taiwan to China.[15] From the Chinese perspective, this reaffirmed the return of Taiwan to China following World War II.[16] Beijing was also pleased that Tokyo, as a major power, took the lead in befriending the PRC. In fact, Japan was the first noncommunist state in the Asian Pacific region to establish diplomatic relations with China.

Since China and Japan were still technically at war, and the peace treaty between Japan and Taiwan was terminated by Japan's Foreign Minister Ohira in a press statement while he was in Beijing in September 1972, steps were taken to negotiate the Peace and Friendship Treaty. In spite of Japan's continued links with Taiwan, as analyzed later in Chapter 3, the Peace and Friendship Treaty was finally signed in August 1978. This not only ended the state of war between the two sides but, from a Chinese point of view, strengthened Sino-Japanese relations at the expense of the Soviet Union, not to say Taiwan. Because of these favorable international developments, Beijing probably calculated that it was an opportune time to launch a "peaceful" offensive and that the KMT would be more inclined to consider the CCP's proposals as Taiwan became more and more isolated from the international community.

By using the typology to survey the circumstances leading to the emergence of a "peaceful" offensive against Taiwan in 1980s, it can be seen that the military option failed in the early years, when Taiwan was backed by the United States. With the subsidence of this military line, the diplomatic offensive seems to have borne fruits, succeeding for quite a while as evidenced by the events starting in the 1970s. The "peaceful" offensive since 1949, however, was not given much of a chance to develop as the dominant line before the 1980s. Consequently, it remains to be tested. As noted from the beginning, these offensives are not mutually exclusive and can be combined to pursue the same goal. In view of the success of the diplomatic option, that will surely be used to complement the "peaceful" offensive which began to emerge as the dominant line in the 1980s. Whether Beijing will opt for the military offensive is still uncertain. However, as analyzed later on, and putting aside for the time being the question of cost and the ability of Beijing to overcome Taipei militarily, Chinese leaders have maintained that the option is still open.

BEIJING'S "PEACEFUL" OFFENSIVE IN THE 1980s

As noted earlier, traces of a new "peaceful" offensive surfaced by late 1978. However, there was still no systematic elaboration of this offensive, and the statements made by Deng in November 1978 and the third plenary session of the 11th Central Committee of the CCP were brief. More revelations of the "new" strategy came about when the Standard Committee of the National People's Congress issued "A Message to Compatriots in Taiwan" on January 1, 1979. In the message, the PRC considered that both the domestic and the international situations were conducive to reunification. It suggested to the people of Taiwan and also to the Taiwan authorities to take concrete steps toward the goal of reunification. On its part, Beijing declared that it would recognize the present condition and respect the opinions of people from all walks of life in Taiwan. It had ordered the PLA to stop bombing Taiwan's offshore islands. In this regard, it suggested that the government of the PRC and the Taiwan authorities should hold talks to end the hostility in the strait, so as to pave the way for more contacts between the two sides.[17] It further suggested that there could be links in trade, post, and transportation—the so-called three exchanges— and other contacts between Taiwan and China.[18]

First, it should be noted that the message was essentially for Taiwan compatriots, although the Taiwan authorities were also egged on by the statement. No word was mentioned about the KMT per se. In fact, as an initial step to end the hostility between China and Taiwan, it was suggested in the message that the PRC government, not the CCP, should hold talks with the Taiwan authorities—presumably not the KMT but its government, the state apparatus supposed to represent the interests of all parties and people in Taiwan. Second, the message revealed that Beijing had, through its National People's Congress, shown its respect for the existence of a separate system in Taiwan. Third, the message made known Beijing's desire to have the three exchanges and other links. First spelled out in the message, the wish to have the exchanges would be used to create the momentum for reunification. It became an important aspect of Beijing's "peaceful" strategy in the 1980s.

The most systematic, elaborate, and authoritative proposal for reunification surely was the nine-point proposal of September 1981 made known by Ye Jianying, chairman of the Standing Committee of the National People's Congress and a leading member of the CCP. By this time, China was prepared to take a closer look at the Taiwan issue. Hua Guofeng and the so-called whateverists had already been eased out, and Deng Xiaoping and his protégés, Hu Yaobang and Zhao Ziyang, managed to reconfirm the concentration on the four modernizations, as demonstrated by the resolution on certain historical questions of the CCP in the sixth plenary session of the 11th Central Committee of the CCP in June 1981. As Deng and others examined the Taiwan issue, they could tell that Taipei did not seem to have responded to "A Message to the Compatriots in Taiwan," released two and a half years ago. Moreover, the Sino–U.S. détente was also not very helpful in tackling the issue. In fact, the United States passed the Taiwan Relations Act and continued to sell arms to Taiwan and it was quite clear that the prospects for the reunification of China were by no means imminent. Consequently, the nine-point proposal was used to reiterate and elaborate on the new "peaceful" strategy. Ye's proposal this time was targeted specifically at the KMT. It suggested that the CCP and the KMT cooperate for the third time to achieve reunification. Although this suggestion was by no means new, the CCP apparently came to the conclusion that it was more realistic to deal with its counterpart, not the compatriots in Taiwan. The cooperation between the CCP and the KMT would also give a sense of parity between the forces.

The proposal reiterated Beijing's desire to have the three exchanges and other links with Taiwan. Most important, the proclamation of respecting the status quo and the opinions of the people was translated into concrete suggestions. As reported by the Xinhua News Agency, these included the following:

1. After the country [China] is reunified, Taiwan can enjoy a high degree of autonomy as a special administrative region and it can retain its armed forces. The Central Government [Beijing] will not interfere with local affairs on Taiwan.

2. Taiwan's current socio-economic system will remain unchanged, so will its way of life and its economic and cultural relations with foreign countries. There will be no encroachment on the proprietary rights and lawful right of inheritance over private property, houses, land and enterprises, or on foreign investments.

3. People in authority and representative personages of various circles in Taiwan may take up posts of leadership in national political bodies and participate in running the state.[19]

Although Ye suggested talks between the CCP and the KMT, Beijing apparently had already had some ideas on how Taipei would come under the central government. The proposals were probably a summation of the experiences and opinions of the CCP leadership after the third plenary session of the 11th Central Committee, and were considered generous enough to serve as a starting point for further discussions between the two sides. Beijing's tactic of giving Taipei some leeway to alter or add terms for the reconciliation of their differences could be detected in the last point of Ye's proposals. It stated that Beijing would welcome "proposals and suggestions regarding affairs of state through various channels and in various ways" by people of "all nationalities, public figures of all circles and all mass organizations in Taiwan."[20] The statement could also be used to lure some interest from Taiwan to start the dialogue between the two sides.

From Ye's proposals, it could be seen that the building blocks of the "one country, two systems" concept were already present. However, the phrase was not used then. Likewise, Deng Xiaoping did not mention the phrase in a meeting with a foreign guest in October 1981, when he talked about reunification and suggested only that Ye's proposals were a "fair and reasonable" policy. And Deng thought that the nine-point proposals should be acceptable to the Taiwan authorities.[21]

According to most Chinese sources, the phrase "one country, two systems" was first used in 1982. One source in the more authoritative *Beijing Review* noted that the phrase was first used by Deng Xiaoping in January 1982, in a meeting with a foreign friend, when Deng said that Ye's nine-point proposal "embodies the 'one country, two systems' principle."[22] Subsequent to that, Deng and others used the phrase on numerous occasions, including Deng's meeting with British Prime Minister Margaret Thatcher, when the latter was in Beijing in September 1982. Deng also elaborated on the concept in various meetings, notably one with a professor from the United States in June 1983. And when the Sino-British negotiations on the future of Hong Kong were conducted in earnest, culminating in the initialing of the Sino-British Joint Declaration on the Question of Hong Kong on September 26, 1984, Deng made many statements in 1984 on the application of the concept. All these statements were eventually summarized and presented systematically in an October 1984 article in *Liaowang Zhoukan* (Outlook Weekly). The article tried to elaborate on the "one country, two systems" proposal by deliberating not only on the concept as a policy but as a foundation for future theoretical treatment and broader applications.

Since the "one country, two systems" proposal was apparently the master plan and the center piece for the CCP's reunification of China in the 1980s, it is of paramount significance that it be dealt with in detail. To do that, the concept is examined from three angles—namely, its meaning, its theoretical basis, and its operation.

The "One Country, Two Systems" Proposal: What It Means for Taiwan

The "one country, two systems" concept was primarily aimed at Taipei but applied first to Hong Kong and later to Macao. It is fair to say that, if not for changes in the domestic and international environments, notably Beijing's desire to concentrate on the four modernizations and the emergence of the Sino–U.S. détente, the policy could not have been developed. Based on its pragmatic calculations or, as they put it in China, "seeking truths from facts," Beijing would like to have a prolonged period of peace to modernize itself. Deng said clearly that "China needs 50 to 60 years to completely modernize."[23] As a result, tension in the Taiwan Strait would be counterproductive and would divert attention from its primary concern—modernization. Deng and other Chinese leaders also seemed to have come to the conclusion that, like it or not, the capitalists have to be accepted to a certain extent. The greater advancement in Western capitalist countries and the four small "dragons" (South Korea, Taiwan, Hong Kong, and Singapore) certainly had impressed Deng and others to concede that capitalism could help China's socialism. This not only had its theoretical implications, as analyzed later, but required tremendous courage on the part of the Chinese leaders. Without the caliber of leadership, as exemplified by Deng and his supporters, it would be difficult to overcome the resistance of others who were still influenced by the leftist line. The triumph of Deng and his associates in the third plenary session of the 11th Central Committee of the CCP was not only a milestone as far as the "one country, two systems" was concerned but it set the tone for a "peaceful" approach toward Taiwan. As mentioned by Deng, "there are two ways to settle the issues [Taiwan, Hong Kong, and Macao]: peaceful and non-peaceful. The non-peaceful way, or the way to settle the issues by force, was deemed inappropriate."[24] As a result, the "peaceful" proposal was "one country, two systems": capitalism in Taiwan, Hong Kong, and Macao and socialism on the mainland in a united China. The coexistence of the two systems does not mean a parity of their forces. Deng did not disguise the idea that socialism on the mainland would be the dominant force and that capitalism would be used to supplement the development of socialism. Because of the preponderance of socialism and the transitional and sub-sidiary nature of capitalism in China, it could be argued that the proposal was a united-front strategy to dilute resistance from other forces. In fact, some Chinese admitted openly that the concept was based on the united-front strategy at home and abroad, only they did not admit that it was a conspiracy as China elucidated the proposal openly. They also emphasized that the proposal was not an expedient because of its factual and theoretical bases.[25] Deng and others were pragmatic enough to realize that it would be difficult for China to absorb these capitalist enclaves, especially Taiwan and Hong Kong, in view of the vast differences. For the time being, they also saw that Hong Kong and Taiwan could be used to beef up the economy in mainland China. To fully utilize the resources in these areas, it was important to preserve their stability and prosperity, thus giving rise to Deng's guarantee that, in the case of Hong Kong, "the social system and life style and its position as an international financial centre and free port will be kept and remain unchanged for 50 years after 1997."[26] Deng's plan for Taiwan was somewhat similar. From Deng's perspective, Taiwan and Hong Kong could be treated with the same formula, since both were pending issues in China's reunification left over by history. Both places have a capitalist system that has to be preserved in order to maintain its prosperity and ensure a peaceful reunification.[27]

It has been pointed out that Taiwan is a de facto independent entity while Hong Kong is a colony. As such, what is considered a compromise in the Sino-British settlement of Hong Kong could not be acceptable to Taiwan.[28] Deng and other Chinese leaders were probably aware of or have been cautioned about the difference. As noted by some Chinese analysts, unlike Hong Kong—a colony under foreign rule—Taiwan is part of China, having its own army, independent international ties, and self-government.[29] Therefore, in the case of Hong Kong, negotiations were between China and Britain on the recovery of sovereignty, whereas in the case of Taiwan, it would be basically between the two Chinese parties, an internal affair. There is also the fact that Hong Kong has always had close communication with the mainland and is geographically linked to China, whereas Taiwan has cut its links with Beijing and is geographically separated from the mainland. Obviously, the problems to be overcome regarding Taiwan will be much more formidable.

In view of this difference, Beijing is seemingly offering more inducements to Taipei than to Hong Kong in its "one country, two systems" proposal to the KMT. One notable difference is that Taipei would be allowed to keep its armed forces, although this could be owing largely to difficulties involved in disarming the KMT and the stationing of PLA troops in Taiwan. The CCP also seems to be ready to give more favorable terms to the KMT in the running of the central government and to Taiwan investors and citizens if and when they return to the mainland. However, in the meeting with Professor Winston Yang of Seton Hall University in June 1983, Deng, according to the official press report in the *People's Daily*, laid down some specific terms for Taiwan. While Deng reiterated that Taiwan, as a special administrative region of China, might retain its independent nature and practice a system different from that of the mainland, he also pointed out that Taiwan could not be completely autonomous.[30] To him, complete autonomy meant the existence of two Chinas. In fact, Deng wanted to emphasize that Taiwan would be a local government and that only a unitary, and not a federal, not to say a confederal, system, with the central government in Beijing, would be allowed. Equally important, Deng made it very clear that only the PRC could represent China under the one-China principle, although there might be two systems in the country. The official press release did not say anything about the ways by which Taipei could play a role in world affairs. However, according to an article by Winston Yang about the same meeting with Deng, it revealed that Deng actually mentioned that Taiwan could use "Zhongguo Taibei" to stay in the Asian Development Bank and "Taiwan, China" as the name for Taiwan after reunification.[31] Yang's impression was that China would give Taiwan some leeway to participate in foreign affairs, especially in international economic relations. Since this was not mentioned in the official press, the Chinese probably thought it was premature and inappropriate to reveal this.

It is interesting to note that, in the same meeting, officially Deng mentioned only that "an independent judiciary and the right of final judgment does not reside in Beijing." He did not talk about an independent legislature. However, according to Winston Yang, Deng said that after reunification Taiwan would have independent legislative power provided it did not go against the Chinese constitution.[32] The fact that this again was not in the official press release creates the suspicion that China will not really grant Taiwan an independent legislature—that it would like to have some way to monitor the legislature for fear that it might hurt the interests of the central government. As for the military and executive power of Taiwan, Deng elaborated in the meeting that "the mainland will station neither troops nor administrative personnel in Taiwan. The party, political, military and other systems in Taiwan will be *administered* by Taiwan itself."[33] It seems that Deng was willing to let Taiwan run its own show provided it did not harm the interests of a reunified China. However, in the case of the armed forces kept and administered by the KMT, the official press release did not mention arms purchase. But according to Yang's report, Deng specifically mentioned that Taiwan could purchase arms from abroad for its own defense.[34] The omission of this from the official report demonstrated China's reservation about endorsing Taiwan's arms purchase. China's displeasure and furor with regard to Dutch and, more important, U.S. arms sales to Taiwan show vividly that China was and is concerned with foreign countries selling arms to Taiwan. Besides, whether the arms sales were for defensive or offensive reasons is very difficult to determine. It can also be argued that a militarily strong Taiwan may tempt it to go independent, the most dreaded outcome and an unacceptable eventuality for Beijing, although others may argue that a militarily strong Taiwan will strengthen the KMT's confidence in coming to the conference table to talk to the CCP about reunification.

The "One Country, Two Systems" Proposal: Its Theoretical Basis and Implications

For the CCP, Marxism, Leninism, and Mao Zedong thought are the political glue that binds the Chinese communists. The "one country, two systems" proposal, however, may cast certain doubts on that ideology, since the new concept admits the positive role of capitalism. As a result, Deng and others had to find a Marxist-Leninist and a Maoist way to rationalize adoption of the proposal. Theoreticians were asked to intellectualize and theorize the compatibility of the concept with Marxism so as to give the former a sense of legitimacy and propriety in a communist system. Deng himself reasoned that the proposal had its international implications, since it could be used to solve some of the international disputes in a peaceful manner.[35] Based on this, he argued that the concept's merit could be deduced from Marx's dialectical materialism and historical materialism; "one country, two systems" was a reflection of the realities of the world. It also coincided with Mao's dictum of "seeking truths from facts," according to Deng.[36] While this may "solve" the methodological problem of justifying the concept, the more difficult part was how to rationalize the place of capitalism within socialism, since the Chinese communists have been attacking the former all the time. Adoption of the concept might thus challenge the very foundation of the CCP's ideology. It could also undermine people's confidence in socialism. More important, perhaps, opposition within the party might query the orthodoxy of such a creation. To alleviate potential opposition and to mobilize support for such a courageous admittance of capitalism, it has been suggested that the two contradictory ideologies can coexist for a while. Marxist dialects and Maoist theory of contradictions were used to rationalize their coexistence. As "reasoned" by some Chinese scholars, "all things in the world are unity of opposites; without contradiction, nothing would exist. . . . Since socialism and capitalism have inhabited the same planet for so long, why should they not be able to operate side by side in one country?"[37] It was further elaborated that for this contradiction, à la Mao Zedong, the principal aspect of the contradiction was socialism.[38] It meant that the main force and the prevailing side, as Deng and others made it abundantly clear, was socialism in the "one country, two systems" proposal; it was precisely because of the dominance of socialism in the proposal that the CCP would allow the existence of capitalism in smaller areas like Taiwan and Hong Kong.[39] The argument was that the preponderance of socialism would make it easier for Beijing to practice "one country, two systems," since it did not feel threatened by the new proposal. As put by Deng himself, "Without the dominance of socialism, capitalism will gobble up socialism."[40] The justification for the dominance of socialism and Deng's worry about capitalist mischief made it all the more important for Beijing to emphasize the subsidiary role of capitalism in China, and consequently the subordinate position of Taiwan, Hong Kong, and Macao. Quite naturally, Beijing would like to reiterate the superiority of socialism; the only concession made by Deng was that "the existence of capitalism in small areas could profit the development of socialism."[41]

For the contradiction between socialism, as represented by the CCP, and capitalism, as represented by the KMT, it was further suggested that it had become a nonantagonistic contradiction in view of new domestic and international developments.[42] Such a contradiction, as students of Chinese politics know too well, is a contradiction among the "people" of China and would be solved by peaceful means.

The above "breakthrough" in Marxism, however, is not without precedent, as argued by some Chinese scholars. They noted that Marx had mentioned the positive aspects of capitalism. More important, perhaps, they argued that Lenin did the same in using capitalism to expedite the development of socialism in the aftermath of the Bolshevik Revolution. Notably, the New Economic Policy launched by Lenin made use of capitalist funds, technology, and managerial know-how under the supervision of the Soviet government.[43] Moreover, Lenin's policy of peaceful coexistence between socialism and capitalism after the Soviet civil war and China's Bandung diplomacy of peaceful coexistence were used by the scholars to rationalize the existence of capitalist Taiwan and Hong Kong. It was suggested that although the theory of peaceful coexistence was applied mainly to foreign affairs, it could be extended to domestic affairs.[44] For the Chinese, just as with Lenin, tolerance of capitalism, however, has its limits. According to Beijing, the system in Hong Kong would remain unchanged for 50 years or more after 1997. And in the case of Taiwan, it could remain unchanged for at least 100 years after reunification, according to Deng in his discussion with Winston Yang in 1983.[45] Although it is difficult to envision what China—or, for that matter, Taiwan and Hong Kong—would be like in the distant future, it should be noted that the Chinese leaders did have a time frame in mind, whether it be 50 or 100 years or more. Quite obviously, the "one country, two systems" concept was meant to apply in the transitional period. The principles that must be kept, at least for present leaders like Deng and others when they mapped out the "one country, two systems" concept, are:

1. There must be one country, one China, which is the PRC.
2. The dominant system is socialism.

As admitted by some, China had been only strategically more flexible under these firm principles. The flexibility of having two systems is meant to exploit capitalism and achieve reunification, not to encourage the integration or convergence of the two systems.[46] As mentioned earlier, it is an example of the united front.

Other than these Marxist-Leninist and Maoist theoretical extrapolations of the "one country, two systems" proposal, the most interesting theoretical justification of the concept is perhaps the adoption of the "primary stage of socialism" in the practice of socialism with Chinese characteristics. Although the theory was mentioned in the sixth plenum of the 11th Central Committee, the 12th Party Congress, and the sixth plenum of the 12th Central Committee, it was only in the 13th Party Congress, held in November 1987, that Zhao Ziyang officially propounded it fully.[47] At the congress, Zhao explained, among other things, that China was only at the beginning of its socialist road and that it would be at least 100 years from the 1950s that socialist modernization would be accomplished. In the meantime, China must emphasize modernization, reform, and open policy, and it must develop diverse sectors of the economy with public ownership playing a dominant role in the primary stage.[48] In other words, public ownership, while dominant, would be accompanied by individual or private ownership, Sino-foreign joint ventures, Sino-foreign cooperative enterprises, and wholly foreign-owned ventures in the primary stage to boost productivity. This new theory in many ways further supports the "one country, two systems" proposal in the sense that it legalizes and enhances the acceptability of special administrative regions where capitalism is practiced under autonomous conditions.

It is interesting to note that some Chinese scholars also elevated the "one country, two systems" concept into a new theory of the state in political science. These scholars emphasized not so much the Marxist-Leninist pretensions of the concept, but its usefulness as a new model with "scientific" meanings. The argument was that the model was new because it was essentially a unitary system structurally, but with characteristics of a composite system. Undoubtedly, the central government was still sovereign, and its sovereignty was not divisible or bargainable under the new proposal. However, the sovereign government authorized the existence of local units with the right to govern and rule certain areas with a different system, so the argument went.[49] It was made very clear that these local governments were not sovereign; they had only the right to govern.[50] As part of the country but not sovereign, these local units, as such, would not exercise the powers of a sovereign state—powers such as diplomacy, defense, declaration of war, and others.[51] Nevertheless, it was argued that the local units under the unitary system would have more power than the constituents of a federal system, because the central government had authorized more judicial, administrative, and legislative powers to the local units. Even in the case of diplomacy, it was argued that local units would have substantial power especially in foreign economic and cultural relations.[52] Whether this is true, of course, is debatable. But the point that should be noted here is that whatever autonomy or residual powers enjoyed by the local units, they must be solely authorized by the central government in Beijing. Moreover, in their ardent support of the new model, these scholars have also overlooked the fact that China has been dominated by the rule of man and not the rule of law. Whether the constitution and the basic law to be enacted for the special administrative regions will be implemented accordingly and fully remains to be seen.

The "One Country, Two Systems" Proposal: Its Practice

While the PRC's record in observing the rule of law does not augur well for respect of constitutionalism in China, it seems that the Chinese leaders are presently trying to grapple with this problem. In implementing the proposal, they adopted a rewritten constitution on December 4, 1982, at the fifth plenum of the Fifth National People's Congress (NPC) that stated in the preamble: "Taiwan is part of the sacred territory of the People's Republic of China. It is the lofty duty of the entire Chinese people, including our compatriots in Taiwan, to accomplish the great task of reunifying the motherland."[53] More important, Article 31 stipulated that the state might establish special administrative regions when necessary, and the systems to be instituted in the special administrative regions shall be prescribed by laws enacted by the NPC "in the light of specific conditions."[54] Likewise, in listing the functions and powers of the NPC, item 13 of Article 62 of the same constitution stated that the congress had, inter alia, the power to "decide on the establishment of special administrative regions and the system to be instituted there."[55] In explaining these stipulations, Peng Zhen, vice-chairman of the Committee for Revision of the Constitution, was at pains to reiterate that while the PRC was "unequivocal on the principle of safeguarding China's sovereignty, unity and territorial integrity," it was at the same time "highly flexible as regards specific policies and measures and gives full consideration to the concrete situation in the Taiwan region and the wishes of the people in Taiwan and those of all personages concerned."[56]

With these adoptions, especially Article 31, the constitutional basis for the "one country, two systems" proposal was laid down. Zhao Ziyang further legitimized the proposal in his Report on the Work of the Government to the second session of the sixth NPC in May 1984.[57]

From Article 31, it is quite clear that special administrative regions will be applied to Taiwan, Hong Kong, and Macao. However, since the law to be enacted by the NPC will be drafted "in the light of the specific conditions," it is also assumed that the law to be applied to Taiwan, Hong Kong, and Macao will not be the same. Having noted that, however, it remains that the principles in the establishment of these special administrative regions will be the same according to the Chinese constitution. This part of the chapter examines these general principles and generalizations, which may help illuminate Beijing's policy toward Taiwan.

As stated clearly in Article 5 of the Chinese constitution, "no law or administrative or local rules and regulations shall contravene the Constitution."[58] It follows that the law to be enacted in special administrative regions will have to follow this stipulation of not contravening the articles in the constitution. Actually this is a well-accepted legal practice. Nonetheless, the problem is that while accepting capitalism in the special administrative regions, it is also stated in the constitution, especially in the preamble and in Articles 1, 5, and 6, that the political, economic, and legal systems are based on socialism.[59] Thus the preamble of the constitution clearly states that "The Chinese of all nationalities will continue to adhere to the people's democratic dictatorship and follow the *socialist* road, steadily improve *socialist* institutions, develop *socialist* democracy, improve the *socialist* system and work hard and self-reliantly to modernize industry, agriculture, national defence and science and technology step by step to turn China into a *socialist* country with a high level of culture and democracy."[60] Moreover, the preamble highlights the siginficance of the four cardinal principles of the CCP—namely, adherence to the socialist road, the people's democratic dictatorship, leadership of the CCP, and Marxism-Leninism and Mao Zedong thought.[61] As explained by Peng Zhen, the drafting of the constitution was done under the overall guidance of the four cardinal principles, and these principles "form the common political basis for the advance of the people of all our nationalities in unity and are the fundamental guarantee for the smooth progress of our socialist modernization."[62] Quite naturally, those in the special administrative regions could fear that the existence of capitalism in their regions would contradict the spirit and stipulations of the constitution. It is possible that when details of the law for the various special administrative regions have been worked out, they may be annulled by the constitution, should the former contravene the latter. And surely the constitution has a higher status than the law of a local government. As a result, it has been suggested that either the NPC or its Standing Committee should clarify this, or Article 31 should be amended to make clear that other articles of the constitution do not apply to the special administrative regions in order to allay the fears and reservations of those who will have to live with these local governments.[63]

It is also noted that, unlike the autonomous areas for the minorities in China, the relationship between the central government and the special administrative regions is not stipulated in the constitution. The constitution states only very briefly that the law of the regions is enacted by the NPC. Therefore, it is possible that the NPC will have more leeway to structure the law or even dissolve the special administrative regions altogether later on.[64]

The ambiguities surrounding Article 31 of the constitution, however, did not move the CCP to amend the constitution, although it is possible that the Standing Committee of the NPC may clarify the article in due course. In the mean time, the Chinese have been painstakingly pointing out that the existence of capitalism in special administrative regions is "guaranteed" by the constitution. As argued by one scholar, "adherence to the socialist system involves the country as a whole, while allowing the special administrative regions to continue the practice of capitalism refers to those few special administrative regions. The two are not at cross purposes."[65] Another also noted that since Article 31 is an inalienable part of the constitution, conformity with it means conformity with the constitution, and not violating Article 31 means not violating the constitution. These arguments, however, did not seem convincing nor logical, although it was conceded by some in China that some form of assurance to the special administrative regions was necessary.[66] With regard to the four cardinal principles, the CCP made it very obvious that it was not negotiable. Deng made it abundantly clear that without the four principles, the "one country, two systems" proposal would not have been born. However, he added that such principles would not be applied to the special administrative regions.[67]

With the establishment of the constitutionality of the "one country, two systems" proposal, the CCP seemed all determined to put it into practice in Hong Kong and Macao. In the case of Hong Kong, the Sino-British Joint Declaration on the Question of Hong Kong were initialed and signed in September 1984 and December 1984, respectively. As explained in Article 3, item 12, and Annex I of the Sino-British Joint Declaration, China's policies regarding Hong Kong will be stipulated in a Basic Law of the Hong Kong Special Administrative Region of the PRC to be enacted by the NPC.[68] For that purpose, the third session of the Sixth NPC established a Drafting Committee for the Basic Law of the Hong Kong Special Administrative Region (HKSAR) in April 1985. Subsequently, the Standing Committee of the NPC in June 1985 passed the membership list of 59 members, among whom only 23 were from the various sectors in Hong Kong. To help the Drafting Committee, however, it was decided that a consultative committee for the Basic Law should be established to solicit opinions from the people of Hong Kong. Eventually, members of the Drafting Committee residing in Hong Kong helped form the Consultative Committee for the Basic Law of the HKSAR in December 1985. The Consultative Committee has a membership of 180 coming from various sectors in Hong Kong. It was expected that a similar procedure would be adopted for the implementation of the Sino-Portuguese Joint Declaration with regard to the return of Macao to China in December 1999. Since both Hong Kong and Macao are colonies to be reunified with the PRC, the details in the Basic Law for each will have fewer implications for Taiwan. As noted earlier, Taiwan is a de facto independent entity, and there are vast differences between Taiwan and Hong Kong. However, it is evident that China is keen to use the Hong Kong case, and to a lesser extent, that of Macao, as an example for the successful implementation of the "one country, two systems" proposal, in an attempt to persuade Taiwan to respond to Beijing's "peaceful" gestures. Consequently, it should be useful to look at the implications for Taiwan from the establishment of the HKSAR. While the details of the Sino-British Joint Declaration and the Draft Basic Law may not be applicable to Taiwan, it is useful to examine the implications for Taiwan in the following areas: (1) the applicability of socialism to special administrative regions (sars); (2) the degree of autonomy of sars; (3) the security of sars; and (4) the foreign relations of sars.

After about three years of work by the Drafting Committee, the Draft Basic Law of the Hong Kong Special Administrative Region of the People's Republic of China (for Solicitation of Opinions) was released in April 1988. The draft, hereafter referred to as Draft I, was used as a basis for consultation with the people of Hong Kong from May to September 1988. As a result of this first round of consultation, the Consultative Committee was able to collect more than 70,000 pieces of opinion from various sources and compile five volumes of consultation reports. These were distributed to the people of Hong Kong for their information, and, more important, submitted to the Drafting Committee in batches in October and November 1988 to refine Draft I. The refined draft, entitled the Basic Law of the Hong Kong Special Administrative Region of the People's Republic of China (Draft), and hereafter referred to as Draft II, was eventually presented to the sixth session of the Standing Committee of the seventh NPC by Ji Pengfei, chairman of the Drafting Committee for the Basic Law of the HKSAR, in February 1989. It was resolved in the session that Draft II should be publicized extensively to solicit opinions in Hong Kong and other regions of China from February to July 1989. The hope was that the second round of consultation in Hong Kong and other regions of China could help the Drafting Committee further revise the Basic Law so that the third session of the Seventh National People's Congress in 1990 could finalize it for promulgation. Although the final draft of the Basic Law was not ready by the end of the 1980s, certain possible implications and consequences for Taiwan of the Sino-British Joint Declaration, Draft I of April 1988, Draft II of February 1989, and the drafting process of the Basic Law of the HKSAR itself could be deduced from Beijing's emphasis in these areas.*

For a start, it should be noted that the Basic Law and the establishment of the HKSAR is done according to the stipulation of the Sino-British Joint Declaration on the Question of Hong Kong. It follows that, in legal terms, and at least theoretically, the HKSAR is protected by an international agreement to have "a high degree of autonomy" under the "one country, two systems" proposal worked out by the PRC. In the case of the KMT, if ever it enters negotiations with the CCP, it will be an internal arrangement between two parties, and whatever agreement reached may not have validity under international law.[69] Moreover, China has always looked upon the Taiwan issue as an internal issue that brooks no outside interference. In fact, Deng had refuted the use of some kind of international guarantee in implementing whatever agreement worked out between the KMT and CCP.[70] At this stage, it is also premature to talk about some kind of international supervision of the implementation of any KMT-CCP agreement. Taiwan still refuses to negotiate with the CCP, since the former is well aware of the loss of its international personality, the confidence of the people on the island, and the KMT regime once it enters negotiations with the CCP, as analyzed in the next chapter.

Since one of the major concerns of the Hong Kong people was whether it was contradictory to have capitalism in a socialist China, it could be seen

---

*For an update through the end of 1989, see the Postscript. The Basic Law was eventually adopted by the National People's Congress in April 1990. The final draft, however, did not really change or affect the following analysis about the Basic Law and its implications for Taiwan.

from Drafts I and II of the Basic Law of the HKSAR that Beijing tried to allay fears in the colony by stating clearly in the preamble of the two drafts that "the socialist system and policies will not be practiced in Hong Kong."[71] In addition, it is stipulated in Article 4 of Draft I, and renumbered as Article 5 in Draft II, that the socialist system and policies shall not be practiced in the HKSAR and the previous capitalist system and way of life shall remain unchanged for 50 years.[72] It could be deduced that socialism will likewise not be applicable to Taiwan and Macao. There also are reasons to believe that the CCP would tolerate such capitalism in China as evidenced by the theoretical and practical arguments for borrowing capitalism to beef up the strength of socialism. But the catch is, of course, that such tolerance is for a limited period. Moreover, the establishment of special administrative regions is on an ad hoc basis. Therefore, it depends very much on Beijing's ruling elite's judgment and thinking at the time. It is also argued that although the Basic Law of a special administrative region enjoys a high legal status in the legal system of the PRC, it is nevertheless still below that of the constitution. As a result, it would help if the Standing Committee of the NPC could make an authoritative statement about the inapplicability of socialism in the HKSAR when the Basic Law is enacted, so as to quash lingering doubts in this regard. Such a statement has legal status in the PRC legal system.[73]

As for the degree of autonomy in the HKSAR, it is again one of the major worries of the Hong Kong people. Clearly, the PRC would treat the special administrative regions as local governments. In the case of Hong Kong, it is stated in the Joint Declaration that the HKSAR will be directly under the authority of the Central People's Government of the PRC, and this is reiterated in Article 11 of Draft I and renumbered as Article 12 in Draft II that the HKSAR shall be "a local administrative region of the PRC."[74] From all indications, the PRC seems to be quite firm that Taiwan be a local government, although the terms for the structuring of the Taiwanese government could be more generous than those for Hong Kong. Even though Hong Kong, just like Taiwan, has been promised "a high degree of autonomy," it should be mentioned that since the Standing Committee of the NPC, according to the constitution, has the right to interpret statutes, it is possible that such power will be used to annul any Basic Law or legislation passed in the special administrative regions.[75] It could also interpret statutes in its favor. And according to Draft I of the HKSAR, it is clearly stated in Article 169 that the power of interpretation of the Basic Law is vested in the Standing Committee of the NPC.[76] It is also stated in Article 16 of Draft I that if the Standing Committee of the

National People's Congress considers any law of the HKSAR not in conformity with the Basic Law or legal procedure, "it may return the law in question for reconsideration or revoke it, but it shall not amend it. Any law returned for reconsideration or revoked by the Standing Committee of the National People's Congress shall immediately cease to have force."[77] Moreover, the power to amend the Basic Law lies with the NPC, according to Draft I, although it is stated in Article 170 that amendment proposals from the HKSAR can be submitted to the NPC "by the delegation of the Region to the National People's Congress *after* obtaining the consent of two-thirds of the deputies of the Region to the National People's Congress, two-thirds of all the members of the legislature of the Region, and the Chief Executive of the Region."[78] All of these stipulations in Draft I would most likely reduce the autonomy of the HKSAR, at least in the eyes of the more "liberal" elements in Hong Kong.[79] The clamor for more autonomy in Hong Kong seemed to have received a receptive ear from Beijing to a certain extent when Draft II was released. Notably, with regard to the interpretation of the Basic Law, Draft II was more willing to delegate some power to the courts in Hong Kong. Thus, it was stated in Article 157 that "the Standing Committee of the National People's Congress shall authorize the courts of the Hong Kong Special Administrative region to interpret on their own, in adjudicating cases before them, the provisions of this Law which are within the limits of the autonomy of the Region."[80] It also states in the same article that "the courts of Hong Kong Special Administrative Region *may* also interpret other provisions of this Law in adjudicating cases before them."[81] It seems that Beijing had conceded in Draft II by allowing Hong Kong to interpret the provisions of the Basic Law on its own domestic issues, essentially those which are deemed to be related to the autonomy of the HKSAR. It also seems to have relatively more respect for the legislative power of the HKSAR in Draft II, when the right of the Standing Committee of the NPC to return any law of the region which was not in conformity with the Basic Law or legal procedures for reconsideration or revocation was not repeated. However, Beijing was careful to state clearly in Draft II that

> If the courts of the Region, in adjudicating cases before them, need to interpret the provisions of this Law concerning affairs which are the responsibility of the Central People's Government, or the relationship between the Central Authorities and the Region, and if such interpretation will affect the judgments on the cases, the courts of the

Region shall, before making their final judgments which are not appealable, seek an interpretation of the relevant provisions from the Standing Committee of the National People's Congress through the Court of Final Appeal of the Region. When the Standing Committee makes an interpretation of the provisions concerned, the courts of the Region, in applying those provisions, shall follow the interpretation of the Standing Committee.[82]

It also reiterates in Article 17 of Draft II that laws enacted in Hong Kong shall be reported to the Standing Committee of the NPC for the record. More important, regarding affairs within the responsibility of the Central Authorities or the relationship between the central authorities and the region again, if the Standing Committee considers "that any law enacted by the legislature of the Region is not in conformity with the provisions of this Law . . . it may return the law in question but it shall not amend it. Any law returned by the Standing Committee of the National People's Congress shall immediately cease to have force. This cessation shall not have retroactive effect, unless otherwise provided for in the laws of the Hong Kong Special Administrative Region."[83] Moreover, with regard to the ways to amend the Basic Law, nothing substantial was changed in Draft II.

From the above stipulations of Draft II, it seems that Beijing, while prepared to relinquish some power to the HKSAR, is firm in retaining its control over what it considers to be the responsibility of the central government, notably foreign and defense affairs, and the relationship between Beijing and the special administrative regions. Beijing is essentially interested in preserving the prosperity and stability, and not so much in developing an autonomous political system in its special administrative regions, be it Hong Kong, Macao, or Taiwan. While it is not the purpose of this study to delve into the other details of the Hong Kong political system as envisaged in Draft I and Draft II of the Basic Law, and the arguments for a more democratic model for the HKSAR, since they may not be directly applicable to Taiwan, suffice it to say that Beijing seems to be keen to have a firm hand in the appointment of the chief executive of its choice in the HKSAR and that it would like to postpone the formation of a more democratically elected legislature as long as possible.[84] This, of course, does not augur well for the so-called democratic forces, be they in Hong Kong or Taiwan. Moreover, from the preliminary drafts of the Basic Law, Beijing seems to be determined to preserve its right to intervene in the special administrative regions if things are not in order from its perspective. Thus, in Draft I, Articles 17 and 22 state respectively the following:

> Laws, enacted by the National People's Congress or its Standing Committee, which relate to defence and foreign affairs as well as other laws which give expression to national unity and territorial integrity and which, in accordance with the provisions of this Law, are outside the limits of the high degree of autonomy of the Hong Kong Special Administrative Region, shall be applied locally by the government of the Hong Kong Special Administrative Region by way of promulgation or legislation on the directives of the State Council, whenever there is the need to apply any of such laws in the Region. ... If the government of the Hong Kong Special Administrative Region fails to act in compliance with the directives given by the State Council, the State Council may decree the application of the above-mentioned law in the Hong Kong Special Administrative Region.[85]

> The Hong Kong Special Administrative Region shall prohibit by law any act designed to undermine national unity or subvert the Central People's Government.[86]

In view of the ambiguities of some of the clauses, such as "laws which give expression to national unity and territorial integrity" and the inappropriateness of using what some considered to be harsh words like "act in compliance with the directives given by the State Council," the articles were changed and renumbered as Articles 18 and 23 in Draft II. The redrafted articles read respectively as follows:

> National laws shall not be applied in the Hong Kong Special Administrative Region except for those listed in Annex III to this Law. ... The Standing Committee of the National People's Congress may make additions or delegations from the list of laws in Annex III after consulting its Committee for the Basic Law of Hong Kong Special Administrative Region and the government of the Region. Laws listed in the Annex III to this Law shall be confined to those relating to defence and foreign affairs as well as other laws outside the limits of the autonomy of the Region as specified by this Law. In case the Standing Committee of the National People's Congress decides to declare a state of war or, by reason of turmoil within the Hong Kong

Special Administrative Region which is beyond the control of the Region, decides that the Region is in a state of emergency, the State Council may decree the application of the relevant national laws in the Region.[87]

The Hong Kong Special Administrative Region shall enact laws on its own to prohibit any act of treason, secession, sedition or theft of state secrets.[88]

The amended articles no doubt are relatively more specific. However, it still gives Beijing a lot of leeway to impose laws on a special administrative region if it sees fit, especially in times it considers "a state of emergency." In fact, Beijing made no bones about its right to station PLA troops in Hong Kong after 1997, and the amended articles undoubtedly will lead to Beijing's right to intervene, militarily or otherwise, if necessary. As far as Taiwan is concerned, any act that defies the wishes of Beijing could be interpreted in such a way that warrants intervention from the mainland. It remains to be noted that although it is understood both in the Joint Declaration, Draft I and Draft II, that Beijing would be responsible for the foreign and defense affairs of HKSAR, the CCP seems to be relatively more generous toward Taiwan, since the latter was allowed to keep its armed forces after reunification provided the armed forces do not pose a threat to the mainland or allow Taiwan to postpone talks on reunification indefinitely or go independent. As for foreign affairs, Hong Kong will be given opportunities to develop economic and cultural relations with the outside world under the name of "Hong Kong, China." Moreover, it was elaborated in Articles 158 and 160 of Draft I and renumbered as Articles 149 and 151 in Draft II with no significant changes, that Hong Kong may participate as members of the delegation of the government of the PRC "in negotiations conducted by the Central People's Government at the diplomatic level and directly affecting the Region" and "in international organizations or conferences in appropriate fields limited to states and affecting the Region."[89] And according to Article 160 of Draft I or Article 151 of Draft II, Beijing also promises to take the necessary steps to ensure that the HKSAR shall "continue to retain its status in an appropriate capacity in those international organizations of which the People's Republic of China is a member and in which Hong Kong participates in one capacity or another."[90] Where necessary, Beijing will "facilitate the continued participation of the Hong Kong Special Administrative Region in an appropriate capacity in those international organizations in which Hong

Kong is a participant in one capacity or another, but of which the People's Republic of China is not a member."[91] It seems that all these provisions will be applicable to all special administrative regions, including Taiwan. As analyzed in the next chapter, the problem is, of course, that Hong Kong, as a former colony, should find the provisions on foreign affairs less difficult to accept, while Taiwan, as a de facto independent entity, will find the provisions disagreeable, since it will lose its international personality to a large extent. Nonetheless, Beijing has been sufficiently tolerant to allow Taipei to take part in international affairs under names such as "Chinese Taipei" or "Taipei, China." As Taipei began to exploit this tolerance by embarking on a more pragmatic line in taking part actively in international affairs, the PRC seems to have second thoughts in giving a blanket endorsement for such a tolerance. As made clear in December 1988 by a spokesman of the Ministry of Foreign Affairs of the PRC, Beijing would not object to nongovernmental economic relations and trade and cultural contacts between Taipei and other countries that have diplomatic relations with China. However, it objects to any such ties raised to the official level. It also objects to the presence of Taipei in intergovernmental international organizations.[92] The spokesperson highlighted the presence of Taipei in the Asian Development Bank (ADB) under the name of "Taipei, China" and maintained that such agreement was done on a case-by-case basis and that it was allowed with the consent of Beijing and after consultation with the relevant international organization. As such, the spokesman emphasized that Taipei's presence in the ADB was a special arrangement that must not be regarded as a model generally applicable to other intergovernmental international organizations.[93] Quite clearly, Beijing would like to maintain its final say on whether to allow Taipei to conduct its international affairs. Moreover, from Article 165 of Draft I and renumbered as Article 156 of Draft II with no significant changes, it can be seen that the establishment of foreign consular and other official or semiofficial missions in a special administrative region requires the approval of Beijing.[94] Nonetheless, for the consular and other official missions established in Hong Kong by states that have formal relations with the PRC, they may be maintained. Otherwise, they may be permitted either to remain or be changed to semiofficial missions. Last but not least, both drafts stipulated that states not recognized by Beijing could establish only nongovernmental institutions in Hong Kong.[95] Again, these provisions, if applicable to Taiwan, would limit the elbow room for the KMT government to maneuver the conduct of its international affairs.

Finally, it should be noted that both Draft I and Draft II did not mention anything about the representation of one special administrative region in another. It only states in Article 21 of Draft I, and renumbered Article 22 in Draft II with minor amendments, that if there is a need for departments of the central government in Beijing as well as provinces, autonomous regions, and municipalities directly under the central government to set up offices in Hong Kong, they must have the consent of the government of the HKSAR and the approval of the Central People's Government (Beijing). Both drafts also stipulate that the HKSAR may establish an office in Beijing.[96] Since other units under the central government could have an office in the HKSAR if approved by Beijing, and that the HKSAR could have an office in Beijing, it could be reasoned that a special administrative region may have an office in another, provided it is approved by Beijing again. Nevertheless, in the case of Taiwan it seems that whether or not it is a special administrative region of China, it will be allowed to stay in Hong Kong if it so wishes provided the former does not undermine the stability and security of the HKSAR. This was clearly stated by Chi Pengfei, chairman of the Drafting Committee, as early as April 1984, that all links between Taipei and Hong Kong would remain unchanged and that KMT members and organizations would enjoy the same privileges as other Hong Kong residents and organizations if they obeyed the local laws.[97] It seems that Beijing sees Hong Kong as a contact point between the two sides of the Taiwan Strait. In fact, Chi also urged the KMT to help keep the stability and prosperity of Hong Kong. This presumably grows out of the CCP's concern for the stability and prosperity of Hong Kong after 1997 and for possible moves by the KMT to sabotage HKSAR. Chi probably also wanted to remind the KMT of the benefits, especially economic ones, that the KMT could derive from Hong Kong after 1997.

CONCLUDING OBSERVATIONS

In its march toward modernization, Beijing realized that it needed a prolonged period of peace and stability. In terms of its relations with Taiwan, the "peaceful" offensive was worked out as part and parcel of this realization and a strategy to reunify China. As embodied in the "one country, two systems" proposal, the strategy is meant to be a united front without really sacrificing its principles of having one China with Beijing as the central government. More important, if we refer back to the typology of offensives at the beginning of this chapter, the ascendance of the "peaceful" offensive in the 1980s has only pushed the diplomatic and military offensives into the background. In actual practice, the diplomatic offensive, as demonstrated by Beijing's insistence on the one-China principle when it establishes diplomatic relations with other countries and in intergovernmental organizations, has been used to add pressure on Taiwan to come back to the fold. As shown later on, when more people from Taiwan began to visit the mainland after November 1987, economic and cultural ties were used by the CCP to build up the momentum to expedite the process of reunification. The CCP also does not seem to have given up the use of force, for fear of a rise of an independent Taiwan or foreign intervention on the island.[98]

It seems that aging leaders in China would like to see Taiwan reunited with the mainland in their life time. Notably before the death of Chiang Ching-kuo in January 1988, the old guard in China reminded its counterparts, especially Chiang Ching-kuo, that they should try to solve their differences so that history will be kinder to them.[99] Their awareness of a sense of history and their place in it no doubt has contributed to the vigor of the propaganda campaign behind the use of the "one country, two systems" concept for reunification and the need to have "three links and four exchanges" (links through trade, mail, and transportation plus economic, technological, cultural, and sports exchanges). China's seeming hurry is also driven by its worry about the rise of an independent Taiwan. As elaborated in the next chapter, the Taiwanization in the pre– and especially post–Chiang Ching-kuo KMT government, the dilution of familial ties between the two sides of the Taiwan Strait, and the fight for independence within and without Taiwan especially by the opposition all pave the way for a Taiwan less attached to the mainland. And certainly, the socioeconomic, not to say the ideological gulfs between the two sides may be reinforced, if not widened, if Taiwan develops in its own way for a longer period. Beijing's dilemma is that the use of the "peaceful" offensive is a long process and not likely to be effective if it is not accompanied by the use of military or diplomatic pressure. However, if this pressure is applied too hard, it will give Taiwan reasons not to talk about reunification. More important, in the case of the use of force, it will disrupt peace and stability in China, thus spoiling not only China's development and its efforts to cultivate the KMT on reunification but also Beijing's relations with the outside world. While the CCP is very eager to talk untiringly about reunification, it probably also realizes that it would not be easy for it to co-opt Taiwan effectively, and that it has to be satisfied with a slow and tortuous process to narrow the vast differences between the two sides before reunification. As such, the experiment in the application of the "one country, two systems" concept in Hong Kong is vital for Beijing; it will provide first-hand experience in the cooptation of a capitalist entity. It is hoped that the HKSAR will not only boost China's economy but, more important, demonstrate to Taiwan that the "one country, two systems" concept will work for China's reunification.

NOTES

1. Allen Whiting, *China Crosses the Yalu, the Decision to Enter The Korean War* (New York: Macmillan, 1960), pp. 49–67.
2. Ralph N. Clough, *Island China* (Cambridge, Mass.: Harvard University Press, 1978), p. 8.
3. For details of the Taiwan crises, see, for example, Harold Hinton, *Communist China in World Politics* (Boston: Houghton Mifflin, 1966), pp. 258–72. See also Hungdah Chiu, ed., *China and the Taiwan Issue* (New York: Praeger, 1979), pp. 157–61 and 167–79.
4. *Peking Review*, 28 February 1972, p. 5.
5. *Xinhua Monthly*, no. 6, 1955, p. 11, as cited in Zhao Chunyi, ed., *Yiguo Liangzhi Gailun* (A General Treatise of One Country, Two Systems) (Jilin: Jilin Daxue Chubanshe, 1988), p. 18.
6. *People's Daily* (PD), 29 June 1956, cited in Zhao, *Yiguo*, p. 19.
7. *PD*, 17 April 1957, as cited in Ziao, *Yiguo*, p. 19.
8. Frank S. T. Hsiao and Lawrence R. Sullivan, "The Politics of Reunification: Beijing's Initiative on Taiwan," *Asian Survey*, August 1980, p. 791.
9. *Peking Review*, 29 December 1978, pp. 8–9. Emphasis added.
10. *Beijing Review*, 4–10 January 1988, p. 17. Emphasis added.
11. Hsiao and Sullivan, "Politics of Reunification," p. 789.
12. *PD*, 1 January 1979.
13. *Peking Review*, 29 December 1978, p. 8.
14. For details of U.S. foreign policy toward Taiwan and China, see Chapter 3.
15. See Chapter 3 for a fuller analysis.
16. *Peking Review*, 6 October 1972, p. 14.
17. *PD*, 1 January 1979.
18. Ibid.
19. See *Beijing Review*, 5 October 1981, p. 10. The three proposals were originally points 3, 4, and 5, respectively, in Ye's interview with a Xinghua correspondent.
20. Ibid., p. 11.
21. *Beijing Review*, 12 October 1981, p. 5.
22. *Beijing Review*, 4–10 January 1988, p. 18. The phrase "one country, two systems" was used as early as late 1981, according to one source. See Zhao, *Yiguo*, p. 33.
23. *Liaowang Zhoukan* (Outlook Weekly), domestic edition, 15 October 1984, p. 9.
24. Ibid., p. 8.
25. See, for example, the article by Qian Junrui, "Cong Xianggang Wenti Yuanman Jiejue Lun 'Yige Guojia Liangzhong Zhidu' Yingming Gouxiang" (A Treatise of the Brilliant Construct of "One Country, Two Systems" Resulting from the Satisfactory Solution of the Hong Kong Question) and Huan Xiang, " 'Yiguo Liangzhi' Fangzhen

32   The Reunification of China

Chansheng Ti Beijing" (The Background for the Birth of the Policy of "One Country, Two Systems") as reprinted in Zhongyang Shehui Zhuyi Xueyuan Tongyi Zhanxian Lilun Jiaoyan Shi, ed., *Yige Guojia Liangzhong Zhidu* (One Country, Two Systems) (Beijing: Shumu Wenxian Chubanshe, 1987), pp. 72, 56.

26. *Beijing Review*, 3 February 1986, p. 25.

27. Deng Xiaoping, *Jianshe You Zhongguo Tese De Shehui Zhuyi* (Building Socialism with Special Chinese Characteristics) (Hong Kong: Joint Publishing, 1985), p. 36.

28. See, for example, C. L. Chiou, "Dilemmas in China's Reunification Policy Towards Taiwan," *Asian Survey*, April 1986, p. 473.

29. See Guo-cang Huan, "Taiwan: A View from Beijing," *Foreign Affairs*, Summer 1985, p. 1066; and Li Shenzhi and Zi Zhongyun, "Taiwan in the Next Decade," a paper presented at the Atlantic Council Working Group on Taiwan in the Next Decade: Western Interests and Options, 11 March 1985, p. 5.

30. *PD*, 30 July 1983.

31. *The Seventies* (Hong Kong), August 1983, p. 19. "Zhongguo Taibei" could be translated into English as "Taipei, China" or some other ways.

32. Ibid.

33. *PD*, 31 July 1983. Emphasis added.

34. Ibid.

35. *Beijing Review*, 3 February 1986, p. 26.

36. Deng, *Jianshe*, revised edition, 1987, p. 80.

37. *Beijing Review*, 3 February 1986, p. 21. See also Zhao, *Yiguo*, p. 83.

38. Ibid., pp. 92–93.

39. Deng, *Jianshe*, revised edition, 1987, p. 83.

40. Ibid.

41. Ibid.

42. Zhao, *Yiguo*, p. 263.

43. Ibid., pp. 98–99.

44. Ibid., pp. 102–103, 236–37.

45. *The Seventies*, August 1983, p. 19.

46. See, for example, Zhao, *Yiguo*, pp. 93–98.

47. Zhao Guoliang et. al., eds., *Shehui Zhuyi Chuji Jieduan Lilun Ziliao Xuanbian* (Selected Materials on the Theory of the Primary Stage of Socialism) (Beijing: Zhongguo Renmin Daxue Chubanshe, 1987), p. 69.

48. *Beijing Review*, 9–15, November 1987, documents, pp. III–XI.

49. See Byron Weng, "Yiguo Liangzhi Chulun" (A Preliminary Analysis of One Country, Two Systems), in *The Nineties* (Hong Kong), December 1985, p. 31.

50. See Yan Jiaqi, "Yiguo Liangzhi De Kexue Hanyi Ji Qi Tezheng" (The Scientific Meaning and Special Features of the "One Country, Two Systems"), in *Red Flag*, September 1985, pp. 17–19.

51. Ibid.

52. Ibid.

53. *Beijing Review*, 27 December 1982, p. 11.

54. Ibid., p. 16.

55. Ibid., p. 19.

56. *Beijing Review*, 13 December 1982, p. 20.

57. *Beijing Review*, 11 June 1984, Documents, p. XVI.

58. *Beijing Review*, 27 December 1982, p. 12.

59. Ibid., pp. 11–12.

60. Ibid., p. 11. Emphasis added.

61. Ibid.

62. *Beijing Review*, 13 December 1982, p. 10.

63. See, for example, Weng, *Yiguo Liangzhi*, p. 35; and Joseph Y. S. Cheng, "The Constitutional Relationship Between the Central Government and the Future Hong Kong Special Administrative Region Government," mimeographed paper, October 1987, pp. 6, 9–10.

64. An-chia Wu, " 'One Country, Two Systems': A Model for Taiwan?," *Issues and Studies*, July 1985, pp. 50–51.

65. *Beijing Review*, 3 February 1986, p. 22.

66. Cheng, *Constitutional Relationship*, pp. 6–9.

67. *PD*, 22 April 1986. See also Zhao, *Yiguo*, p. 10.

68. *Beijing Review*, 1 October 1984, Documents, pp. IV–V.

69. Hungdah Chiu, "The 1984 Sino-British Agreement on Hong Kong and Its Implications on China's Unification," *Issues and Studies*, April 1985, pp. 14–15, 20.

70. *Taiwan Yanjiu Jikan* (Taiwan Research Quarterly) (Amoy), No. 2, 1986, p. 95.

71. The Drafting Committee for the Basic Law, *Draft Basic Law of the Hong Kong Special Administrative Region of the People's Republic of China (for Solicitation of Opinions)*, Hong Kong, April 1988, p. 29; and *Basic Law of the Hong Kong Special Administrative Region of the People's Republic of China (Draft)*, Hong Kong, February 1989, p. 1. The former document, as stated earlier in the text, is cited as Draft I and the latter as Draft II.

72. Draft I, p. 30 and Draft II, p. 2.

73. Cheng, *Constitutional Relationship*, p. 10.

74. See *Beijing Review*, 1 October 1984, Documents, p. III; Draft I, p. 32; and Draft II, p. 4.

75. See Article 67 of the Chinese constitution in *The Constitution of the People's Republic of China* (Beijing: Foreign Languages Press, 1983), pp. 52–55.

76. Draft I, p. 75.

77. Ibid., p. 33.

78. Ibid., p. 75. Emphasis added.

79. For details, see, for example, Martin Lee and Szeto Wah, *The Basic Law, Some Basic Flaws*, June 1988.

80. Draft II, p. 45.

81. Ibid. Emphasis added.

82. Ibid.

83. Ibid., p. 5.

84. For details of the proposed methods in the selection of the chief executive and the formation of the Legislative Council in the HKSAR, see, for example, Draft I, pp. 78–90 and Draft II, pp. 48–52. See also *Reference Materials of the Basic Law of the Hong Kong Special Administrative Region of the People's Republic of China (Draft)*, published by the secretariat of the Consultative Committee of the Basic Law in February 1989, pp. 71–77.

85. Draft I, p. 34.

86. Ibid., p. 36.

87. Draft II, p. 6. For the laws listed in Annex III, see Ibid., p. 53.

88. Draft II, p. 8.

89. Draft I, p. 71 and Draft II, p. 42.

90. Draft I, p. 71 and Draft II, p. 42.

91. Draft I, pp. 71–72 and Draft II, pp. 42–43.

92. *Ming Pao* (Hong Kong), 20 December 1988.

93. Ibid.

94. Draft I, p. 73 and Draft II, p. 44.

95. Ibid.

96. Draft I, p. 35 and Draft II, pp. 7–8.

97. Li Da, ed., *Yiguo Liangzhi Yu Taiwan* (The One Country, Two Systems and Taiwan) (Hong Kong: Wide Angle Press, 1987), p. 93.

98. For details see Chapter 4.

99. Deng, *Jianshe*, revised edition, 1987, p. 16.

2

Taipei's Changing Policy

THE SETTING

In view of the CCP's "peaceful" offensive in the 1980s, it is quite natural that the pressure was on Taipei to respond. The seeming reasonableness of Beijing's "one country, two systems" proposal, and its growing influence in world affairs as a result of its open door policy, forced Taiwan to consider the initiatives from the other side of the Taiwan Strait. To understand fully the way Taipei has responded and the strategy mapped out by the KMT government to counteract pressure for reunification from Beijing, it is important to note not only external but also internal factors shaping the options for Taiwan.

Over the years, the KMT government has gradually realized that its chance to make a comeback to the mainland or to recover the mainland has become more and more slim. This was especially true after the loss of its right to represent China in the United Nations in 1971 and, more important, the emergence of the Sino–U.S. détente in the 1970s. The two events heralded the isolation of Taipei diplomatically. In 1979, even the United States established official ties with the PRC, although the Taiwan Relations Act was passed by Congress to safeguard the security of the island. As Taipei became more and more isolated from world affairs, it began to adopt a more flexible approach in the conduct of its international relations. Since it could not change the mood of dropping Taipei in favor of Beijing diplomatically, the KMT government began to promote what it called substantive relations with countries that had cut off official ties with

Taipei. By and large, Taipei tried to salvage its diplomatic setbacks by maintaining semi-official or unofficial relations with other countries. While this way helped Taipei's sagging diplomatic fortune to a certain extent, the fact remains that the KMT government's influence and presence in world affairs is dwindling. Moreover, Beijing kept on pressing other countries and international organizations to adopt a one-China policy, although in a number of occasions it had no objection if Taipei was represented by designations like "Chinese Taipei" or "Taipei, China." The KMT's perspective took it that Beijing was squeezing Taipei out of international affairs and that Beijing was using its diplomatic influence to pressure Taipei to talk about reunification. The fact that other divided states such as Korea and Germany had already begun to talk and had institutionalized exchanges between the two sides probably reflected negatively on Taipei's continuous refusal to have a dialogue with its mainland counterpart. After the conclusion of the Sino-British Declaration in Hong Kong in 1984 and the Sino-Portuguese Declaration on Macao in 1987, it was obvious that more pressure would be exerted by Beijing for Taipei to consider the "one country, two systems" proposal, since the "world community" had accepted the proposal for Hong Kong and Macao.

It should be noted that Taiwan has always maintained a one-China policy. It has been emphasizing that Taiwan is part of China and has rejected pressure for the separation of Taiwan from the mainland, whether for self-determination or independence. In fact, within the island, all forces for self-determination and independence have been clamped down by the KMT government. Even the CCP has acknowledged that the KMT has contributed its share to reunification by maintaining that there is only one China and that Taiwan is part of China.[1] However, to keep this one-China policy at home, the KMT has, among other things, structured its government to represent the whole of China. The constitution of the KMT government adopted in 1946 provides for a National Assembly to elect the president and vice-president and amend the constitution, a Legislature Yuan to pass the laws, an Executive Yuan to implement legislation, a Judicial Yuan to interpret legislation, a Control Yuan to supervise officials, and an Examination Yuan to conduct civil service examinations. Of the five pillars of power, three are elective bodies—namely, the National Assembly, the Legislative Yuan, and the Control Yuan, whose deputies were elected on the mainland in 1947 and 1948. Because the KMT government maintains that it is the legitimate government of China, the constitution has not been changed, even after its retreat to Taiwan. As it has been impossible to hold new elections on the mainland since 1949, the terms of the original members of the elective bodies were extended indefinitely. As more and more of the original members died, it was evident that new members would have to be added. To bypass the constitution and enhance the powers of the president, "Temporary Provisions Effective During the Period of Communist Rebellion" were adopted in 1948 and applied in Taiwan after 1949. Martial law was also decreed in Taiwan after the KMT had moved to the island.

With unambiguous diplomatic, economic, and military support from the United States, the KMT government in Taiwan, composed primarily of mainlanders at the top, was able to establish its base in a new home. However, it was obvious that the old political structure would eventually fail to meet the needs and rising expectations of a changing society. While it is not within the scope of this study to survey the progress in Taiwan since 1949 and the changes in the social fabric of Taiwanese society over the years, suffice it to say that Taiwan has been transformed by the 1980s from a primarily agrarian entity to a more commercial and industrial society with a strong middle class. The social and economic successes of Taipei ironically have produced a yearning for political participation and liberalization that quite naturally questions the stringent government limitations. Under the instruction of Chiang Kai-shek, and later on Chiang Ching-kuo, the KMT had already introduced supplementary elections to increase the number of delegates from Taiwan. A process of localization, or Taiwanization, also began under Chiang Ching-kuo. These changes were made at a time when the KMT was fizzled out of the international community, as a result of Beijing's diplomatic successes. The decreased international support and the fear of not getting enough domestic support to stay in power in Taipei certainly propelled the KMT to adjust its policies at home. With a growing desire for democratization and a fading away of many members of the old guard from the mainland, adjustments were necessary to accommodate new demands, as elaborated upon later on. It is pertinent and significant to note at the very beginning, however, that many of the adjustments and policies toward the mainland mapped out by the KMT in the 1980s were more a reflection of the needs of the Taiwan polity at home than a response to the "peaceful" offensive of the PRC.

TAIPEI'S RESPONSES TO BEIJING'S OVERTURES

To the KMT government, one of the heaviest blows after 1949 was certainly the decision of the United States to establish diplomatic relations with Beijing and to cut off official ties with Taipei, as made known on

December 16, 1978. The sense of despair, disappointment, betrayal, and anguish could be vividly noted in the two statements made by Chiang Ching-kuo about this event on the same day.[2] To preempt Beijing from advocating its plan for reunification in view of Taipei's diplomatic setback, Chiang made it very clear that Taipei would under no circumstances negotiate with "the communist bandits" or compromise with communism and forsake its plan to "recapture" the mainland. He further noted that the CCP would lure Taiwan with its "peace talks" and reiterated that Taipei would resolutely not enter any peace talks with the "communist bandits."[3] Quite obviously, the basic line of the KMT remained unchanged.

After the launching of the "peaceful" offensives, as noted by the release of "A Message to Compatriots in Taiwan" by the standing committee of the NPC and the cessation of the bombing of Quemoy and Matsu in January 1979, the KMT felt compelled to react to all these united-front activities of the CCP. The KMT's response was perhaps best summed up by the then-Premier Sun Yun-suan's declaration "On Recent Chinese Communist United Front Activities At Home and Abroad," issued on January 11, 1979.[4] From the declaration, Taipei rejected the three exchanges with the mainland and peace talks from Beijing. To the KMT, these gestures were intended primarily to soften U.S. support of Taiwan and weaken Taipei's determination to fight against the communists. Ultimately, according to Sun, Beijing was interested in communizing Taiwan by means of the peace talks.[5] To the CCP, Sun suggested the following so that the people in the mainland could also enjoy the "freedom and prosperity" developed in Taiwan:

1. Forsake Marxism-Leninism and give up world revolution.
2. Abolish communist dictatorship and safeguard the rights and freedom of the people.
3. Disband the people's communes and return properties to the people.[6]

These unrealistic proposals, especially the first two, betrayed an inability or unwillingness to negotiate and the uncompromising attitude of the KMT government. Notwithstanding, it was noted by some, and judging from statements made by Sun on other occasions, that the premier could be less repugnant to Beijing's "peaceful" overtures. It was noted that the KMT government, as represented by Sun's statement, did make a tactical change in declining the peace feeler from Beijing with an uncharacteristic moderate tone, leading some to speculate that the KMT was trying to salvage its damaged international image after the U.S. derecognition of Taipei.[7] Moreover, there were suggestions elsewhere in Taiwan to have a more pragmatic approach toward the mainland. Notably, several well-known academics at a major conference of scholars and officials in July 1979 proposed that Taiwan consider some kind of commercial contact with the mainland.[8] While these suggestions did help build momentum for changes that came later, the KMT stuck officially to what was dubbed the "three-no" policy: no contact, no negotiation, no compromise. The KMT government evidently was not in a mood to negotiate with Beijing when it was trying to repair damages done by the U.S. derecognition and to restore normalcy to Taiwan as soon as possible.

As U.S.–Taiwan relations gradually began to return to normal, as evidenced by the adoption of the Taiwan Relations Act by the U.S. Congress, the establishment of the American Institute in Taiwan, and Taipei's Coordinating Council of North American Affairs in the United States, it seems that Taipei also reappraised its relations with Beijing, leading a "new" line—namely, "reunifying China under the three principles of the people." While there were precedents in Taiwan when both Chiang Kai-shek and Chiang Ching-kuo were said to have used this slogan, it was officially adopted only at the 12th KMT Congress held in March–April 1981.[9] From this, the KMT would probably emphasize the invincibility of ideology—the three principles of the people pioneered by the founder of the Republic of China, Sun Yat-sen—rather than repeat the previous futile and unrealistic doctrine of launching an attack against the mainland or recapturing the mainland by force. To a certain extent, this new slogan could be a departure from the KMT's past policy toward the mainland. More important, it was also more of a response to Beijing's "peaceful" offensive and its domestic and international pressure. However, the KMT probably also knew too well that the CCP could not accept this, and as such the sincerity regarding reunification was very much doubted, especially by Beijing.

When Yeh's nine-point proposal of September 1981 was made known, the KMT had to deal with this new move, which sparked lively discussions in the island. As noted in the last chapter, the nine-point proposal embodied what was later known as the "one country, two systems" proposal, and it called for a third alliance between the CCP and KMT. Some reckoned that this proposal could be aimed at the United States as well as Taiwan. But Taipei's reaction was predictably a flat repudiation. As revealed by Chiang Ching-kuo in his address to the standing committee of the Central Committee of the KMT on October 7, 1981, the proposal to have a third alliance between the CCP and KMT was a nonstarter. From his perspective, previous alliances were used by the CCP to infiltrate the ranks of the KMT and expand the CCP's influence. To him, the proposal for a third united front was a reaction to Taipei's reactivation of the reunification idea under the three principles of the people. Chiang noted that, from past experience, all these proposals for peace talks were just another round of warfare launched by the communists, and that it would not be wise for the KMT to negotiate with the CCP. As usual, he reiterated that the only way to unify China was to get rid of communism and to adopt Sun Yat-sen's three principles of the people.[10] To expose this "united front conspiracy" of Yeh's nine-point proposal, KMT sources further noted that it was a plot to gobble up the KMT government and relegate it to a local government. They regarded Beijing's offer to help Taiwan financially as a joke, since Taiwan was doing well economically. They also took the promise to allow Taiwan's status to remain unchanged after reunification a farce, especially when they looked at the fate of Tibet on the mainland.[11] Though they rejected the offer, it is interesting to note that Premier Sun, in an address to a conference in June 1982, did suggest that if the political, economic, social, and cultural gaps could be narrowed, the conditions for reunification would be more mature and the obstacles would be lessened at that time.[12] This time, he did not reiterate that Taiwan would never negotiate and that Beijing had to abandon communism. The sense of realism, however, might have been aimed, not so much at the other side of the Taiwan Strait, but more to gain more support from the United States and to court world opinion. It should also be noted that while Sun might have held the view that Taiwan should not permanently reject the peace talks, that opinion might not have been shared by the more conservative members of the KMT. Nonetheless, in early 1984 Premier Sun had to retire from politics prematurely because of poor health.

The KMT's reactions toward the "one country, two systems" proposal were also negative. For example, it was noted that the proposal contained many irreconcilable contradictions and difficulties, and that Taiwan was different from Hong Kong, making it impossible for Taipei to accept the same plan.[13] As far as the Sino-British Declaration on Hong Kong was concerned, Premier Yü Kuo-hwa declared in September 1984 that Taipei would not recognize the agreement on Hong Kong, since the KMT government and not the CCP government should represent China in the talks with Britain. However, he promised to extend his government's support and assistance to the people of Hong Kong in various ways, although he did not make any policy statement on the position of the KMT government with regard to the blossoming trade and other links with Hong Kong after 1997.[14] Chiang Ching-kuo, in his speech on the eve of the National Day of his government in 1984, also attacked the "one-country, two systems" proposal as a "united front conspiracy." According to him, what the Chinese wanted was a China under the three principles of the people, with freedom, democracy, and equality of wealth. He reiterated Premier Yu's rejection of the Sino-British Declaration and promised to support the Chinese in Hong Kong.[15]

In view of the persistent and seemingly obstinate attitude of the KMT toward the "peaceful" initiatives from Beijing, it begs the question of the real reasons for such a posture. From a broader perspective, the principal reason for Taipei's refusal to accept the peace talks is the conflict over the right to rule China.[16] Simply put, any indication to negotiate with the communists would challenge what Taipei calls its legally constituted authority to rule all of China. Thus Sun Yat-sen's three principles of the people have been used by the KMT to counteract the CCP's moves on reunification. As the hope of "recovering the mainland" dwindles, the KMT feels it all the more important to guard jealously its sovereignty over Taiwan. And Taipei knows very well that whatever "benefits" Beijing may bestow upon the KMT, Taiwan will be looked upon by China as a province, with bargaining power accordingly limited in reunification negotiations. It also knows very well that by accepting Beijing's "peace" proposals, Taiwan would lose its international personality and sovereignty; without an international personality and sovereignty, Taiwan fears there would be no legal restraints to prevent Beijing from taking away whatever it promises Taiwan at the time of reunification.[17] To be sure, the KMT had collaborated with the CCP in two united fronts, one in 1924–1927, the other in 1937–1945. However, as noted earlier in Chiang Ching-kuo's comments, the KMT experience in the cooperative effort was a bitter one and the two united fronts ended in bloodshed. In the first united front, the CCP no doubt was more or less decimated by the KMT under Chiang Kai-shek. However, the KMT claimed that the communists were sabotaging the front, thus asking for reprisals. The second united front allowed the CCP to expand its influence in the vacuum left by the KMT in the Second World War. That was decisive in giving the CCP the influence to turn against the KMT after the war. Therefore, the CCP's calling a third united front would just remind the KMT of its humiliation and embarrassment in the hands of the communists in 1949, when it had to retreat to Taiwan. To the KMT leaders, it would be naïve and fruitless to negotiate with the CCP, since the latter could not be trusted to act as agreed. Thus all of Beijing's promises of granting legislative, judicial, administrative, and military autonomy to Taipei are viewed with great skepticism by Taipei. This is especially true when Taipei looks at the example of Tibet, which was taken over by force by the PRC in 1959 despite the promise of regional autonomy. Beijing's use of force to restore law and order in Tibet in October 1987, and again in March 1989 in response to the demonstrations in Lhasa and an upsurge in Tibetian nationalism, certainly was a reminder to Taipei that the proposals from the PRC were mere bait to abosrb Taiwan into the PRC and that force could be used in the process. As far as Hong Kong is concerned, the KMT has great doubts about whether Hong Kong would be given much freedom in the implementation of the "one country, two systems" concept. Beijing's tactics in pressing concessions from London during the Sino-British talks have reinforced Taipei's convictions that to negotiate with the CCP could only bring disaster to Taiwan. As remarked by Taipei's foreign minister Chu Fu-sung, "during the process of negotiations, the British Government was in a posture of concession, retreat and abandonment. It accepted all demands set down by the Chinese communists and disregarded the wishes of the Hong Kong residents."[18] While this may not be a totally accurate description of the Sino-British talks, Taipei's perception clearly suggests that it was unproductive, if not dangerous, to negotiate with the communists. Moreover, even though the CCP has outwardly shown reasonableness in its proposals to court Taipei, it has never ruled out the use of force in reunifying China. It is also pressurizing the United States to cut back its arms sales to Taipei and to isolate Taipei diplomatically. As a result, Taipei does not have much confidence in CCP sincerity. Finally, the ups and downs of the political careers of many Chinese leaders, and the related problems of succession and the four modernizations, have cautioned the KMT that it is not useful to negotiate, at least for the time being, with Chinese leaders who may not be around physically or politically.

Taipei's rejection of Beijing's offer is also based on the domestic situation in Taiwan. Any indications of a willingness to consider the "peaceful" proposals would create great anxiety among the people on the island. For the economy, the fear of a communist takeover might engineer a flight of capital from Taipei to other places. The impact on the financial market in Hong Kong at the time of the Sino-British negotiations probably was a good reminder that this could happen to Taiwan too, if and when there are talks between the two sides. For the military and civilian officials in Taiwan, especially the mainlanders, their worry is what would happen to them if the CCP gains control over the island. Many Taiwanese would like to have an independent Taiwan, if possible. Since this is not feasible, they would like to increase their influence in a Taiwan that remains free of communist control. Their fear is that reunification with the PRC could greatly diminish their impact on the politics of the island. While the CCP may emphasize the feelings and wishes of the Taiwanese, it is possible that it may ignore them in negotiating with the KMT. This is especially true if the CCP senses that the Taiwanese may ask for independence or self-determination leading to independence. The negotiations between Beijing and London on Hong Kong without any representation from the Hong Kong people certainly does not seem to be very encouraging for the Taiwanese.

With an increasingly diversified and pluralistic society in Taiwan, it is quite natural that more and more Taiwanese are entering the KMT government. Notably, the gradual democratization of Taiwan, as analyzed later, would give more opportunities to the Taiwanese, or for that matter, the mainlanders, to take part in the political process. From the KMT's point of view, it is necessary to "Taiwanize" the government; until a sufficient number of Taiwanese are in key positions, it would be unwise to negotiate with the PRC, since this would give rise to suspicions that Taiwanese interests will not be taken into account by the KMT. In fact, high on the KMT agenda is a set of political reforms to consolidate the power of the KMT. Changes in its policy toward the mainland can only be understood in light of the KMT's desire to transform itself into a forward-looking party based on support by the people. The growing pluralistic nature of the Taiwanese society requires that the KMT spend some time at home, rather than thinking about reunification. It may also limit the KMT leaders' freedom of choice, since they will have to take into account the feelings of competing interests, making it more complicated for the Taiwanese government to respond to the proposals from Beijing.

TAIPEI'S STRATEGY TOWARD THE MAINLAND

From Taipei's response to Beijing's "peaceful" overtures, one gets the impression that Taipei has been evasive and that it is not really interested in reunification, at least for the time being. Taipei's seeming rigidity should not, however, disguise the fact that it has become relatively more flexible, starting from the last years of Chiang Ching-kuo. This has been evidenced by the tacit approval of many people-to-people contacts between the two sides in third countries, especially after the U.S. derecognition of Taipei.[19] Taiwan's people have also been visiting the PRC quietly and keeping postal contacts with their relatives via third countries; scholars and scientists from both sides also share membership in international bodies. Taipei apparently has encouraged active participation, even agreeing not to use its official state name or fly its national flag, in *nongovernmental* international organizations in the hope of keeping links with other countries.[20] This has been demonstrated in various events, like the participation of Taiwan in international athletic competitions under the name of "Chinese Taipei." And in the case of the Asian Development Bank, the last major international organization to which Taipei still belongs in its governmental capacity, the KMT decided to stay in the institution after a period of absence and protest despite the bank's ruling to grant entry to China and force Taiwan to change its name to "Taipei, China." Such a move demonstrated the prevalence of the pragmatists in Taipei. It seems that the long-time policy of rejecting dual membership with China in intergovernmental organizations was changing even in the twilight years of Chiang Ching-kuo. This was probably propelled by Taipei's enhanced confidence in its dynamic economic development and its improved military capability. More important, Taipei should be able to see that it would be unwise to walk out of an organization whenever China is present. This would give China the forum and isolate Taiwan further from the international community. More signs of flexibility were detectable when there were negotiations between Taipei's China Airlines (CAL) and Beijing's China Civil Aviation Administration of China (CAAC) officials, when a CAL cargo plane was diverted to China by its captain in 1986. Taipei's decision to allow CAL—a company controlled by the Taipei government—to negotiate with CAAC must have come from the top leadership. The direct talks, and not through an intermediary, demonstrated Taipei's flexibility and willingness to soften its consistent rejection of PRC offers to talk. The talks were a success, with the captain staying behind in China and the return of the two crew members and the aircraft to Taipei. The favorable public opinion on the KMT government's handling of this case probably diluted its negative response to talks with Beijing and reinforced the argument of pragmatists that contact with Beijing can work to Taipei's advantage. As such, Taipei would probably accept talks with the PRC by adopting a case-by-case approach.

More dramatic changes in Taipei's relations with the mainland took place in 1987. First, after lifting martial law in July 1987, Taipei announced that it would relax its ban on importing PRC publications that did not promote communism. The publications could not be imported directly from China, but had to be imported through a third country, probably Hong

Kong, and be reprinted in Taiwan using the traditional, not the simplified, characters. Second, and more important, Taipei dropped its ban on direct travel to Hong Kong and Macao in July 1987, and announced in October 1987 that family visits to the mainland via third countries would be allowed. However, the mainland remained off-limits to serving soldiers and civil servants, at least for a while. In addition, tourism, direct trade, and reciprocal participation by athletic teams in sports events on both sides of the Taiwan Strait were still banned. Taipei also reaffirmed its policy of only granting entry to mainland Chinese who had lived in noncommunist countries for five years or more.[21] Although the KMT still maintained that there was no change in its "three-no" policy, and that permission for family visits to the mainland were based on humanitarian reasons, it was obvious that, in the last years of Chiang Ching-kuo's life, he must have thought of changing Taiwan's policy toward the mainland. As far as the family visits were concerned, Taipei was responding, to a certain extent, to reality. An estimated 10,000 Taiwan people had been visiting the PRC annually before the official approval; the announcement in October 1987 just recognized a fait accompli. More important, Chiang seemed to have come to the conclusion that reunification under the three principles of the people would have to be supplemented, if not modified, by more concrete measures. In view of the rapid socioeconomic changes and the evolving desire to have a more open and democratic society, steps had to be taken to cope with its newly industrializing economy. As always, U.S. pressure to democratize Taipei's political system was present. In addition, the February Revolution in the Philippines overthrowing President Marcos served as a reminder to Chiang of the need to cope with rising expectations. In the sunset of his life, in April 1986, Chiang set up a twelve-man task force of Standing Committee members of the KMT to work out the party's political reforms.[22] The task force was asked to address sensitive issues such as martial law, the ban on new political parties, a rejuvenation of central elective bodies, and a strengthening of local government. These initiatives were aimed not only at improving the KMT influence in Taiwan but probably also at paving the way for a post–Chiang Ching-kuo Taiwan. The task force subsequently proposed a general but still bold six-point reform in the following areas:

1. To conduct large-scale supplementary elections to the central representative organs (the Legislative Yuan, the Control Yuan, and the National Assembly) in order to address the problem of super-annuation and deaths of members.

2. To put local self-government on a legal basis.

3. To simplify the national security laws.

4. To provide a legal basis for formation of new civic associations.

5. To strenghen public order.

6. To strengthen party work.[23]

Chiang, however, asked the task force to work on points three and four first, in view of the great dissatisfaction with martial law and the apparent participation explosion on the island. Notably, the Tang-wai had already founded a quasipolitical party called the Research Association on Public Policy. And despite warnings from the government and Chiang's directive to have dialogues with those from the opposition, leading Tang-wai personalities defied the government by forming the Democratic Progressive Party (DPP) in September 1986. Nonetheless, the KMT did not arrest the DPP leaders, but chose to declare the party illegal and, more important, to expedite reforms on the martial law system and no-new-political-parties ban. Chiang was not unopposed in these moves. Apparently, he was able to have his view prevail, as demonstrated by the decision of the Central Standing Committee, and subsequently the Executive Yuan in October 1986, to draw up plans to replace martial law with a national security law and to allow establishment of new political parties.[24] It is significant to note that the political reforms did not focus on Taiwan's relations with the mainland per se. Apparently, that was not really a priority of the KMT leadership. Also, the KMT leadership could not stop—and chose not to act against—the emerging opposition. Instead, it bowed to the inevitable by expediting reforms in at least these two areas. While this may improve the KMT image at home and abroad, the KMT could not but be concerned with likely consequences that could threaten the KMT's power and the security of Taiwan. With the lifting of martial law and the new political parties ban, the KMT would have to face challenges from emergent forces. More pertinent to this study, the years of separation from the mainland— ironically the KMT's own doing—would also dilute, if not change, the desire of the people in Taiwan to look at the mainland as part of their body politic. The danger was that the opposition or other emerging forces and separatist movements might be intertwined or combined, making them not only a formidable challenge to the KMT but shattering its long-held one-China policy. As Chiang surveyed the situation on the island, he, just as his adversaries on the mainland had, would be concerned with possibilities of independence or self-determination for Taiwan. And the trend is that, whether they are mainlanders or Taiwanese, the people's identification with the mainland would be nebulous, making it plausible for an independence movement to gain momentum. As a result, lifting martial law in July 1987—the first of the political reforms implemented—could not be introduced without other precautionary measures to preserve the KMT's power. It is in this light that permission for family visits to the mainland can be understood as other than for the humanitarian reasons cited by KMT officials. For one thing, the family visits were a way to rekindle the ties between Taiwan and the mainland before the two sides drifted too far apart. As the first major KMT move toward the mainland, the family visit rule could dilute the influence of the independence movement and consolidate or perpetuate KMT rule in Taiwan. In addition, Chiang probably did not want to be remembered as a leader who was responsible for the separation of Taiwan from the mainland. Since the infuence of the Chiang family would be diluted (Chiang Ching-kuo had said that Taiwan after him would not be headed by any member of the Chiang family), it was possible that Chiang took the initial steps to link the two sides of the Taiwan Strait so that history would be kinder to him. And if ever there was to be a change in Taiwan's mainland policy, it would be easier to do under Chiang, in view of his dominance in the politics of the island. Chiang's stature proved to be most useful in overcoming the opposition, especially from the still-powerful security agency officials and conservative party leaders. Chiang might also have sided with the so-called liberals, who would like to adopt a more pragmatic policy toward the mainland. Notably, the reform-minded secretary-general of the KMT, Lee Huan, tried to tone down the rhetoric about "recovering" China under the banner of the three principles of the people. Instead, Lee remarked in September 1987 that the KMT did not intend to replace the communists on the mainland. According to him, the strategy henceforth was to launch a "political offensive" to demand the democratization of politics, freedom of the press, and the opening of the economy on the mainland.[25] This no doubt reflected a realistic assessment of the ability of the KMT and the place of the CCP on the mainland. It was probably clear to Lee Huan and others that it was not likely the KMT would be able to recapture the mainland, at least not in the near future.[26] With enhanced confidence as a result of Taiwan's remarkable economic performance and with plans to liberalize the polity and economy, pragmatists such as Lee Huan intended to compete with the mainland by demonstrating the success of the "Taiwan model." Renewed contacts with the mainland via allowing family visits was just one step in this direction, as the Chinese on both sides of the

Taiwan Strait would surely find out for themselves which system had done better since 1949.

As Taiwan eased its policy on family visits to the mainland, practical arguments to link up even more with the other side came forward. Notably, some businesses in Taiwan would like to branch out into China. The rise of protectionism in the West, including Taiwan's major trade partner, the United States, has forced the business community to look for alternatives. Taiwan's huge trade surplus with the United States has strained Taipei-Washington relations as well as put pressure on Taiwan to increase the value of the Taiwan dollar, open its market to the outside world, and decrease its exports to the United States. To be sure, the Taiwan dollar had been appreciating, putting pressure on Taiwan's export industries. In addition, increasing labor costs, a lack of natural resources, and surplus capital have induced businesses in Taiwan to look for new trade and investment opportunities. And China, in the midst of the four modern-izations, probably could offer such opportunities if not for the restrictions of the Taipei government. No doubt, businesses could conduct trade with and invest on the mainland, especially through third areas like Hong Kong; but these actions risk incurring the wrath of the KMT government. Thus the hope was that trade with and investment on the mainland, especially through third countries, would be condoned officially later on.

The death of Chiang Ching-kuo in January 1988 no doubt ended an important chapter in Chinese history, especially in Taiwan. In the case of the KMT, it marked the end of the Chiang command. The problem of succession had to be faced squarely. As it turned out, the change of guard was conducted quite smoothly, without chaos and uncertainty. Vice-President Lee Teng-hui was sworn in four hours after the death of Chiang. Despite efforts to delay or derail the selection of Lee Teng-hui as acting chairman of the KMT, notably by the so-called palace faction including Yu Kuo-hwa and Madam Chiang Kai-shek, he stepped into the shoes of his mentor. However, Lee, the first native-born Taiwanese to head the KMT, not only had to establish his rapport with the other power blocs headed by Lee Huan, secretary-general of the KMT; Premier Yu Kuo-hwa of the conservatives; and General Hau Pei-tsun from the military, but he had to continue Chiang's unfinished reform initiatives and his new direc-tions toward the mainland.

Apparently, Lee was not in a hurry to introduce more measures to ease relations between the two sides of the Taiwan Strait, although he had headed the five-man task force that worked out the family visitation policy.[27] In fact, the major concern of the new president and acting KMT chairman was to tackle domestic issues. Faced with public unrest, the KMT government had to deal with what the spokesman of the Taipei government called the "labor pains" of introducing political democraticization, which included termination of martial law and the relaxation of restrictions on foreign exchange in July 1987 and the lifting of restrictions on newspapers and new newspaper registrations in January 1988.[28] The 13th KMT Congress, held in July 1988, also required immediate attention to the transfer of power in the party. As a result, amidst the delicate situation in post-Chiang Taiwan in 1988, the KMT could not possibly ponder its strategy toward the mainland. While it is beyond the purview of this study to examine in detail the power politics in post-Chiang Taiwan, it is significant to note that the July 1988 KMT congress gave Lee and his reform-minded colleagues a clear endorsement. Inner-party democracy also seems to have been respected to a certain extent when grassroots party members voted in delegates to the congress. This was also evidenced in the election of the central committee members, where at least half of the candidates were nominated by the delegates.[29] The result of the election witnessed a rise from 20 to 45 percent of Taiwanese in the central committee. More important, the number of Taiwanese in the Central Standing Committee changed from 14 to 16, a simple majority. The average age of the Central Standing Committee also fell from 70.67 to 63.68, as a result of retirement by some of the old guard.[30] The subsequent cabinet reshuffle retained the unpopular conservative, Yu Kuo-hwa, as premier. However, in what was lauded as the "Lee Teng-hui Era," there was new blood in the cabinet. Of the 15 new appointees, 8 were Taiwanese—the first time Taiwanese ever formed a majority in the cabinet. A woman, Shirley Kuo, was appointed as a minister for the first time.[31] In addition, President Lee seemed keen to rely on some forward-looking technocrats in their mid-50s to carry forward the political reforms mapped out by the late Chiang Ching-kuo.

As far as the KMT's strategy toward the mainland was concerned, the government finally allowed letters from the mainland to be delivered in Taiwan starting from March 1988, and it lifted a 39-year-old ban on sending mail from Taiwan to the mainland in April 1988.[32] The letters from China were delivered after the Taiwan post office stamped the words "Reunification under the Three Principles of the People" on the envelopes, while those from Taiwan to the mainland would be forwarded by the Red Cross Society in Taipei through Hong Kong.[33] The KMT also decided, in its 13th Party Congress and its aftermath, to gradually broaden its contacts with the mainland. Notably, it decided to condone Taiwan investments on the mainland via third areas. In that connection, it legalized the two-way trade with China through Hong Kong and other third countries, and it officially approved a list of commodities that Taiwan could import indirectly from the PRC. Policy guidelines on visits between the two sides of the Taiwan Strait also seemed to have been relaxed considerably. As analyzed in Chapter 5, among these was the disclosure that Taiwan would review requests from mainland Chinese to visit Taiwan for funerals or when direct relatives were seriously ill. Eventually, a plan allowing mainlanders to visit dying relatives or to attend funerals of family members in Taiwan went into effect in November 1988.[34] Intellectuals who "denounce Marxism-Leninism or who have fought to maintain academic freedom" might also be allowed to visit Taiwan.[35] These measures included mainland Chinese who previously were barred from entering Taiwan under the National Security Law unless they were at least 75 years old or under 16 and had relatives in Taiwan, or unless they had lived as a permanent resident in a "free country or area" for at least five years.[36] And for visits to Taiwan by intellectuals from the mainland, a first group of five mainland graduate students studying in the United States came to Taiwan in December 1988, under Taipei's program to give intellectuals, athletes, and other outstanding Chinese personalities opportunities to observe Taiwan first hand.[37] The KMT also agreed that it would study the possibility of allowing participation by its athletes in international competitions sponsored by international organizations on the mainland. Finally, it would consider allowing its journalists to go there on assignment. This last consideration was probably necessary in view of the fact that some journalists had already gone to the mainland in defiance of the ban, notably the first-ever open reporting trip to China by two reporters from the *Independence Evening Post* in September 1987. It was obvious that the KMT would have to adopt face-saving measures to meet the demands of journalists on the island. Other guidelines from the KMT congress included permission to import academic, technological, literary, and artistic publications from the mainland via third areas after screening. Copyright of mainland authors would be protected according to the KMT.[38]

From events later on in 1988, it seems that more people from Taiwan, other than those for family visits, were allowed to go to China. Notably, and as analyzed in Chapter 5, three scientists from Taiwan were sent to attend the annual conference of the International Council of Scientific Unions in Beijing.[39] It was also known that the KMT government was considering allowing private citizens to attend conferences on the mainland sponsored by international organizations.[40] As more and more such measures were introduced, the KMT, as noted in the introduction, finally formed a nine-member group and a cabinet-level task force to coordinate these activities.

The documentation of these piecemeal measures introduced by the KMT around the 13th Party Congress is meant to demonstrate that although the KMT was preoccupied with its own reforms and reorganization so as to meet future challenges, it also selectively broadened contacts with the mainland. The KMT's assessment of its overall open-door policy toward the mainland evidently had produced optimism that such contacts would promote the "Taiwan model." More important, they would not pose a threat toward the security of the island. Thus, in the case of the family visitation program, it was concluded after a six-month study that such a program did not present any security problems for Taiwan.[41] Taipei's increasing confidence in dealing with the other side was evident. In fact, such confidence had prompted some in the KMT old guard, notably Chen Li-fu, to come up with an unrealistic suggestion of offering U.S. $10 billion from Taipei's enormous foreign exchange reserves to help the mainland, provided the latter would renounce the use of force in the reunification of China and give up the CCP's four cardinal principles.[42]

The steps taken by the KMT and its government in easing its relations with Beijing have been guided by a number of criteria in its mainland policy. First, it is significant to note that the KMT has ruled out official links with Beijing. Thus, although follow-up measures gave practically all Taiwan residents, including those who had no real family roots in China, the right to visit the mainland, senior government officials, security and intelligence personnel, and members of the elective bodies were in principle banned from these visits. To make its point, the KMT expelled Hu Chiu-yuan, a senior member of the Legislative Yuan from the party in September 1988 because he made an unauthorized trip to Beijing and, more seriously, he had discussed the reunification issue with leaders of the CCP.[43] Second, and in connection with the first point, the KMT restricted the contacts to the people-to-people level. Civic organizations like the Red Cross were asked to handle the increasing contacts. It would even create unofficial organizations to do it, if necessary; for example, it created the Union of Scientific Societies for the three scientists to attend the International Council of Scientific Unions in Beijing in 1988 so that Academia Sinica, an official institution, would not be involved. The extra precaution taken by the KMT to relegate these contacts to the unofficial level allowed the party to adopt a more detached position to monitor the consequences of such encounters. It would, of course, allow the KMT to claim that the "three-no" principle remains untainted and it would not give the impression to the CCP, and especially to some political forces at home, that it has compromised with the other side. Third, the contacts made were conducted via third areas. This indirect route again allows the KMT to claim that it still adheres closely to the "three-no" policy. However, it could also be that such a communication pattern tones down the "China fever" in Taiwan and lessens the direct impact on Taiwan to a certain extent. The extra precautions in indirect communication links may also be considered necessary for the security of the island, where there is still a sense of threat from the communists. As such, the use of third areas like Hong Kong will be continued for quite some time. And as far as Hong Kong is concerned, it seems that after a careful reassessment, the KMT had decided that its organizations would stay in the colony until 1997.[44] The KMT probably had concluded that it would be difficult to replace Hong Kong's role completely because of the latter's geographical proximity to the mainland and its wide range of networks and connections with the PRC. For practical purposes, Hong Kong will, at least in the near future, continue to serve Taiwan and other countries as an attractive base for moves into China. Fourth, the KMT evidently is interested only in having incremental changes in its policy toward the mainland. The readjustment is also selective, depending on whether it is helpful to the KMT and how strong the pressure is at home to change the policy.[45] Such strategy is evidenced by the family visitation program. As analyzed in detail in Chapter 5, this was a response to domestic pressure, to a certain extent. Many of the mainlanders and old soldiers who followed the KMT to Taiwan were homesick. They wanted to return to their hometowns and the mainland during their life time. Moreover, academics and the opposition had been criticizing the government's "three-no" policy as cruel and inhumane. These domestic pressures subsequently helped force the KMT to lift the ban on direct visits to Hong Kong and Macao in July 1987. This was a precursor for family visits, since most Taiwanese went to Hong Kong so as to visit the mainland. Official approval for such visits via third areas eventually came in November 1987. Even KMT cadres and public servants would eventually be considered for approval to make a trip to the PRC. This incremental strategy again demonstrated the KMT's caution. Too big a step might result in irreparable damage, beyond the control of the KMT. As disclosed by a KMT source, Taipei's policy toward the mainland was divided into stages, and every stage was examined and adjusted. It was designed to give the KMT more initiatives and flexibility in dealing with the CCP.[46] Finally, the contacts were more from one direction—namely, from Taiwan to the mainland and not the other way round. At the very beginning, the contacts actually were all from Taiwan to the mainland. The primary concern was and is the security of the island. As Taipei began to see that the visitation program was not a threat to its security, some people from the mainland, such as those attending funerals or visiting sick relatives and selected intellecutuals, were allowed to visit Taipei. Still, it was only a trickle and the KMT exercised extreme caution. With more self-confidence and with the realization that it could be useful to promote the Taiwan experience, the KMT may allow more people from the mainland, such as the Taiwanese living in the PRC, to visit Taiwan in the future.

Although the KMT reiterates that it is still holding the "three-no" policy in dealing with the mainland, it is obvious that the policy has been modified, if not changed, by the developments after November 1987. However, it is significant to point out that the "three-no" policy is only part of Taipci's attitude toward the other side. In conjunction with it, and actually in contrast to it, Taipei is launching a political offensive to promote the "Taiwan model" on the mainland. In many ways, the "three-no" policy, the promotion of the "Taiwan model," and its related sanctioning of contacts with the mainland have consolidated the KMT's rule on the island. As revealed by Lee Teng-hui, Taipei's policy toward the mainland aims primarily to preserve the stability and security of Taiwan. It is a means to an end not directly related to reunification.[47] Quite clearly, the KMT was under domestic pressure to introduce new measures in dealing with the mainland. Since it cannot stop the flow of the Taiwan people going to China for family reunions, pleasure, trade, and investments, it may as well make use of the situation and make the best of it. It is also pragmatic enough to fine-tune its policy to a level that could help it politically and economically. As far as reunification is concerned, the KMT is trying its level best to stall the move in that direction so that it can strengthen its bargaining position. For the time being, the KMT under Lee Teng-hui is essentially more concerned with its agenda for political reform and other issues at home. And as far as political reforms are concerned, party organization, democracy, and discipline in the KMT will have to be emphasized to strengthen the KMT's ability to meet future challenges. The KMT government under Lee also has been preoccupied with introducing a program of political reforms including legalization of new political parties and registration of civic organizations; retirement of old deputies of the Legislative Yuan, the Control Yuan, and the National Assembly representing constituencies on the mainland; and giving Taiwan's provincial government and its assembly more autonomy. This preoccupation of the KMT highlights its governance in Taiwan; whatever changes come in its mainland policy are relegated to secondary importance.

CONCLUDING OBSERVATIONS

It is important to note that, in spite of all the changes in its policy toward the mainland in the last years of Chiang Ching-kuo and early years of Lee Teng-hui, the KMT still clings to its own one-China policy. As noted, these changes were made on the principle that the security of Taiwan and power of the KMT would not be affected. As for the contacts between the two sides, dialogues between the CCP and KMT at the top level were absent, although there were some low-level or unauthorized contacts. The KMT continues to reject the "one country, two systems" proposal, notwithstanding its sanctioning of some practical steps to ease relations. In principle, it remains anticommunist. The "China fever" in Taiwan, as exemplified by the barrage of discussions and demands to open Taiwan to the mainland and introduce more contact with the mainland, no doubt has acted as a catalyst for such changes. However, this fever may not necessarily reflect a desire for reunification by the people of Taiwan; it may only show that there should be a period of peace and communication between the two sides. Whether this might eventually lead to reunification remains to be seen. In fact, it is possible that such contacts have reminded many in Taiwan that there is a wide gap between the two sides. Whether this may strengthen the latent or overt desire to have an independent Taiwan, free to deal with the mainland and other nations and enjoy the fruits of progress, remains to be seen. It is also possible that such gaps may strengthen support of the KMT and its efforts to postpone the talks on reunification.

Toward the end of the 1980s, Taiwan had moved itself from a society with a per capita income of U.S. $50 in 1949 to about U.S. $6,000 by late 1988.[48] Taiwan's remarkable economic success story no doubt has emboldened the KMT to face the challenges of political democratization at home. It has also enhanced its self-confidence in the conduct of its international relations. In terms of its strategy toward the mainland, the KMT feels relaxed enough to allow indirect contact, provided the security of Taiwan is not threatened. Based on this assumption, and provided that the KMT finds it necessary, further measures will be introduced. In this connection, Taipei has found it necessary to work on a special law to govern contacts between the two sides by late 1988. This law to be drafted by the Taipei government will address disputes and problems related to marriage, property ownership, and inheritance in view of the many communications and people-to-people contacts between the mainland and Taiwan.[49] But as highlighted by President Lee, Taipei will "seek better methods of building a consensus among the different sectors of Taiwan's society before instituting additional measures to control the development of Taiwan-mainland relations."[50] As such, Taipei certainly is not in a hurry to move its society closer to the mainland.

In the conduct of its foreign relations, Taipei's enhanced confidence and the rise of pragmatism in the KMT have led Taiwan to adopt a flexible diplomacy toward participation in world affairs, as analyzed in detail in Chapter 4. Suffice it to note at this point that President Lee Teng-hui declared, in a conference held in Taipei in November 1988, that Taiwan "is now sufficiently armed with economic muscle to take its place in international organizations and make a meaningful contribution to the world."[51] That was in fact the first public declaration by the president that Taipei was set to assume a major role in key international organizations. Earlier, the Taipei delegation reappeared at the Asian Development Bank meeting. Although it protested the designation of "Taipei, China" to its delegation, Taipei's decision to return to the ADB suggested that it would later seek membership in other international organizations such as the General Agreement on Tariffs and Trade (GATT), as part of Lee's call to play a role in key international bodies. In addition, Taipei had set up a U.S. $1 billion Overseas Economic Cooperation and Development Fund in late 1988 for economic aid to developing countries friendly to Taiwan.[52] It has also sent more than 30 agricultural aid teams to about 20 countries in the past three decades to build good-will with other states. Moreover, Taiwan businesses have been broadening their trade markets in view of the West's protectionism and have directed their capital abroad because of a rise in production costs at home in recent years. As a result, there has been a need to broaden Taipei's contacts, and the Taipei government is prepared to do so. Notably, although Taipei had established diplomatic relations with only 23 countries by early 1989, its wealth and aid programs would prove to be major inducements for other countries to make friends with Taiwan.[53] Besides, it has established what is called "practical and substantive" relations with more than 120 countries.[54] More interestingly, President Lee paid a visit to Singapore in March 1989, his first trip abroad since succeeding Chiang Ching-kuo and the first such trip abroad by a Taipei head of state in 12 years.[55]

President Lee went to Singapore as planned despite the remark made by Goh Chok Tong, first deputy prime minister and minister for defense of Singapore, in an interview just before the visit. Goh said that Singapore would establish diplomatic ties with Beijing after Indonesia had resumed its official ties with the PRC, as revealed by Jakarta's agreement to start the negotiations to do so in February 1989 when President Suharto attended the funeral of Japan's Emperor Hirohito.[56] In that regard, Singapore's prime minister Lee Kuan Yew reiterated toward the end of President Lee's visit that Singapore had a one-China policy; he estimated that Indonesia would take a year to resume official ties with Beijing, and his government would follow suit in a few months after that.[57] Nonetheless, President Lee was given an official reception in Singapore, which had no diplomatic relations with Taipei or Beijing. He was addressed as "President Lee from Taiwan" in public, notably in the well-briefed mass media in Singapore. Taipei's official reaction, as disclosed by President Lee in the press conference when he went back to Taipei, was that his government should not be too fuzzy about its name. And although he was not satisfied with the term "President Lee from Taiwan," he thought it should be accepted.[58] As to whether he would like to have similar visits, he was unequivocal in stating that if there were a need for it, he would go out "one hundred times" visiting other countries for the sake of Taiwan.[59] Lee mentioned specifically that he did not care if Singapore had formal ties with Beijing as long as the former continued to upgarde its relations with Taipei.[60] He also said that he would visit Singapore or any other friendly nation with a Chinese embassy if he were invited.[61] As regards Taipei's "flexible diplomacy," he emphasized that such a policy should not be carried out in leaps and bounds, but rather step by step.[62] It was apparent that President Lee did not fall for a high-level, idealistic type of flexible diplomacy. A sense of realism seemed to have prevailed again in his government's efforts to carve out for itself a place in diplomacy, as analyzed further in Chapter 4. Taipei's renewed activism and pragmatism in international affairs no doubt has created misgivings from the PRC, culminating in the latter's charge that Taipei was trying to promote "two Chinas."[63] Predictably, this was refuted by Taipei. From all indications, it seems that Taipei will continue to make efforts to strengthen ties with other countries, even if they have diplomatic ties with Beijing, so that Taipei can play a more active role internationally and can defuse Beijing's efforts to isolate Taipei or downgrade it to a local government of China.

NOTES

1. See, for example, *Taiwan Yanjiu Jikan* (Taiwan Research Quarterly), No. 4 (1986), p. 66.

2. For the full text of the statements, see *Zhongyang Yuekan* (Central Monthly), 16 January 1979, pp. 7–15.

3. Ibid., p. 9.

4. For a full text of the declaration, see *Central Monthly*, 16 February 1979, pp. 7–9. The text was translated into English and published in the same issue, pp. 174–179.

5. Ibid., p. 8.

6. Ibid., p. 9.

7. See, for example, *Far Eastern Economic Review* (FEER), 26 January 1979, p. 26.

8. Far Eastern Economic Review, *Asia Yearbook 1980* (Hong Kong: Far Eastern Economic Review, 1980), p. 288.

9. See, for example, Lu Keng, ed., *Zhonguo Tongyi Wenti Lunzhan* (Debates on Problems of the Reunification of China), Hong Kong: Baixing Wenhua Shiye Pte. Ltd., 1988, p. 86; *Central Monthly*, 16 January 1980, pp. 22–23, and 16 December 1981, p. 23.

10. *Central Monthly*, 10 October 1981, pp. 6–9.

11. See, for example, Ibid., p. 13.

12. Paraphrased from Sun's speech quoted in Li Da, ed., *Meitai Guanxi Yu Zhongguo Tongyi*, (U.S.–Taiwan Relations and the Reunification of China) (Hong Kong: Wide Angle Press, 1987), p. 92.

13. See, for example, Yu-ming Shaw, "An ROC View of the Hong Kong Issue," *Issues and Studies*, June 1986, pp. 21–30.

14. For details, see Ibid., pp. 23–24.

15. For details, see *Central Monthly*, October 1984, pp. 6–8.

16. The following is partially extracted from Lee Lai To, "The PRC and Taiwan—Moving Toward a More Realistic Relationship," in Robert Scalapino, et al., eds., *Asian Security Issues: Regional and Global* (Berkeley, Calif.: Institute of East Asian studies, 1988), pp. 172–74.

17. See, for example, the argument put forward by Hungdah Chiu, "The 1984 Sino-British Agreement on Hong Kong and Its Implications on China's Unification," *Issues and Studies*, April 1985, p. 19.

18. Quoted in Hungdah Chiu, Ibid., pp. 21–22.

19. *FEER*, 20 July 1979, p. 21.

20. Yu-ming Shaw, "Taiwan: A View From Taipei," *Foreign Affairs*, Summer 1985, p. 1054.

21. The five-year period was changed to three to four years, starting in late 1988. See *United Daily Press* (Taipei), 22 September 1988.

22. *Central Daily* (Taipei), 10 April 1986.

23. Yangsun Chou and Andrew J. Nathan, "Democratizing Transition in Taiwan," *Asian Survey*, March 1987, p. 286.

24. Far Eastern Economic Review, *Asia Yearbook 1987*, Hong Kong: Far Eastern Economic review, 1987, p. 249.

25. Li Da, ed., *Kaifang Taiwan* (The Opening of Taiwan) (Hong Kong: Wide Angle Press, 1988), p. 36.

26. The following analysis is extracted from Lee Lai To, "Taiwan and the Reunification of China," *Pacific Review*, Vol. 2, No. 2, 1989, p. 135.

27. For Lee's role in the visitation program, see Li Da, ed., *Lee Teng-hui Yu Taiwan* (Lee Teng-hui and Taiwan) (Hong Kong: Wide Angle Press, 1988), pp. 68–73.

28. *Free China Journal* (FCJ), 19 December 1988, p. 5.

29. See *FCJ*, 18 July 1988.
30. Ibid.
31. For details, see *FCJ*, 25 July 1988, p. 1.
32. *Straits Times* (Singapore), 17 April 1988.
33. Ibid.
34. See *FCJ*, 7 November 1988.
35. Ibid., 18 July 1988.
36. As noted in footnote 21, this was shortened to three to four years in 1988. The permanent residency requirement was also scrapped. See *United Daily News*, 22 September 1988.
37. *FCJ*, 26 December 1988.
38. Ibid., 18 July 1988.
39. Ibid., 17 October 1988.
40. Ibid.
41. Ibid., 1 August 1988, p. 2.
42. Ibid., 18 July 1988, and *The Nineties* (Hong Kong), October 1988, p. 48.
43. *FCJ*, 24 October 1988.
44. *The Nineties*, April 1988, pp. 42–44.
45. See the remarks of Ma Yinjeou in *Qingnian Ribao* (Taipei), 12 November 1988.
46. See the interview of James Soong, then deputy secretary-general of the KMT in *Chaoliu Yuekan* (Tide Monthly), 15 August 1988, p. 32.
47. *The Nineties*, February 1989, p. 51.
48. *FCJ*, 19 December 1988.
49. Ibid.
50. Ibid., 9 January 1989.
51. *FCJ*, 21 November 1988.
52. Ibid., 9 January 1989.
53. Ibid., 12 January 1989.
54. Ibid., 6 March 1989.
55. Ibid., 23 February 1989.
56. *Straits Times*, 2 and 3 March 1989.
57. Ibid., 10 March 1989.
58. *Hong Kong Times* (Hong Kong), 10 March 1989.
59. Ibid.
60. *FCJ*, 13 March 1989.
61. Ibid.
62. Ibid.
63. Ibid., 23 January 1989.

3

A Role for the Other Major Powers?

Although Beijing reiterates that reunification of China is a domestic issue which brooks no outside interference, and that Taipei certainly does not like outsiders to egg it on to talking about reunification, it is obvious that the international environment, especially the politics of the major powers, could wield considerable influence on the development of the Taiwan Strait. In the case of the major powers, the United States has undisputable links with China and Taiwan, and it could play a role in reunification. In fact, Beijing is interested in asking the United States to promote the reunification of China, as noted in Chapter 1. However, unlike the reunification of the other divided or formerly divided nations—Korea, Germany, and Vietnam—reunification of China directly involves a major power—the PRC—and an economic upstart friendly toward the United States—Taiwan—making it an extremely delicate and sensitive situation. As all students of international relations know too well, the foreign policy of a nation, be it the United States or another, is defined in terms of its national interests. It is the purpose of this chapter to examine, from this perspective, the U.S. policy in the 1980s toward reunification of China. In that connection, the position of the other major powers—the Soviet Union and Japan—will also be scrutinized to ascertain to what extent major power politics are of relevance.

THE U.S. STRATEGY

Ever since President Truman's historic decision in June 1950 to reverse the hands-off policy in Taiwan and declare that the determination of the future of Taiwan "must await the restoration of security in the Pacific, a peace settlement with Japan, or consideration by the United Nations," the Taiwan issue has become a bone of contention in Sino–U.S. relations.[1] The consolidation of Washington-Taipei relations after the Korean War in fact became one of the cornerstones of U.S. policy toward the Far East. However, with changed international developments, especially with the growing desire to disengage at least partially from abroad as exemplified by the Nixon Doctrine and the need to build a constructive relationship between Washington and Beijing to counter Moscow, the United States under Richard Nixon began to build its rapport with the PRC. The problem for the United States was that, while it had to break the ice in its cold war with China as the latter emerged as a major power in a multipolar world, it did not want to be seen as leaving an old ally in the lurch. This was particularly true because Taipei had been a successful example of U.S. aid and support. The United States would like to continue its commitment to Taipei, especially in security matters, but often-times it finds it difficult to do so under the critical eyes of Beijing. While it would like to leave the Chinese on both sides of the Taiwan Strait to settle their differences, it does not want to give undue advantage to the PRC by withdrawing completely from Taiwan.

The dilemma of the U.S. normalization policy with China could be detected in the Nixon administration. While it was clear that Nixon was keen to promote the Sino–U.S. rapprochement, his administration fought to keep a seat for Taipei in the United Nations at the time when Secretary of State Henry Kissinger was in Beijing, arranging President Nixon's visit to China. When the Shanghai Communiqué was signed in February 1972, the United States acknowledged and did not challenge that "all Chinese on either side of the Taiwan Strait maintain there is but one China and that Taiwan is a part of China."[2] It reaffirmed the U.S. intention for "a peaceful settlement of the Taiwan question by the Chinese themselves."[3] The emphasis on "a peaceful settlement of the Taiwan question by the Chinese themselves" actually has become the cornerstone of U.S. policy toward the reunification of China, although the term *reunification* was not used by the United States. On the surface, it seems that the United States would like to adopt a detached attitude toward reunification. However, the very fact that the United States had asked for a "peaceful settlement" made U.S. detachment from the Chinese civil war impossible, as analyzed later on.

The Shanghai Communiqué did not really indicate when or on what other terms the United States expected to normalize relations with the

PRC. It also did not mention the Washington-Taipei diplomatic relations and the Mutual Defense Treaty, although Washington did declare its ultimate objective to withdraw its military forces and installations from Taipei. In actual practice, Washington-Taipei relations did not seem to have changed much in substance immediately, although Taipei was shocked and alarmed by the détente. To calm the KMT government, Washington repeatedly tried to assure Taipei that the United States would honor its commitments, including the Mutual Defense Treaty before and after Nixon's visit to China.[4] However, it was obvious that the United States was determined to continue to normalize relations with the PRC. This was demonstrated by the establishment of liaison offices in each other's capitals before full-fledged diplomatic relations would be formed. The United States, nonetheless, was not willing to forsake Taiwan. In fact, instead of allowing Taipei's representation in the United States to decrease, it authorized Taipei to open three new consulates. Naturally, the PRC was displeased and considered progress in U.S.–PRC normalization too slow.

When Jimmy Carter became president in 1977, he made it clear that normalization with China should not endanger the security of the people of Taiwan and that the United States did not want to see the Taiwanese people punished or attacked.[5] However, because of his wider strategic concern, especially the triangular relations among the United States, the USSR, and the PRC, Carter eventually decided to establish diplomatic relations with Beijing in January 1979, as announced by the United States and by the PRC in December 1978. By that time, many of the noncommunist states had moved faster than the United States in establishing formal ties with Beijing. The U.S. announcement thus was not a big surprise to its allies. In the announcement, the United States recognized the PRC as the sole legal government of China. The United States reiterated its stand that it "acknowledges the Chinese position that there is but one China and Taiwan is part of China."[6] In that connection, the United States would sever diplomatic relations with Taipei, terminate its Mutual Defense Treaty with Taiwan a year from January 1979, and withdraw U.S. forces from Taiwan within four months. The announcement did not mention a unilateral U.S. commitment to Taipei's security nor did it require the PRC to refrain from the use of force in reunifying China. However, it did reiterate that the "United States *continues* to have an interest in the peaceful resolution of the Taiwan issue and expects that the Taiwan issue will be settled peacefully by the Chinese themselves."[7] This was apparently rebuffed by the Chinese in a statement accompanying the announcement. In it, Beijing stated that "as for the way of bringing Taiwan back to the embrace of the motherland and reunifying the country, it is entirely China's internal affair."[8] However, it was clearly understood that the United States could maintain unofficial relations with Taipei and the PRC would not object to that. As stated in the joint communiqué, "the *people* of the United States will maintain cultural, commercial and other unofficial relations with the *people* of Taiwan."[9] The condonation of people-to-people and unofficial relations between Washington and Taipei did not conceal the fact that there were serious differences between Beijing and Washington on arms sales to Taiwan. As disclosed by Premier Hua Guofeng in a press conference, "the U.S. side mentioned that after normalization it would continue to sell limited amount of arms to Taiwan for defensive purposes. We [the PRC] made it clear that we absolutely would not agree to this."[10] The difference on arms sales to Taiwan proved to be a major conflict between China and subsequent U.S. administrations.

To maintain its unofficial ties with Taipei, Washington finally set up the American Institute in Taiwan (AIT), staffed by diplomats or other civil servants "temporarily" on leave of absence from the U.S. government. As a concession to Taiwan, the United States also allowed the KMT government to create a Coordination Council for North American Affairs with several branches as a counterpart of the AIT. As it turns out, the two organizations perform most of the functions of a diplomatic mission. More important, the Taiwan Relations ACT (TRA) was approved in April 1979 after extensive discussions between congressional leaders and the Carter administration. The act stated clearly that the policy of the United States "to establish diplomatic relations with the People's Republic of China rests upon the expectation that the future will be determined by peaceful means."[11] It stated also that the United States would "consider any effort to determine the future of Taiwan by other than peaceful means, including by boycotts or embargoes, a threat to the peace and security of the Western Pacific area and of grave concern to the United States."[12] Finally, the act allowed the United States to provide Taipei with arms of a "defensive" character. Indeed, the act almost revived pledges of the Mutual Defense Treaty, which would expire on December 31, 1979, and even went further in extending coverage to protect Taiwan from boycotts and embargoes not mentioned in the treaty. To a large extent, it went to the very edge of undoing the goodwill built up in the normalization of relations with the PRC, which objected vehemently to this act since it considered it interference in the domestic politics of China and a restoration of a two-China policy. Naturally, Beijing called for its abrogation. But for Washington, the act was a clear example of the impact of bipartisan politics on its policy toward China. It substantiated and satisfied the need to fulfill U.S. moral obligations to a friend.

When Ronald Reagan became president in January 1981, his pro-Taipei orientation, notably his campaign speech calling for the reestablishment of official ties with Taipei, did not stop him from being pragmatic enough to notify Beijing of his desire to maintain close relations with China and that he supported the joint communiqué of December 15, 1978. The early years of the Reagan administration apparently still banked on building a strategic alliance with Beijing to counter the perceived Soviet threat. Among other things, Reagan authorized Secretary of State Alexander Haig to notify the Chinese that the United States was willing to consider requests for U.S. weapons on a case-by-case basis. Washington indicated that it would also liberalize technology exports to China. Reagan probably hoped that, by doing this, it would soften Beijing's opposition to U.S. arms sales to Taipei and his pro-Taipei statements. However, the Chinese were not really at ease when Reagan and some of his subordinates stated that the TRA would be implemented fully. Of special concern to Beijing in early 1981 was the possible sale of FX jet planes to Taipei. The United States finally decided in January 1982 not to sell the FX planes but to coproduce the F-5E with Taipei. While the Reagan administration, in deference to Beijing, considered the decision not to sell FX planes to Taiwan a concession to the PRC, the Chinese, however, were not satisfied and reiterated their demand that the United States specify the qualitative, quantitative, and time limits on arms sales to Taiwan.

After intensive negotiations between Beijing and Washington, a joint communiqué was signed on August 17, 1982. In it, Washington declared that it "does not seek to carry out a long-term policy of arms sales to Taiwan, that its arms sales to Taiwan will not exceed, in either qualitative or quantitative terms, the level of those supplied in recent years since the establishment of diplomatic relations" in 1979 and that the United States "intends to reduce gradually its arms sales to Taiwan, leading over a period of time to a final resolution."[13] As far as U.S. policy toward the reunification of China is concerned, it is interesting to note that the August 1982 communiqué stated that the United States had no intention of "interfering in China's internal affairs, or pursuing a policy of 'two Chinas' or 'one China, one Taiwan.' "[14] It continued to say that the United States "understands and appreciates the Chinese policy of striving for a peaceful resolution of the Taiwan question as indicated in China's Message to Compatriots in Taiwan issued on January 1, 1979 and the Nine-Point Proposal put forward by China on September 30, 1981."[15]

From these quotes, it should be noted that the August 1982 communiqué was most vague on the cut-off dates and the kind of arms the United States might sell to the KMT government. As testified by John Holdridge, then assistant secretary of state for East Asian and Pacific Affairs, the United States agreed to reduce arms sales to Taiwan gradually on the premise that Beijing's pursuance of a *fundamental* policy of using peaceful means to resolve the long-standing dispute between the two sides of the Taiwan Strait.[16] He added that the United States did not agree to set a date for ending arms sales to Taipei and the term *final resolution* did not have an exact meaning but rather "a variety of different formulae that one might consider in reaching a final solution."[17] Holdridge, in fact, refused to be specific on whether the term final resolution referred to arms sales or differences between Taipei and Beijing. However, he emphasized that the TRA would still be Washington's guiding principle to "make appropriate arms sales to Taiwan based on our [U.S.] assessments of the defence needs, as specified by the act."[18] In that connection, Holdridge reiterated that as far as the reunification of China was concerned, the U.S. interest was that its resolution should be by peaceful means, and it was a matter to be worked out by the Chinese themselves. He stated clearly that Washington saw "no mediation role for the United States, nor will we [United States] attempt to exert pressure on Taiwan to enter into negotiations with the People's Republic of China."[19] Holdridge's testimony also coincided with the assurance given to Taipei at the time the August 1982 communiqué was about to be announced. According to a statement by the Ministry of Foreign Affairs in Taipei on August 17, 1982, the United States made the following points to the KMT government on July 14, 1982:

1. The U.S. side has not agreed to set a date for ending arms sales to the Republic of China.

2. The United States has not agreed to hold prior consultations with the Chinese Communists on arms sales to the Republic of China.

3. The United States will not play any mediation role between Taipei and Peking.

4. The United States has not agreed to revise the Taiwan Relations Act.

5. The United States has not altered its position regarding sovereignty over Taiwan.

6. The United States will not exert pressure on the Republic of China to enter into negotiations with the Chinese Communists.[20]

Quite obviously, as far as the United States was concerned, the August 1982 communiqué was consistent with and did not contradict the TRA. In fact, Holdridge in the same testimony emphasized that the communiqué was "not a treaty or an agreement but a statement of future U.S. policy" and that the United States intended to implement that policy "*in accordance with our [U. S.] understanding of it.*"[21] The Reagan administration also made it clear that, in terms of legal precedence, the TRA would supersede the August 1982 communiqué if there were any conflicts between the two.[22] As argued by a legal expert of the U.S. State Department, the communiqué under U.S. domestic law was that of a statement by the president of a policy which he intended to pursue, whereas the TRA was and would remain the law of the United States unless amended by Congress.[23] The communiqué's statement on U.S. arms sales no doubt was linked to Beijing's pursuance of a peaceful policy toward reunification of China. As long as Beijing was continuing this peaceful policy, it seems that Washington was willing to decrease its arms sales gradually. In this connection, Washington welcomed the "peaceful" gestures made by Beijing, as exemplified by the January 1979 message to the people in Taiwan and Yeh's nine-point proposal of September 1981. However, the United States had only shown its "understanding" and "appreciation" of such moves by Beijing but did not really endorse them. Likewise, Reagan earlier in his letters to the Chinese leaders had welcomed and recognized the significance of the January 1979 message and the nine-point proposal, although he again did not really endorse the plan.[24]

From the 1972, 1979, and 1982 Sino–U.S. communiqués, it could be seen that the United States had deliberately veered from involvement in the reunification issue. It had only stated that it would like the Taiwan question resolved peacefully by the Chinese themselves. It had not advocated any particular solution to the issue, although it had welcomed but not endorsed the peaceful initiatives from Beijing. It should be noted that the United States has not recognized Beijing's sovereignty over Taiwan nor even committed itself to *recognizing* the Chinese position that Taiwan is part of China. It has only *acknowledged* that the Chinese on both sides of the Taiwan Strait maintain that there is but one China and that Taiwan is part of China. Surely it has recognized the PRC as the sole legal government of China, but it still maintains unofficial ties with Taipei and had adopted the TRA to ensure the security of Taiwan.

From Beijing's perspective, U.S. policy toward Taiwan was clearly unacceptable. China has all along considered the Taiwan issue, particularly the TRA, as the obstacle in improving Sino–U.S. relations, as analyzed in

Chapter 1. It is interesting to note that shortly after the 1982 communiqué, Beijing began to pursue what it called an "independent" foreign policy, signaling that it would be following a more even-handed policy toward the two superpowers. And it seems that Beijing's disappointment with Washington's stand on Taiwan could have contributed to the PRC's "new direction" in its foreign policy. It remains to be noted that Beijing actually had been able to gain more concessions from the Reagan administration than it expected. It was probably appeased to a certain extent by the more relaxed U.S. policy on technology exports and military and economic cooperation between the two sides. As far as arms sales were concerned, the United States did not sell Taipei the promised FX advanced fighters and the August 1982 communiqué, though vague, did state the intention of Washington to decrease its supply to Taipei in due course. The Reagan administration in fact hoped that by making these concessions, a strong and lasting strategic relationship with China could be advanced. With the intransigence of the Chinese attitude and, more important perhaps, a rise of realism in the later years of the Reagan administration with regard to China's place in world affairs, Washington was led to reassesss and finally to shift its strategic focus in Asia from China back to Japan.[25] Beijing, henceforth, was treated as a regional and not a global power, making the United States less willing to make more concessions over the Taiwan issue. However, it is important to point out that Washington's policy toward reunification remains unchanged. In concert with its earlier gesture welcoming the peaceful initiatives from Beijing, the United States reacted favorably to the Sino-British Declaration on the future of Hong Kong.[26] In view of this, the PRC probably sensed that the United States might be persuaded "to do something" to help Beijing tackle the remaining Taiwan issue in China's reunification. That was done first by Deng's request to Reagan through the service of British Prime Minister Margaret Thatcher when the latter visited the United States in December 1984. According to the interviews conducted by Martin L. Lasater in Washington between December 1984 and February 1985, there were arguments favoring U.S. involvement with the issue as well as with maintaining the status quo in the Reagan administration at that time. Eventually, Reagan decided in early 1985 to turn down Deng's request since any involvement in the issue would reopen the divisive Taiwan issue in U.S. domestic politics. It was argued that the present policy satisfied the bipartisan nature of U.S. politics and it was doubtful if U.S. involvement would substantially help Sino–U.S. relations. Moreover, Asian countries would feel more insecure with the rise of an united and stronger China.[27] For these reasons and Reagan's own personal relations with Taiwan, the U.S. policy toward reunification of China remained unchanged.

However, China seemed undeterred by the U.S. refusal to cooperate. Thus, Deng suggested in an interview with CBS's Mike Wallace in September 1986 that "the United States can encourage and persuade Taiwan first to have 'three exchanges' with us [the PRC], namely, the exchange of mails, trade and air and shipping services."[28] In the mean time, Chinese relations with the Soviet Union began to change for the better. Concrete steps were taken by Mikhail Gorbachev to ease tensions along the Sino-Soviet border, to withdraw troops from Afghanistan where eventually the Soviet troops left totally in February 1989, and, last but not least, to help in the Cambodian conflict by adding pressure on Vietnam to withdraw from Cambodia so as to improve relations between Moscow and Beijing. With these steps taken by Moscow to tackle what Beijing called the three major obstacles in Sino-Soviet relations, a summit meeting between Gorbachev and Deng would be held in May 1989 in Beijing. The warming of relations between Moscow and Beijing no doubt requires a close examination by the United States on the new strategic implications of improved Sino-Soviet relations. Although Beijing still clings to what it calls its independent foreign policy and that China would not really go so far as to form an alliance with the Soviet Union as it did in the 1950s, the United States evidently was concerned that its interests, particularly in Asia, would be damaged by such a development. The conclusion of the final years of the Reagan administration was that Washington should not overreact, and that, by and large, the U.S. position in Asia was still strong save for the areas neglected by it, notably the South Pacific. With regard to the Taiwan issue, again the conclusion was that any U.S. effort to help Beijing resolve the reunification issue would be counterproductive.[29] From all indications, the last years of the Reagan administration did not alter its policy toward Taiwan and the government was unmoved by Beijing's urge to help resolve the reunification issue and its criticisms of U.S. relations with Taipei. The United States, nonetheless, welcomed a continuing evolutionary process toward a peaceful resolution of the Taiwan issue. Such contacts, such as indirect trade and family visitation to the mainland, were welcomed by the United States because they were considered to contribute to the relaxation of tension in the Taiwan Strait. However, the United States sticked steadfastly to adopting its own one-China policy and a peaceful resolution of the Taiwan question by the Chinese themselves.

With the election of George Bush as president, there were reasons to suspect that Bush, as a former chief of the U.S. Liaison Office in China in 1974–1975, could be quite close to leaders in the PRC. Although the China question was not much of an issue during his presidential campaign, one of Bush's first acts was to pay a visit to China and Korea after the president had attended Emperor Hirohito's funeral in February 1989. The trip, however, was more of a symbolic gesture to emphasize the significance of the Asian Pacific region in the foreign policy of the new administration. The trip did not result in any noticeable change in U.S. policy toward the region. As far as China was concerned, there was no change in U.S. policy toward Taiwan.[30] However, the trip was marred by the U.S. invitation of Chinese dissident Fang Lizhi to its reception in Beijing, and the Chinese refusal to allow Fang to attend. In spite of this and other irritants in Sino–U.S. relations, it seems that the Bush administration will continue the policy toward reunification worked out by the previous administrations. And as far as Taiwan is concerned, Bush has made clear that he believed in the TRA. Likewise, his secretary of state, James Baker, has said that he would support the TRA.[31]

From the foregoing review, it would be very difficult for the United States to say that it is not involved in the reunification issue. It has laid down the condition that the resolution of the matter be by peaceful means, worked out by the Chinese themselves. This clearly prevents Beijing from exercising the option of using force—the military offensive. The insistence in pursuing a peaceful approach to reunification actually helps Taiwan to a large extent. If Taiwan turns down the "peaceful" initiatives from Beijing, and this is precisely what is happening, Beijing will not be able to press any further. At most, it could use the diplomatic offensive to isolate Taipei in international affairs. The United States will not help in any way, and it has not really advocated any form of reunification except that it be by peaceful means. The emphasis on solving the issue by the Chinese themselves also gives the United States plenty of reasons for not getting involved. In fact, this coincides with the KMT's request for not pushing for reunification and, perhaps more important, the U.S. determination of turning down all suggestions from Beijing to "do something" about the issue. In the mean time, Taipei should have breathing space to strengthen itself before it meets the other side at the conference table.

Washington's involvement in the reunification is also quite clear from the TRA. The United States, however, argues that the TRA is necessary to maintain peace in the Taiwan Strait and to prevent Beijing from adopting the military option. Through the TRA, the United States could provide arms to Taipei for a prolonged period, thus enhancing Taipei's security. The act and other statements from Washington supporting the KMT government are deemed necessary to demonstrate to Beijing that the PRC cannot rule out possible U.S. intervention in the event of a PRC-Taiwan conflict. No doubt Sino–U.S. relations may be tarnished by the TRA. However, the United States tried to placate Beijing's anger with the August 1982 communiqué. Moreover, it still has good working relations with Beijing. Besides, the Taiwan issue has not prevented military, economic, cultural, and other relations between Washington and both sides of the Taiwan Strait. And it seems that, in the case of Beijing, its strategic calculations of aligning with the United States to dilute the Soviet threat and the U.S. contributions to its four modernizations are important enough to caution it not to sour Sino–U.S. relations because of the Taiwan issue.

The "one foot in, one foot out" approach adopted by the United States toward the Taiwan issue would not be able to satisfy the Chinese on both sides of the Taiwan Strait. In fact, Washington is often attacked by Beijing and Taipei for doing nothing, doing too little, or acting too late. It is also accused by Beijing of interfering in the internal affairs of China, for hampering the process toward reunification, although the PRC has asked the United States to promote reunification. As the drama between Beijing and Taipei continues to unfold, the United States may be caught in the cross fire between the two antagonists.

In spite of these, the U.S. policy toward the reunification of China seems to have served its own interests. As noted earlier, the Taiwan question is a very divisive one in the domestic politics of the United States. If Washington is seen to be promoting reunification, which the KMT definitely does not want, at least for the time being, it will reopen the China issue at home, thus endangering the political equilibrium, if not the consensus, built up in the way Washington should approach China. The present policy toward the Taiwan issue has satisfied the sense of moral obligation to Taiwan that most Americans—conservatives and liberals alike—share, by supporting Taipei in arms for the time being and allowing Taiwan to determine what is best for itself. Pushing Taiwan to talk to the communists probably would not be acceptable to most Americans. Although the PRC has its supporters in the United States, Taiwan also has strong U.S. support, which would make it difficult for the PRC to ask the United States to change its present U.S.–Taiwan relations without damaging Washington's domestic political scene.

In terms of its interests abroad, it is obvious that Washington–Taipei relations would be strained if the United States nudged the KMT government to the conference table with the CCP. And certainly noncommunist countries in Asia would have increased doubts about U.S. support for the region. Moreover, a reunified China would have strategic implications for both the United States and Asian countries. The smaller Asian states would have to deal with a stronger and probably more assertive communist China, and the United States may lose its political leverage, particularly on Taiwan, a place of strategic importance to the United States. In the case of the PRC, the United States is not sure if Sino–U.S. relations will improve substantially even if the Taiwan issue is resolved to Beijing's satisfaction. Beijing is presently pursuing an independent policy and Sino-Soviet relations are warming. Chances are, it will follow an equidistant policy toward the superpowers in the future. As far as Sino–U.S. relations are concerned, it seems that the Taiwan issue has not substantially hurt the working relationship between Washington and Beijing. And for the United States, it is still able to maintain its contacts with both sides of the Taiwan Strait. In short, working for the reunification and the emergence of a reunified China may not be in the interest of the United States.

It has also been argued that the present U.S. policy toward the reunification of China is very flexible, since it leaves open the possibility that Washington might not oppose independence for Taiwan. The argument is that Washington has not recognized Chinese sovereignty over Taiwan, but only acknowledged that the Chinese claim that Taiwan is part of China. While it is following a one-China policy and it declares that it has no intention of pursuing a policy of two Chinas or one China, one Taiwan, the argument continues that it cannot be concluded that the United States is in fact against Taiwan's independence or is seeking to prevent such a move. Moreover, the TRA, according to Section 15, is considered to be applicable to "the governing authorities on Taiwan recognized by the United States as the Republic of China prior to January 1, 1979, *and any successor governing authorities* (including political subdivisions, agencies, and instrumentalities thereof)."[32] As a result, the argument is that it seems that "the guarantees of support for the ROC, as mandated by the TRA, would apply equally to an independent Taiwan republic so long as the law remained in effect."[33] Although the argument is one way of interpreting the *intention* of the U.S. policy toward Taiwan, it is obvious that the official U.S. position does not support this. The realities of international relations also may not permit the independence of Taiwan, as analyzed in the next chapter. For Washington, maintenance of the status quo and pursuit of its present policy toward Taiwan works well for U.S.

interests. The stabilization of the situation in the Taiwan Strait is in the interests of the United States and its allies, and any effort to change the status quo may damage U.S. interests.

THE SOVIET OPTION AND JAPANESE FORMULA

The United States remains a critical factor in the development of the Taiwan Strait. For the Soviet Union and Japan, their relevance dwarfs considerably when compared with the United States. To be sure, both the Soviet Union and Japan also do not want to get involved in the reunification issue. But in view of the fact that both in their own ways exercise leadership roles in global and regional affairs, a succinct analysis of their position on the Taiwan issue is useful.

For the Soviet Union, the more interesting aspect has been the talk of the so-called Soviet option by some in Taipei. Moscow, however, has been unequivocal in the reunification issue by consistently supporting the PRC's one-China policy. Even with the outbreak of the Sino-Soviet conflict, Moscow maintained the same stand. It seems that as long as Moscow is keen to improve its relations with Beijing, and especially with the warming of Sino-Soviet relations in recent years, it is unlikely it will jeopardize such an important relationship by building substantial ties with Taipei. Besides, having ties with Taipei would lead the Soviet Union into the same problem of the "Taiwan question" from which the United States is having a hard time extricating itself. Thus the release of the remaining members of a Russian tanker in August 1988 seized by Taipei in the 1950s for humanitarian reasons was not greeted with enthusiasm by Moscow. In fact, *Pravda* reported that these crewmen were tortured and held in Taipei against their will.[34] Likewise, Moscow did not really give the first Taiwan mission to the Soviet Union in October 1988 a very warm reception.[35] Nonetheless, Moscow under Mikhail Gorbachev is interested in promoting economic cooperation with the Asian Pacific region. In the case of Taipei, Soviet officials actually have proposed a barter trade system with Taiwan businesses keen on breaking into the Soviet market.[36] Apparently, Moscow would like to keep its ties with Taipei at a low and unofficial level, primarily in the trade area. From Taipei's record in the past, it would also be difficult for Moscow to build up its ties with the KMT government even if Moscow were interested in it. No doubt it was known that Soviet journalist Victor Louis visited Taiwan way back in 1968. Taipei's foreign minister Chou Shu-kai also indicated after Taipei's departure from the United Nations in 1971 and again after Nixon's China visit that he anticipated further development of Taipei-Moscow relations.[37] In fact, according to an analyst, there were sufficient interactions between the Soviet Union and Taiwan in the late 1960s and early 1970s to justify the statement that there were substantive but nonmilitary ties between the two sides.[38] However, it is highly debatable if there were "substantive" ties between Moscow and Taipei even though there were occasional contacts between Moscow and Taipei in the Soviet Union or elsewhere.[39] Taipei's hardliners who were most firmly against contact with the Soviets seemed to have rejected Chou Shu-kai's advocacy of flexibility in Taipei's foreign policy, since Chou lost his position as foreign minister. The argument was that such contacts would be morally wrong. But, more important, it would undermine support for Taipei in the United States.[40] Nonetheless, there were still other occasional reports of contacts between the two sides, including meeting between Soviet and Taiwan diplomats and Soviet warships passing through the Taiwan Strait.[41] Indeed, it has been noted by Beijing at one time that Taiwan would be most useful in encircling the PRC and for the operation of the Soviet navy in the Asian Pacific region if Moscow were able to establish a foothold in Taiwan.[42] With normalization of relations between Beijing and Washington in the offing, there were also discussions on Moscow-Taipei rapprochement in the Taiwanese press.[43] After the Sino–U.S. normalization, Taipei revealed that it would trade with the Soviet Union and Eastern Europe.[44] It seems that the pragmatists might have been able to exert some influence to have a more flexible posture in handling trade with Moscow and other Eastern European states. Such trade, however, was conducted indirectly. It was not until March 1988 that Taipei removed restrictions on direct trade with Eastern European countries. As for the ban against direct trade with the Soviet Union, together with Albania and North Korea, it was not lifted although the KMT government was considering allowing Taiwan businesses to trade directly with Moscow by the end of 1988.[45] The move to expand into the Soviet market no doubt was prompted more by economic realism. With the rise of protectionism in the United States and heavy dependence on the U.S. market, it was only wise that Taipei should try to diversify its markets. As a result, the move for Soviet trade is part of a larger effort to find new supplies of raw materials, to diversify markets, and preferably to cut down the trade surplus with the United States. Still, the move was opposed by the diehard anticommunists in Taipei. Notably, Shen Chang-huan, President Lee Teng-hui's conservative secretary-general at the time, vehemently criticized Taipei's clearance of a trade mission to the Soviet Union in October 1988 to promote Taipei-Moscow economic cooperation.[46] Shen eventually resigned after his outspoken comments about the mission were criticized.[47]

It remains to be noted that Taipei is still cautious in approaching the Soviet Union, since trade between Taipei and Moscow was conducted by third parties like Japan and countries in Eastern Europe. More important, Taipei reiterated that it considered the "Soviet card" a red herring.[48] No doubt there were discussions of the "Soviet option" when U.S.–PRC relations were warming. But it was more of a move to caution the United States and the PRC from pushing Taipei too far. For the pragmatists in the KMT government, Taipei's low-level contacts with Moscow could be useful not only for economic purposes but perhaps also in enhancing its international status in view of Beijing's efforts to isolate Taiwan diplomatically. It is obvious that there is a limit to how far Taipei would move toward Moscow. For one thing, the leadership still holds deep suspicions against the Soviets and communists. More important, too close a relationship with Moscow would work against its present policy of having the closest possible relations with the United States. It would also provoke the PRC to take drastic action against Taipei. After all, Beijing has said that one of the conditions under which it will use force in the reunification of China is when Taipei leans toward the Soviet Union.

As regards Japan, its relevance to the reunification issue lies in the fact that it has been heavily involved with both the PRC and Taiwan all along.[49] Japanese diplomatic finesse and shrewdness have enabled Tokyo to benefit economically from both sides of the Taiwan Strait. At the very beginning, Tokyo's relations with Beijing and Taipei were governed by the cold war until the Sino–U.S. détente. Under U.S. pressure, Japan concluded a peace treaty with Taipei but not Beijing in 1952. In the years that followed, Japan supported Taipei in the United Nations together with the United States until 1971 and maintained diplomatic relations with Taipei until 1972. As such, Japan followed closely the China policy of the United States. However, Japan did not ignore China. In the absence of official relations, Japan and China developed novel channels to conduct trade.[50] As China resumed its role in international affairs after the CCP's ninth congress in 1969, Japan under Sato was under pressure to rethink Tokyo's China policy. Such pressure was increased after the Nixon "shocks" and the seating of the PRC in the United Nations. Sato, however, was not regarded by Beijing as the right candidate to normalize relations between Beijing and Tokyo; his pro-Taipei stand probably made him unacceptable to China. Nonetheless, China would welcome Sato's successor provided he accepted three basic principles. They were: (1) that the government of the PRC was the sole legitimate government of China; (2) that Taiwan was an inseparable part of China; and (3) that Tokyo-Taipei peace treaty was illegal and must be abrogated.

By the time Tanaka took over as prime minister of Japan, Tokyo's recognition of China was a foregone conclusion. The Shanghai communiqué of 1972 also gave Tokyo a clear indication that the United States was on the way to normalize its relations with Beijing and that the Taiwan issue would be best left for the Chinese to tackle. Tanaka finally visited Beijing in September 1972, and a joint statement between Japan and the PRC was signed on September 29, 1972. As far as the Taiwan issue was concerned, Japan recognized the government of the PRC as the sole legal government of China; that Japan fully understood and respected the PRC's view that "Taiwan is an inalienable part of the territory of the PRC" and promised to comply with Article 8 of the Potsdam Proclamation; and that the PRC and Japan agreed to establish diplomatic relations. The Tokyo-Taipei peace treaty was not mentioned in the joint statement. Foreign Minister Ohira, however, announced after the release of the joint statement that the treaty with Taiwan was "understood as having ended." Tanaka also made it clear that establishing formal relations with Beijing would mean ending diplomatic relations with Taipei. As a result, the Sino-Japanese détente was achieved by Japan's acknowledgement of China's demands on Taiwan. It accepted with no reservation that the PRC was the only legal government of China, expressed its "understanding and respect" for China's claim that Taiwan was part of China, and complied with the abrogation of Japan's treaty with Taiwan by means of a press statement.

Although Taipei was angry with Tokyo, relations were patched up as shown by the agreement in December 1972 on the establishment of an office in Japan by Taiwan's East Asian Relations Association (EARA) and in Taiwan by Japan's Interchange Association (ICA). The functions of the ICA and EARA included those normally carried out by diplomatic missions. By this arrangement, Japan hopes to maintain close ties with both sides of the Taiwan Strait. While this approach may work well most of the time, problems do crop up once in a while. Notably, in the various negotiations with Beijing on trade, aviation, shipping, fishery, and a formal Treaty of Peace and Friendship, Japan encountered complications in some of these because of its Taipei connections. Notably, in the case of aviation, Beijing stressed that while it did not oppose the continuation of the Japan-Taiwan air route, it would object to the continuation of service by China Airlines (CAL) and Japan Airlines (JAL) as national carriers, and allow CAL planes to use the same airport as the ones from Beijing's Civil

Aviation Administration of China (CAAC). Taipei in turn threatened that it would not allow Japanese planes to land in Taiwan and use its airspace if Japan accepted China's conditions. The issue was resolved only when Japan Asia Airways (JAA), a subsidiary of JAL, would fly from Japan to Taiwan. Flights of Taipei's CAL and Beijing's CAAC were scheduled in such a way that both airlines would not have planes at Haneda Airport at the same time. JAA would serve as the sole agent for the ground operations of CAL in Japan and the public address system at Haneda Airport called CAL as "China Airlines based in Taiwan." With the opening of the Narita Airport, CAL began to use Haneda Airport while the CAAC used the Narita Airport. As such, JAL, just like some other Japanese companies, was able to maintain its business ties with both Beijing and Taipei by setting up a second company, JAA.

Since the conflict in the aviation issue was averted, Japan still encountered protests from Beijing, especially when the latter considered that Japan was conferring official standing to the activities conducted by Taipei or followed a one-China, one-Taiwan policy. For example, Beijing protested against the participation of Japanese parliamentarians in meetings commemorating the centennial of Chiang Kai-shek's birth. It was also unhappy about the Japanese court decision in early 1987 favoring Taiwan over the ownership of a student dormitory in Kyoto. But on the whole, they did not produce irreparable damages to Tokyo-Beijing relations. China is still keen to strengthen its relations with Japan at the expense of the Soviet Union, as demonstrated by the 1978 Treaty of Peace and Friendship between Beijing and Tokyo. Moreover, Japan has been regarded by China as a major supplier of industrial hardware and technology and a source of finance in China's four modernizations. Taiwan also seems to be more realistic in maintaining practical relations with Japan. Its ties with the pro-Taipei LDP Dietmen and Japanese-Chinese Parliamentary Association are useful in circumventing bureaucratic obstacles to its interests in Tokyo. As such, the Japanese formula in dealing with both the PRC and Taiwan has by and large worked. As noted by an analyst, Japan has been quite successful in having back-door relations with Beijing and front-door relations with Taipei before 1972. After 1972, the relations were reversed.[51]

The success of the Japanese formula has demonstrated to other states that a similar approach would be acceptable to both sides of the Taiwan Strait when they establish diplomatic ties with the PRC.[52] In fact, President Ford mentioned that the Japanese was "a possibility" for consideration when the United States normalized relations with the PRC. But of course, the United States, unlike Japan, has to sort out its security relations with Taipei, resulting in the adoption of the TRA. Still the "American formula," as noted, was to establish a similar unofficial organization, à la Japan, the AIT. This reinforced the impression of other states that a de facto one-China, one-Taiwan policy would be tolerated by Beijing after it had set up an embassy in the PRC.

CONCLUDING OBSERVATIONS

On the whole, the other major powers are not interested in being directly involved in the reunification issue. The United States actually could be most useful in helping the Taiwan question. But owing to its own interests, it has refused to help and it wants to keep clear of the issue. The Soviet Union has little sympathy for Taipei, and it could not really gain much practical benefits from Taiwan, whose development has been to a large extent very much linked to U.S. support. With the warming of Sino-Soviet relations, it remains to be seen if Moscow will "do something" to help Beijing in the reunification of China.

Tokyo did not really advocate any form or way to reunify China. Its interests were and have been to maintain ties, especially those of an economic nature, with both sides of the Taiwan Strait. The success of the Japanese formula, reinforced to a certain extent by the U.S. example, has inspired other states to follow its way in dealing with Beijing and Taipei. From the dual-track policy of the United States and Japan, it would be clear to smaller states in Asia that a de facto one-China, one-Taiwan policy would be most useful in getting the best of the two sides of the Taiwan Strait. Some of these smaller states also may consider that the emergence of a reunified China could be a threat to their security.

For Taipei, it has gradually learned by the end of the 1980s that acceptance of this dual-track policy adopted by other states could be to its advantage. Notably, besides the existence of the AIT, France opened the "French Institute" in Taipei in February 1989.[53] It is possible that other countries such as Britain may follow suit.[54] Noncommunist Southeast Asian states are also interested in upgrading their relationship with Taipei. Notably, the Philippines is even considering adopting its own version of the TRA, the Philippines-Taiwan Beneficial Act to protect Taiwan investors in the Philippines in early 1989.[55] The act, if adopted, will give de facto recognition to Taiwan. In addition, Singapore, as noted in the last chapter, invited President Lee Teng-hui to visit the republic in March 1989. It seems that Taipei's flexible diplomacy has paid off. In the case of

Beijing, it is naturally not satisfied with the United States, Japan, and other states that are following a de facto one-China, one-Taiwan policy. For example, it has threatened to cut off its diplomatic ties with the Philippines if the Philippines-Taiwan Beneficial Act is passed by the Filipino Congress and signed by President Aquino.[56] Apparently, Beijing is getting very uneasy about the dual-track policy pursued by others, since this will lessen the diplomatic pressure on Taipei to negotiate. But then the threat to cut off diplomatic ties or lower the state of official ties with other states actually does not help much in the reunification issue per se. In fact, it may work to Taipei's advantage, since it could enhance its own presence in these countries. As such, Beijing will continue to be plagued by its "helplessness" in inducing Taipei to initiate negotiations on reunification.

NOTES

1. Ralph N. Clough, *Island China* (Cambridge, Mass.: Harvard University Press, 1978), p. 8.

2. *Peking Review*, 3 March 1972, p. 5.

3. Ibid.

4. Hungdah Chiu, ed., *China and the Taiwan Issue* (New York: Praeger, 1979), p. 180.

5. The following survey of the policies of Presidents Carter and Reagan toward China is based partly on Lee Lai To, "The PRC and Taiwan—Moving Toward a More Realistic Relationship," in Robert Scalapino, Seizaburo Sato, Jusuf Wanandi, and Sung-joo Han, eds., *Asian Security Issues: Regional and Global* (Berkeley, Calif.: Institute of East Asian Studies, 1988), pp. 182–186.

6. The word *acknowledges* in the communiqué was translated as *cheng-ren*, which, if retranslated into English, means "recognizes." However, the United States did not challenge this linguistic discrepancy.

7. *Peking Review*, 22 December 1978, p. 12. Emphasis added.

8. Ibid., pp. 8–9.

9. Ibid., p. 8. Emphasis added.

10. Ibid., p. 10.

11. Chiu, *China and Taiwan Issue*, p. 267.

12. Ibid.

13. *Beijing Review*, 23 August 1982, p. 14.

14. Ibid.

15. Ibid.

16. Committee on Foreign Affairs, *China-Taiwan: United States Policy, Hearing Before the Committee on Foreign Affairs, House of Representatives, Ninety-Seventh Congress* (Washington, D.C.: U.S. Government Printing Office, 1982), pp. 5–6.

17. Ibid., p. 20.

18. Ibid., p. 7.

19. Ibid.

20. *Free China Journal* (FCJ), 5 September 1988.

21. Committee on Foreign Affairs, *China-Taiwan*, p. 6. Emphasis added.

22. Martin L. Lasater, *U.S. Policy Toward China's Reunification* (Washington, D.C.: Heritage Foundation, 1988), p. 52.

23. Ibid., pp. 51–52.

24. For the contents of the letter, see Ibid., pp. 34–38.

25. For a detailed analysis of this shift, see Lasater, *U.S. Policy*, pp. 25–59, especially p. 55.

26. Ibid., p. 112.

27. For details, see Ibid., pp. 112–18.

28. *Beijing Review*, 22 September 1986, p. 5.

29. Lasater, *U.S. Policy*, pp. 127–29.

30. *FCJ*, 2 March 1989.

31. Ibid., 6 February 1989.

32. Dennis Van Vranken Kickey, "America's Two-point Policy and the Future of Taiwan," *Asian Survey*, August 1988, pp. 891–92.

33. Ibid., p. 892.

34. *FCJ*, 10 November 1988.

35. Ibid., 24 October 1988.

36. Ibid., 12 December 1988.

37. John W. Garver, "Taiwan's Russian Option: Image and Realty," *Asian Survey*, July 1978, pp. 765–66.

38. Ibid., pp. 751–57.

39. Ibid.

40. Clough, *Island China*, p. 169.

41. Ibid.

42. Chiu, *China and Taiwan Issue*, pp. 191–92.

43. Garver, "Taiwan's Russian Option," p. 169.

44. Far Eastern Economic Review, *Asia Yearbook 1981* (Hong Kong: Far Eastern Economic Review, 1981), p. 253.

45. *FCJ*, 18 August 1988 and 15 September 1988.

46. Ibid., 20 October 1988.

47. Ibid., 12 December 1988.

48. Yu-ming Shaw, "Taiwan: A View From Taipei," *Foreign Affairs*, Summer 1985, pp. 1055–56.

49. The following is extracted from parts of Lee Lai To, "The PRC and Taiwan," pp. 174–79.

50. For details, see Ibid.

51. Clough, *Island China*, pp. 178–94.

52. Similar arrangements were later made by other noncommunist Southeast Asian states. For details, see Lee Lai To, "Taiwan and Southeast Asia: Realpolitik Par Excellence?," *Contemporary Southeast Asia*, December 1985, pp. 209–20.

53. *FCJ*, 19 January 1989.

54. *The Nineties* (Hong Kong), March 1989, p. 9.

55. *FCJ*, 9 March 1989, and *South China Morning Post* (Hong Kong), 15 March 1989.

56. *South China Morning Post*, 15 March 1989.

4

In Search of a Solution

To break the impasse in the reunification issue, might the CCP resort to some other means? If we return to the typology of strategy used by Beijing, as analyzed in Chapter 1, it is evident that the "peaceful" offensive, and to a certain extent the diplomatic offensive, has not yielded the intended momentum for negotiations. While there has been progress, it has been too slow from Beijing's perspective. The question is: Will the CCP use the military offensive? Beijing has after all reiterated that it will not abstain from the use of force in the reunification. Taipei is preoccupied with its political reforms, and work toward reunification will take a back seat for quite some time. Is Taipei creating conditions that will strengthen the desire to go independent? How strong is the movement for independence in Taiwan? Or is the KMT government really looking for other viable options to reunify China? These are some of the questions that this chapter tries to answer.

THE USE OF FORCE BY BEIJING

In the pursuit of a "peaceful" offensive against the KMT government, the CCP has not been tempted to use its military to enforce its plan for reunification. In fact, Beijing stopped the bombing of Quemoy and Matsu in January 1979. The KMT subsequently responded by stopping its bombing of the mainland, too. Distribution of propaganda materials by both sides was also discontinued in the early 1980s.[1] Most important, Beijing withdrew most of its troops from Fujian, and the Foochow Military

District, the main force to be used in case of an attack on Taiwan, was withdrawn and absorbed by the Nanking Military District in 1987.[2] With this Chinese military disengagement, the cut of the PLA troops by 1 million, and the relatively low priority accorded to defense by Beijing, it seems that the threat against Taiwan has diminished. While the PLA is still superior in quantitative terms compared to Taiwan, its quality lags behind that of Taiwan, especially in the air force.[3] Besides the PLA is spread thin to defend the whole nation, particularly the border areas, and not just the coastal areas facing Taiwan. It remains to be pointed out that although the PLA was not able to launch a military attack against Taiwan, the CCP general secretary at the time, Hu Yaobang, revealed in May 1985 that China could do it in four to five years or, at the most, seven to eight years.[4] More important, perhaps, Taipei still has a "seize" mentality in spite of its relatively well-trained and well-equipped military; its primary target of defense is against the mainland. There is, as reiterated by the Taipei government, a strong sense of an ever-present danger from the communists.[5] This perception of threat no doubt is a more important factor in assessing the security situation in the Taiwan Strait than in an analysis of the military capabilities of Beijing and Taipei. Such perceptions no doubt has been reinforced by the fact that Beijing has never renounced the use of force in reunifying the country, as noted earlier.

According to Hu, there was no way that China would renounce the use of force. If it did, so the argument went, the KMT would be more at ease and reluctant to open negotiations on reunification.[6] In fact, Deng Xiaoping did lay down at one time five conditions under which force would be used in the reunification of China: if Taiwan (1) leaned toward Moscow instead of Washington; (2) decided to go nuclear; (3) lost internal control as a result of the succession process; (4) claimed to be an independent state; or (5) continued to reject reunification talks for "a long period of time."[7] As noted in the last chapter, Taipei is not likely to play the "Soviet card." It is also unlikely that Taipei would openly manufacture nuclear weapons, although it has the technology and could take contingency measures to transform its nuclear research program for military purposes. Nonetheless, Taipei's nuclear capability is well demonstrated by the existence of a Nuclear Energy Research Institute (NERI), a key component of the much larger Chungshan Institute of Science and Technology, operating under the Ministry of Defense. It is an open secret that the NERI is involved in researching and developing sophisticated weapons, perhaps including nuclear weapons.[8] This had, in fact, caused some concern from the United States, which has repeatedly advised Taiwan to adhere to its nonproliferation commitments as a signatory to the Non-Proliferation of Nuclear Weapons Treaty.[9] The disappearance of one of the deputy directors of the NERI and his subsequent appearance in the United States, allegedly with the help of the Central Intelligence Agency in early 1988, promoted speculations that Washington could be alarmed with Taipei's developments of its nuclear program.[10] Although the United States subsequently stated that Taipei was not engaged in developing nuclear weapons, the comments were laced with reminders to Taipei that Washington remained concerned about and watchful over Taipei's nuclear program. The official line of the KMT government is still that it has long rejected the nuclear option, since choosing the option would invite PRC military retaliation against Taiwan. Also, it would not use nuclear weapons to hurt its own people on the mainland. Lastly, the cost involved would be tremendous and burdensome.[11] Under these circumstances, and more important perhaps, under the watchful eyes of both Washington and Beijing, it seems that it would be difficult, although not impossible, for Taiwan to produce nuclear weapons.

The relatively smooth constitutional succession in the government and the KMT by Lee Teng-hui after the death of Chiang Ching-kuo squashed Deng's third condition for the use of force. Consequently, Taiwan's endeavor to go independent and its refusal to accept reunification talks for a long time seem to be the more important factors for Beijing's possible use of force in the Taiwan Strait. However, judging from discussions on the topic among the mainland Chinese themselves in 1988, it seems that these two factors were expanded or modified to a certain extent. Three articles in *Liaowang Zhoukan* (Outlook Weekly, overseas edition) published in 1988 provide some clues to these modifications. The first was published in April 1988, in response to President Lee Teng-hui's first press conference held in February of the same year. As a reaction to Lee's demands that Beijing renounce the use of force, the article tried to explain why Beijing could not, listing three reasons: (1) the existence of separatist forces in Taiwan; (2) the existence of the U.S. TRA, and (3) the "three-no's" policy of the KMT.[12] A second article published in June 1988 engaged itself primarily in a debate on the problems involved in the reunification of China. When discussing the use of force by China, the author maintained that Beijing would not unless the following occurred: (1) the peaceful formula did not work and the Taiwan authorities postponed and blocked reunification of the country indefinitely, disregarding nationalism; (2) military intervention by a foreign country in Taiwan, infringing the sovereignty of China and blocking the reunification; (3)

advocacy of the independence of Taiwan was put into action, threatening the sovereignty and territorial integrity of China; and (4) Taiwan authorities carried out military actions that endangered the fundamental interests of having a reunified China.[13] Although the author implied that the list might not be exhaustive, the four conditions for Beijing's use of force apparently were the more important ones. Finally, an article elaborating the author's thoughts on the proposal of some members of the KMT old guard, notably Chen Lifu, to provide economic help to the PRC, published in September 1988, argued that Beijing had all along advocated peaceful reunification and would not use force if Taiwan (1) insisted that China be reunified and headed in that direction; (2) opposed and stopped any comment and action leading to the independence of Taiwan; (3) did not experience domestic chaos resulting in a loss of control and making it impossible to restore normalcy to the island; and (4) did not give rise to conditions leading to foreign military intervention. In a summary fashion, the article highlighted that if Beijing had to use force, it would be used against the invaders and people who had committed acts of treason and not the patriots and supporters of reunification.[14]

Missing from these articles was mention of Taipei's going nuclear, choosing the Soviet option, or succession crisis as reasons for use of force. Most prominent of the reasons or conditions for the use of force were those focused on foreign military intervention and the independence of Taiwan. It could also be surmised that these two conditions were essentially referring to a loss of control in Taiwan by the KMT government, making it impossible to restore normalcy to the island and thus endangering the precondition for talks on reunification.[15] On top of this, it is possible that Beijing might lose its patience and use force to reunify the country if Taipei were seen to be taking action, military or otherwise, to delay or block the reunification to safeguard the KMT's fortunes on the island. Thus there could be three major circumstances in which Beijing might use force in the future: (1) foreign military intervention, probably engineered by the United States from Beijing's perspective, blocking the reunification; (2) independence for Taiwan, with or without foreign support; and (3) refusal of the KMT to talk or work toward reunification for a long time.[16]

Since the present emphasis is on the "peaceful" offensive, Beijing does not want to give the impression that it is keen to use force against the KMT. It tried to soothe Taipei's fear by emphasizing that "not discounting the use of force in resolving the Taiwan question is aimed primarily at the foreign powers and the independent movement."[17] The CCP's head of the United Front Work Department, Yang Mingfu, also disclosed in August

1988 that the use of force was a question affecting both sides of the Taiwan Strait, thus requiring the KMT and CCP to work out the agreement on this.[18] Apparently, Yang wanted to make ues of this issue to lure the KMT to the conference table. This, of course, was a nonstarter, and the KMT government would not be interested in it. In fact, the KMT had rejected similar suggestions from its own members of the Legislative Yuan.[19]

Thus it seems that it will be very difficult for the CCP to renounce the use of force unilaterally. To Beijing, a unilateral renouncement would mean that its hands and feet were bound and lessen its freedom of action in dealing with Taipei.[20] It is also feared that such a move would give the KMT reasons to go slow when coming to reunification, as the threat to its security lessened. Moreover, the CCP may have to use the military option under certain circumstances, as analyzed earlier. Nonetheless, it seems that Beijing's use of force is negotiable. It is part of the united-front strategy by which it hopes to start a dialogue with the other side of the Taiwan Strait.

THE INDEPENDENCE OF TAIWAN

Beijing and Taipei are adamant that Taiwan remain part of China. They have all along refuted the independence of Taiwan. Yet both sides are afraid of such an eventuality, since the independence of Taiwan stirs the hearts of many a Taiwanese. As a result, Beijing has been most consistent in insisting that Taiwan is part of China in all joint communiqués signed at the time of establishing diplomatic relations with other countries. The CCP government, just as the KMT government, claims that Taiwan has been Chinese territory since ancient times.[21] Although Taiwan became a Japanese colony for 50 years, both Taipei and Beijing took it that the Chinese government under the KMT regained it from Japan in 1945, in accordance with the Cairo Declaration of 1943 and confirmed by the Potsdam Declaration of 1945. To the CCP and KMT governments, the Cairo Declaration was an international agreement that gave the Chinese the right to take back Taiwan.[22] Even if the San Francisco Peace Treaty of 1951 and the peace treaty between Japan and Taiwan of 1952 only stated that Japan renounced its sovereignty over Taiwan, and did not provide for the explicit transfer of Taiwan to China, it has been argued in Taipei that Taiwan belonged to China since the KMT government had declared its incorporation into China and since it had effectively controlled the island for a long period.[23] As a nonsignatory of the two peace treaties, Beijing naturally rejected the treaties. However, it pointed out that no state had objected to the Chinese sovereignty over Taiwan, as demonstrated by the documents signed by these states at the time diplomatic relations with China were established. Although most states used words like *acknowledge* or *understand* or *respect* Beijing's stand on Taiwan, the interpretation of the CCP government is that its sovereignty over Taiwan in these documents is not disputed and in fact has been accepted by many, including Japan and the United States.[24]

These arguments, however, have been refuted by others, especially those who favor the independence of Taiwan. Their argument is that Taiwan's relations with China have historically been nebulous. While they may admit that the Qing government proclaimed Taiwan to be a province of China in the late 19th century, Taiwan was ceded to Japan by the Shimonoseki Treaty in 1895.[25] From then onwards, Taiwan was under Japanese rule until the end of the Second World War. When Japan surrendered, it did not really return Taiwan to China. The argument is that the Cairo Declaration and the Potsdam Declaration were not in a formal sense legal documents. They were only "statements of intent."[26] Moreover, according to some analysts, the Cairo Declaration was superseded by the San Francisco Peace Treaty of 1951, which stated the renouncement of Taiwan by Japan but did not transfer ownershp of the island to China.[27] Likewise, the peace treaty between Japan and Taiwan in 1952 had the same ambiguity, thus rendering the legal status of Taiwan uncertain. As such, KMT control over Taiwan after the Second World War had not been accepted, so the arguments go.[28] The fact that most nations have kept away from the issue and only "acknowledged" or "taken note of" or "respected" Beijing's stand on Taiwan tends to give this argument some credence. For those who argue that the status of Taiwan is unsettled, they further note that the KMT government in Taiwan has never been representative of the people of Taiwan, not to say the Chinese people as a whole. According to them, the majority of the population in Taiwan, the Taiwanese, seem to have developed their own identity and rightly should be allowed to shape their own destiny.[29]

It is clear that both Beijing and Taipei have not accepted these arguments, and it is most unlikely that both would bring the issue to the International Court of Justice for adjudication, since they consider this unnecessary; the issue has been settled in their favor. However, it does not mean that they could easily brush aside these arguments, and, more important, ignore trends toward independence of Taiwan. In fact, one of the major reasons for Chiang Ching-kuo to introduce political reforms, as noted before, was to forestall the move toward independence by some

Taiwanese. And in the case of Beijing, it has threatened to use force if Taiwan goes independent. Thus the fear and anxiety on both sides of the Taiwan Strait is apparent. What is disturbing is that the advocacy of an independent Taiwan has become more obvious among the opposition, especially the newly formed Democratic Progressive Party (DPP). Ever since its illegal formation in 1986, the DPP has not disguised that the party would seek Taiwan's independence. The major difference between the two principal factions in the party—the radical new movement faction and the relatively more moderate Formosa group—is that the former is advocating freedom to promote independence, while the later wants to take a more pragmatic approach to securing Taiwan's future via reforms and liberalization. However, it was agreed in the DPP that it would adhere to the cause of independence for Taiwan in general. It has also adopted a resolution, though it is not in the party platform, stating that "people have the freedom to advocate Taiwan independence."[30] In fact, it has laid down four conditions under which it would demand independence: (1) if the KMT sought a "compromise" with Beijing; (2) if it "sold out" the interests of Taiwanese people; (3) if China took Taiwan by force; (4) if the KMT failed to implement genuine political reforms.[31] After its third party congress held in October 1988, Huang Hsin-chieh, a veteran political dissident from the moderate Formosa group, or "pan Formosa group" if less faction-oriented leaders were included, became the party chairman. According to Huang, what the DPP wanted to pursue was not independence based mainly on slogans but "substantive independence" based on the election to all the seats of an elective body like the National Assembly. To him, there was no point in sloganeering for independence, since this would not be allowed by either the KMT or the CCP.[32] If Huang were able to hold the quarrelsome party together, it would seem that the DDP has recognized that it is not wise to challenge the one-China policy; that it would be "safer" for it to take part in the politics of a more or less autonomous Taiwan, at least for the time being. In the mean time, the party is trying to broaden its base by advocating not only the interests of the Taiwanese but all the people in Taiwan. Its social basis of support has been primarily the middle class and small- or medium-size enterprises.[33] In spite of the conflict-ridden nature of the party, it was successful in the last national elections of December 1986. A prominent feature of the elections was the strong performance of individual DPP candidates. Although only 23 of its 44 nominees were elected, this represented a remarkable change for the DPP, since the Legislative Yuan in 1987 had 13 DPP members compared to 6 earlier. Of these 13, 12 were elected in December 1986, while the remaining one, Fei

Hsi-ping, was the sole opposition member elected on the mainland in 1947. Opposition representation in the National Assembly was also increased from 5 to 11 DPP members as a result of the December 1986 elections.[34] The electorate also seems to have given the DPP more encouragement, since the latter's electoral support was increased by about 5 percent. While the KMT was by no means threatened, since it came away with more than 80 percent of the seats contested and its popular vote only took a slight dip, the elections demonstrated that the still-illegal DPP had a solid place in Taiwanese politics. The electoral pattern in December 1986, with the DDP having 22.17 percent and 18.90 percent and KMT having 69.87 percent and 68.31 percent in Legislative Yuan and National Assembly elections, respectively, showed that the electors in Taiwan concentrated on only two major parties.[35]

The DPP may not be able to threaten the power base of the KMT, but certainly the former has become a force to be reckoned with and the latter would have to grant legal recognition to the DPP, like it or not. With the political reforms introduced by the KMT initiated by Chiang Ching-kuo and continued by Lee Teng-hui, representation of the Taiwanese electorate will be increased, albeit gradually. This will probably increase the DPP's chances of establishing a niche for the party in Taiwanese politics.

The fight for independence in Taiwan is further supported by the activities of overseas Taiwanese. Notably, some overseas Taiwanese have been campaigning for the independence of Taiwan in places like the United States and Japan. Admittedly, it is difficult for these overseas Taiwanese to exert their influence on Taiwanese politics from abroad. The eagnerness of some of those wanting to go back to take part in Taiwan elections is a case in point. However, the DPP seems to have started to see the usefulness in maintaining such overseas contacts. While recognizing that the center-stage of its politics is still in Taiwan, the DPP, as reviewed by Chairman Huang Hsin-chieh after the third party congress, has recognized the need to strengthen its ties with overseas Taiwanese organizations.[36] However, the foreign connection is further complicated by the attitude of host countries. Notably in the United States and Japan, there are politicians who may be sympathetic toward the independence of Taiwan. Nonetheless, it is safe to say that there is no evidence to show that the official policy of the United States or, for that matter, Japan, is supporting the independence of Taiwan, especially after the Sino–U.S. détente. Overseas Taiwanese advocating independence for Taiwan also have not been able to exert much influence on the foreign policy of their host countries toward China. In fact, they were seen more as a disruptive or negative influence in the case of Sino–U.S. relations and Sino-Japanese relations.[37] Notwithstanding, Beijing's anxiety or suspicions that there could be foreign intervention in support of an independent Taiwan is still present, as noted in the analysis of Beijing's conditions for the use of force against Tawian. Also it has been speculated that the United States has been using the yearn for independence by some Taiwanese to check the KMT authorities.[38] This suspicion or fear by some no doubt is to a certain extent reinforced by the U.S. noncommittal policy toward the legal status of Taiwan and the push on Taiwan to democratize its polity so that more Taiwanese can participate in politics. And it is obvious that the process of democratization in Taiwan has helped raise demands for self-determination and independence of Taiwan, especially from the opposition.

From all indications, the KMT government seems to have come around to recognizing that the opposition will be a permanent feature of Taiwanese politics. The eventual passing of the civic organization law by the Legislative Yuan in January 1989 would pave the way for legalization of the DPP or other opposition parties.[39] The KMT also seems to have relaxed slightly its policy toward some former opposition figures residing abroad, by allowing some of the latter to come back to Taiwan for short or long stays.[40] The hope is probably to let off some of the opposition's steam. Moreover, it hopes to improve its image, especially among the Taiwanese residing abroad. In concert with its moves to dilute the independence movement by sanctioning contacts between the two sides of the Taiwan Strait, the KMT probably wants to use these image-improving measures to tone down its conflictual relationship with the opposition. Its hope is to build up a consensus in combating communism on the mainland; it would be ideal if the target of attack could be shifted partially, if not totally, from the KMT to the CCP.

It remains to be noted that the move toward independence is not necessarily from the opposition alone. As a de facto independent political entity, Taipei could well be breeding the independence ideas among some other people in Taiwan. The generational change in Taipei's society and leadership will detach it from the mainland. The younger generation of mainlanders, not to say those of Taiwan, do not have the sentimental attachment to the mainland as do their parents. The wide gap in the standard of living and in other socioeconomic and political terms may put off some people in Taiwan from reunifying with the mainland. For the KMT itself, it no doubt sees it wiser to denounce independence and keep a one-China policy, since this could allow it to continue to develop in its own way without much disturbance from the other side and legitimize its rule, as noted before. However, there is an increasing number of Taiwanese moving into the decision-making level of the party and its government. Localization seems to be the wave of the future if the KMT wants to get more support from the native-born. It is possible that some of these Taiwanese leaders and the new generation of pragmatic KMT leaders will, with the support of a new generation of electors in Taiwan, look upon the independence of Taiwan favorably, especially if Beijing chooses to increase pressure on Taiwan. As a result, while the present politics on both sides of the Taiwan Strait and the international environment make independence improbable, the emergence of an independent Taiwan in the future cannot be ruled out.

ONE CHINA, TWO GOVERNMENTS

Ever since the departure of the KMT government from the mainland in 1949 and its subsequent rooting in Taiwan, there have been in actual practice two governments in China—one in Beijing and one in Taipei. However, both sides were not willing to come to terms with reality and both harbor the hope that the other side will lose out in the battle to be sole representative of the one China they have in mind. With the help of the United States and its allies, Taipei managed to gain the upper hand initially, until the end of the 1960s. Taipei's policy of "noncoexistence of Hans [read the KMT] and bandits [read the CCP]" worked for the KMT in the cold war environment, although it did not, by and large, diminish the effective rule of the CCP on the mainland. With the unseating of Taipei in the United Nations and, more important, the Sino–U.S. détente, Taipei's subsequent isolation from the international community was a foregone conclusion. But like the CCP in the 1950s and 1960s, the ouster of Taipei from a large number of international organizations and the derecognition of the KMT government by others did not reduce the dominance of the KMT on the island.

To a certain extent, Taipei's isolation from the international community was a result of its own doing. It claimed it was the sole representative of China, it insisted on the correct use of its name, Republic of China, and it refused to accept dual membership with Beijing in international organizations. This unbending policy of rejecting the CCP failed to work as many countries, including the United States, came to realize the utility of maintaining official ties with Beijing. To salvage its diplomatic isolation and to counter the "peaceful" offensive by the PRC on reunification, Taipei was forced to opt for "substantive diplomacy." Essentially, this develops practical relations in the absence of official ties with other countries. It could be pursued by means of economic, technological, cultural, and even semi-official links with as many countries as possible. Since Taipei has diplomatic relations with only slightly more than 20 countries, a majority of which are small states, its "substantive diplomacy" plays a very significant part in maintaining and broadening its links with the international community for the political and economic well-being of the island. To make such an approach a success, all available resources other than the official channels are mobilized by Taipei. These may include the use of trade and investment aids, technological cooperation, and academic activities. Taipei also knows very well that such an unconventional diplomacy depends to a large extent on the economic health of Taiwan. Fortunately, Taipei has been most successful economically. A per capita income of U.S. $50 in 1949 has been increased by the late 1980s to about U.S. $6,000.[41] Its foreign reserves of about U.S. $70 billion by the late 1980s is the second largest in the world. With its economic strength, it is obvious that Taipei could make use of economic diplomacy to upgrade its international status, especially its relations with smaller states eager to build economic links with Taiwan. In addition, it is Taipei's hope that such emphasis on practical relations could help upgrade its ties—if possible, even its official links— with other countries. In diversifying its relations with other countries, Taipei is probably also trying to decrease its heavy dependence on the United States and Japan for trade and investments.

Taipei's coordinated effort, sometimes dubbed "macro diplomacy" (*zongti waijiao*), emphasizing practical relations with the outside world without the usual official recognition or protection by others, certainly has modified if not changed the out-of-date stand of nonexistence with Beijing in international affairs. Forced into it by Beijing in order to have breathing space in international relations, this move was initially tested, notably in the Japanese case when both sides agreed at the end of 1972 to establish the East Asian Relations Association by Taipei in Tokyo and the Interchange Association by Tokyo in Taipei as analyzed earlier. By the time the United States established diplomatic relations with the PRC in January 1979, and set up the subsequent American Institute in Taiwan and Taiwan established the Coordination Council for North American Affairs in Washington, it was obvious that the KMT government had established a pattern, adopting a more flexible approach in its conduct of international relations. Thus, in the case of the countries of the Association of Southeast Asian Nations (ASEAN), it was noted that in the 1970s Taipei tried to salvage its diplomatic setbacks in the region by maintaining semi-official or unofficial representations in all the ASEAN states. In return, the ASEAN states also had their own semi-official or unofficial representations in Taipei.[42]

While the "substantive diplomacy" was essentially bilateral relations between Taipei and other countries, the approach had also implications for and impact on Taipei's relations with Beijing and the reunification issue. This became more obvious after the establishment of diplomatic relations between Washington and Beijing, when it was known that Taipei, as revealed by Premier Sun, would adopt a policy of "no retreat, no avoidance" if and when it met its counterpart from Beijing in international activities.[43] However, because of its emphasis on the one-China principle and the insistence on the correct use of its name in official functions, Taipei's policy of "no retreat, no avoidance" was more applicable to unofficial gatherings. Thus Taipei accepted a new name—"Chinese Taipei"—to join the Olympic Committee in 1981 and participated under the new name in the 1984 Olympics together with Beijing. The KMT government rationalized that such a meeting was not official and that even if it participated under the name "Chinese Taipei," it had the rights and privileges of any other country, including the PRC. The simultaneous appearance of Beijing and Taipei delegates in the same function apparently had indicated that such an arrangement would be acceptable to both sides. It gave rise to the question of whether this could also be applied to the reunification of China. However, Taipei insisted that the formula would be applicable only to international functions hosted by third countries at the "people-to-people" level. To Taipei, the label was ambiguous and did not delineate clearly the sovereignty of the KMT government. More important, the name was not acceptable in official functions. Because of this, Taipei's thinking on its relations with the mainland is reflected more in its move toward retaining a role in other international organizations based on official capacity. Of the ten remaining international organizations of which Taipei is a member, the Asian Development Bank (ADB) is most significant in terms of its official representation for Taiwan. As a founding member of the ADB, Taipei's membership in the organization was based on its own population and not that of the whole of China. When Beijing was admitted into the organization in 1986, Taipei's name in the ADB was changed to "Taipei, China." Because of its dwindling membership in international organizations and possibly the utility of staying in ADB, Taipei decided to remain in the organization but requested that Beijing's name be changed to "Peking, China." That was rejected by the ADB. Since Hong Kong would be designated as "Hong Kong, China" after 1997 by the PRC, Taipei refused to accept the name change; it considered the change a denigration of itself into a local government of China. Taipei's dilemma was that it could not afford to withdraw from such an important international organization. The initial decision was to boycott the annual meetings of the ADB. Despite this, it was quite clear that Taipei intended to favor continual participation. It seemed that the pragmatic argument for acceptance of dual representation of China in international organizations had won the battle, since participation in these organizations was too important to be sacrificed for the sake of principles that no longer served the interests of the KMT government. Such pragmatism led to Taipei's reappearance at ADB annual meetings starting in 1988. The Taipei delegation attended the 1988 meeting with its "Taipei, China" name tag covered and placed a sign "Under Protest" alongside the sign "Taipei, China" at the conference table. Apparently, Taipei would not accept the notion of Taiwan being a local government of China. More interesting was the decision to send its minister of finance, Shirley Kuo, to head the delegation to attend the ADB meeting in Beijing in 1989. For the first time, the KMT government in Taiwan had a high-ranking official attend a meeting where there were official representatives from Beijing. Moreover, the official delegation from Taipei attend a meeting in Beijing and not in a third country. Although in 1988 a group of scientists attended an annual meeting of the International Conference of Scientific Unions in Beijing under the name of a newly created unofficial organization and it was known that Taipei could take part in international sports competitions in China in early 1989, under the English name "Chinese Taipei" and the Chinese name "Zhonghua Taibei" (Chong-hua Tai-pei), Taipei's arrangement to send a minister to China was far more important, not only in terms of the calibre of people sent but its implications for Taipei's policy toward the mainland. Taipei pointed out that its finance minister would be in Beijing as Taiwan's representative to the ADB's board of governors, and it would again protest the use of "Taipei, China." It also emphasized that the delegation would not be attending the meeting sponsored by Beijing but one by an international organization in Beijing.[44] Still, it was a bold move that set a significant precedent for Taipei's officials to travel to the other side of the Taiwan Strait to attend meetings. In fact, Premier Yu clearly indicated that Taipei would consider attending all official and unofficial meetings on the mainland under the auspices of international organizations according to the "ADB model." He further added that for similar meetings held in Taiwan, delegates from the mainland could attend and the KMT government would act according to the decisions of the international organizations concerned.[45] Although Taipei in principle still rejected the bilateral meetings with Beijing on the mainland, and it would not discuss bilateral relations with Beijing in international meetings held on the mainland, the simultaneous appearance of officials from both sides of the Taiwan Strait at the ADB meeting signaled that the policy of accepting dual representation in international organizations had advanced one major step forward in Taipei's "flexible diplomacy." This gave rise to the hope in some quarters that Taipei might be admitted or readmitted into more international organizations, including the United Nations eventually.[46] The indication by President Lee on his Singapore trip that the name was not that important also signaled that Taipei would accept a name change that did not downgrade it to a local government. More important, Taipei's use of the "ADB model" indicated that it would like to test the idea of "one China, two governments" proposed for the conduct of its international relations. In fact, Premier Yu did not hide the fact that such a proposal was worth investigating and had asked the Ministry of Foreign Affairs to conduct research for future references.[47] The revelation of Taipei's serious consideration of the "one China, two governments" proposal was made at the time when it was known that an official delegation would be attending the 1989 ADB meeting in Beijing. It suggested that the KMT government considered it mature and opportune to make a comeback in international politics. It had taken a very cautious, step-by-step, yet pragmatic approach in assessing the ways to overcome its diplomatic isolation and had come to the conclusion that the "one country, two governments" proposal might be worth considering. To be sure, there has been no lack of suggestions from various quarters over the years. Quite obviously, those proposals that would compromise its international personality and that were aimed primarily at the reunification of China have been brushed aside as too high-sounding, academic, and idealistic to be of any use, since, rightly so, the preconditions for reunification were not imminent and that Taiwan was not ready and interested in such a move. The rejected proposals may include the formation of a federal, confederal, or coalition government between the two sides. Even existing "models" like Germany, Korea, or Singapore had not struck a responsive chord, since the KMT government considered its situation different from those other countries. Besides, Beijing had rejected all these other proposals and reiterated the use of the "one country, two systems" proposal for the reunification. It simply was not practical to give the rather academic proposals any serious consideration.[48]

However, the proposals that suggested ways for Taipei to take part in international activities under the one-China principle may not have been totally unheeded by the KMT government, although the latter probably still considered them premature. These may have included the suggestion of "one country, two seats" concept of some academics advocating a period of peaceful coexistence and peaceful competition before reunification. Probably inspired by the "Olympic model," this was suggested as acceptable to Beijing and one that would allow Taiwan to maintain or return to many international organizations as a full member. Under such an arrangement, Taiwan's name could be changed to other names that did not contradict the one-China principle.[49] The argument for the proposal was that Taipei's changed name in the international organizations was not really related to its "proper" name elsewhere.[50]

A related proposal was for a "one country, two administrations" concept advocated notably by Shen Chun-shan, an academic who became a Minister Without Portfolio in the KMT government in 1988. In a nutshell, this proposal suggested that both the PRC and Taiwan exercise sovereign rights jointly. The two separate but not independent entities would administer and govern their own areas of influence and compete with one another peacefully under the one-China principle.[51] In terms of international relations, this proposal emphasized that Taipei strive for an international personality as a separate political entity.[52] In view of Taipei's diplomatic isolation, it advocated separation of cultural (nonpolitical) and political encounters with Beijing in international functions and encouragement of Taiwan's participation in the former. However, Taipei's participation, according to Shen, should be conditioned by four principles: (1) no indication of a political compromise; (2) no influence on the stability of Taiwan; (3) no way of leading to the dependence on the mainland economically; and (4) no sacrifice of Taipei's team as a separate and equal opposite of that from Beijing.[53] Premised under these "four-no" principles, Shen's argument in fact further suggested as early as late 1983 that there not be deliberate moves on the part of the people from Taiwan to avoid interacting with students from the mainland studying overseas, and that Taipei consider liberalizing contacts with people on the mainland by making them legal, based on humanitarian and national grounds.[54] Shen emphasized that the proposal was only a transitional arrangement allowing peaceful competition and mutual impact between the two sides of the Taiwan Strait in an abnormal period. The proposal was aimed at the evolution of a system suitable for all of China, and the eventual goal was for a China reunified under one system and one administration.[55]

A third proposal, which might have attracted some attention, was one advocating a "multisystem nation." Again, the proposal recognized the existence of two separate political entities in China. Working under the one-China principle, the proposal underscored the point that there was only one country, which had two competing political systems with their own international personalities. Taiwan not only had not announced its withdrawal from China and independence from the mainland but had also not forsaken its wish to reunify.[56] It was argued that this proposal came closest to Beijing's "one country, two systems" concept, since both upheld the one-China principle and accepted "peaceful coexistence" as a basis for the gradual reunification of China.[57] However, it was noted that the "one country, two systems" proposal differed from the "multisystem nation" proposal in at least two important aspects. First, Beijing's proposal would designate places such as Hong Kong and Taiwan as local governments. The latter had no international personality and they were not equals of Beijing, where the central government was located. Second, Beijing's proposal was based on its unilateral move to amend the constitution and policy to have a "one country, two systems" structure. It could amend the constitution again and change the policy with no restraint and protection from international law and the international community.[58] It was clear that the "multisystem nation" proposal could be useful for Taipei to break its diplomatic isolation. Thus the proposal suggested that the KMT government separate the reunification issue from the diplomatic issue. For the former, it was a domestic issue that should be deliberated and solved gradually by the Chinese people from both sides of the Taiwan Strait; it was not really related to the international community. For the latter, the "multisystem nation" proposal would provide a way for divided countries with two effective governments to exercise their rights and duties as independent international personalities; it would solve their diplomatic problems without really touching on the domestic issues of reunification and other political conflicts. It was also noted then that the two parts of divided countries like Korea and Germany had successfully been accepted internationally, even though the domestic conflicts, especially the reunification issue, were unsolved.[59]

These proposals, as far as Taiwan's international relations are concerned, were put forward to suggest ways by which Taiwan could return to more international organizations when many countries had already derecognized Taipei. After Taipei had managed to do so successfully in unofficial organizations à la the "Olympic model," and as Taipei began to regain its confidence, proposals addressing the question of international recognition came forward from various quarters in Taiwan, particularly how to reestablish diplomatic relations with countries that had official ties with Beijing. The most discussed proposal was probably that on dual recognition. Simply put, the suggestion was to consider reestablishing diplomatic ties with countries willing to do so, even if they had official ties with Beijing. Again, reunification was considered a domestic issue separate from dual recognition in international affairs. For this rather realistic proposal, it was argued that the measure could stop or delay the remaining countries which had diplomatic ties with the KMT government from dropping Taipei in the future. By using Taipei's economic strength, it was suggested that Taiwan could also "tempt" some states to establish official ties with Taipei if these states could not profit from official relations with Beijing.[60] As disclosed by Yung Wei from the Research, Development and Evaluation Commission of the Executive Yuan of the KMT government in early 1988, in reply to questions from a member of the Legislative Yuan, the question of dual recognition should not have been a surprise to Premier Yu Kuo-hwa and Foreign Minister Ding Mou-shih, although the foreign minister had earlier pointed out that dual recognition for the KMT government was a "pure hypothesis."[61] Yung Wei pointed out the positive results of the Korean and German examples in separating the recognition question from the reunification question. Moreover, he noted that there had been precedents of dual recognition during the times of Sun Yat-sen, Chiang Kai-shek, and Chiang Ching-kuo.[62] Yung Wei suggested that the KMT government might consider various options, including dual recognition, to make a comeback in international politics. As the 13th largest trading nation in the world, Taiwan might also establish or reestablish diplomatic relations with countries that had formal ties with Beijing, if only to keep growing as a major economic power in the Asian Pacific region.

It is unknown to what extent these proposals have influenced or will influence the KMT government. Nor is it clear if these proposals were merely floated by policy-makers in Taipei. However, it is clear that such proposals depended on acceptance not only by the international community but even more so by Beijing. The KMT government and the advocates of these proposals could not but be weary of critical commentaries from Beijing. They have been attacked for creating "two Chinas" or "one China, one Taiwan," with the conclusion always that the "one country, two systems" concept should be feasible for reunification and a solution to Taipei's diplomatic problems.[63] It should be noted that the commentaries from the mainland, while refuting all these proposals, did in a few instances agree with selected points. The notable example was the proposal by Shen Chun-shan, on "one country, two administrations."

Thus in a fairly thorough treatment of this proposal in *Taiwan Yanjiu Jikan* (Taiwan Research Quarterly) from Xiamen University, the author conceded that the proposal had rejected the traditional anticommunist stand. It had shaken off the independence and self-determination of Taiwan by advocating a more rational approach toward the mainland. Moreover, the article agreed with Shen's point about the inapplicability of the Korean and German models to China.[64] Another article in *Liaowang Zhoukan* (Outlook Weekly, overseas edition) conceded that Shen's proposal had two correct prerequisites—namely, the need to ascertain the sovereignty of a reunified country (China) as soon as possible in a complex international environment and the basic stand in Taiwan-mainland China relations as for the benefit of the people of Taiwan, the country, and the Chinese people as a whole. As expected, these concessions were made because they coincided with the official Beijing policy. However, the mainland articles rejected Shen's proposed "two administrations" for China, because they felt that it would lead to the creation of two Chinas, or one China, one Taiwan. According to them, it would also consolidate and legalize the separation of Taiwan from the mainland.[65]

The KMT government was more concerned with the way to break its diplomatic isolation than the reunification of China. As a result, it could not but be concerned that these proposals were criticized by commentaries on the mainland. More important, its pursuit and practice of "substantive diplomacy" or "flexible diplomacy" had also been under attack from the other side. These criticisms again reflected Beijing's fear of the KMT government creating two Chinas or of going for the so-called B-type of independence.[66] The criticisms were also used to put pressure on Taipei to work for reunification by making it difficult for the KMT government to conduct its official activities in the international community. Beijing, however, did not object to the economic and cultural links between Taipei and the outside world at the people-to-people level, since it realized that the KMT government needed such links to maintain its prosperity and stability. Without these links, Taipei would not have the confidence to further relax its contacts with the other side. However, it would not be acceptable to the CCP if Taipei used its strengthened links with Beijing to bargain for a return to the international community.[67] Beijing watched with unease Taipei's moves to make its unofficial links with other countries more "official." To Beijing, such moves by Taipei in its "flexible diplomacy" were the legalization and consolidation of a partitioned China. These were regarded as an infringement of the territorial integrity and sovereignty of China.[68] To be sure, in the 1980s Taipei upgraded and diversified its links with the outside world by rallying all its resources available, in conjunction with its "macro diplomacy." Even under the watchful eyes of the PRC, and with the reluctance of many countries to resume official ties with Taipei for fear of offending Beijing, Taipei has been quite successful in building economic links with other countries because of its economic strength.

As Taipei established mutual unofficial offices with other countries and gradually rejoined some international organizations, it became clear to the KMT government that it would be desirable and inevitable to upgrade its bilateral ties with other countries and to explore ways to rejoin even more official international organizations. For the upgrading of bilateral relations, the important thing for Taipei was of course to maintain its official ties with the 23 countries with which it was already linked. However, Taipei could not but be concerned that 2 of those 23 countries—South Korea and Saudi Arabia—were building ties with Beijing. As a result, Taipei's diplomacy was to prevent these remaining states from dropping official ties. In addition, for those countries with which it already had unofficial ties, Taipei wanted to upgrade those relations into semi-official or even official ties. Finally, Taipei also intended to establish ties with countries where ties with Taipei were absent.[69] This could be done by economic diplomacy, people-to-people exchanges, connections with "overseas Chinese," and even party-to-party diplomacy, namely the links between the KMT and other political parties. While Taiwan previously was most concerned with use of its official name, "ROC," and has been able to use that name for some sociocultural or economic offices in a few states, the name used has not been as important since Lee Teng-hui's rise to power. This change was clearly shown by Lee's visit to Singapore in March 1989. As noted earlier, Lee was addressed as "President from Taiwan." Lee accepted the name, although he was not satisfied with it. Apparently, what was important was not so much the name but the substance of the relationship. Besides enhancing economic cooperation between Taiwan and Singapore, as evidenced by the drafting of two economic agreements, the two sides consented in principle to hold a ministerial-level meeting each year to deliberate bilateral cooperative projects. It seems that Taipei would, as a whole, pursue a policy of arranging ministerial-level visits with countries that have no official ties with Taipei.[70] It was also interesting to note that, after his visit, President Lee mentioned ministerial-level meetings with Singapore would be held even if the latter had diplomatic ties with Beijing.[71] He further stated that he did not care whether Singapore had formal ties with Beijing, as long as it continued to upgrade its relations with Taiwan. His point was that "Singapore's normalizing ties with Peking [Beijing] is one thing. Our [Taipei's] relationship with it [Singapore] is another."[72] To make himself clear, he said he would visit Singapore or any other friendly nation with an embassy from Beijing if he were invited.[73] These remarks showed clearly that Taipei's deemphasis of a proper name would not affect the sovereignty of the KMT government. Also, in its pursuit of "flexible diplomacy," Taipei had accepted Beijing's relations with other countries and Taipei's relations with those same countries. The acceptance of two sets of relations demonstrated that the policy of dual recognition would be considered seriously and tested, although its success depended very much on the countries concerned, as noted by President Lee, and, more important, on Beijing.[74] As a result, Lee was realistic enough to note that such diplomacy could not take place in leaps and bounds, but would happen step by step. The gradualist approach would start from an unofficial and move to a semi-official or even official level. Formalities might not be as important as substantive relations worked out independently by Taipei with other nations.

Taipei's upgrading of its presence in international organizations was demonstrated vividly when it declared that it would take part in the ADB meeting in Beijing. As discussed earlier, it was clear that pragmatism had ruled the decision to take part in the meeting, with a ministerial-level team in an official capacity. Taipei's willingness and ability to attend other such official international functions, of course, depends on the organizations and on Beijing. It is clear that whenever possible, Taipei will participate in such functions provided it is not downgraded to a local government of China. That was why the name "Taipei, China" was not acceptable, protested at the ADB meeting in Manila in 1988 and again in Beijing in 1989. Taipei probably is flexible enough to accept some other names that have no such implications. In fact, some Taiwan officials suggested that, in the case of the 1988 ADB meeting in Manila, Taipei might accept "China, Taipei," "China Taiwan," or "Chinese Taipei," as those names imply Taiwan is still somehow connected to China.[75] Judging from events in early 1989, notably the debate on the "one country, two governments" formula in Taiwan, what Taipei is fighting for is to have the same standing with Beijing in the international community. It is easier in the case of the ADB, since Taiwan's full membership is based on the population in Taiwan and the shares committed by each member. As such, the "ADB model" may not be applicable to other international organizations whose membership is based on the sovereignty of a nation. Since both Beijing and Taipei claim that there is only one China, and as far as Beijing is concerned it is the sole representative of China and that sovereignty is indivisible, it is difficult, if not impossible, for Taipei to carve a niche for itself in official international occasions. As a result, the "one country, two governments" proposal in early 1989 in Taipei, as disclosed by Premier Yu, is interesting. What this proposal entailed was the coexistence of the two governments in international affairs. In a way, it was a concession on the part of Taipei, since it recognized the CCP government as the other part of China, thus giving up its long-held *fatong* (constitutional rule) over the whole of China. It also recognized the division of China into two parts, a reality. To underscore the parity of Taipei and Beijing in this arrangement, the suggestion was also dubbed the "one country, two *equal* governments" proposal. Quite clearly, Taipei would like to emphasize that it will not accept the debasement that is implied under the "one country, two systems" approach.[76] It seems that Taipei was prepared to fight for some kind of official standing in the international community under such a proposal, and was quite confident that its effective rule in Taipei would not be challenged. By using the phrase "two governments," it is far more obvious and formal than earlier suggestions of having "two seats," a "multisystem," or "two administrations." This concept coincides with the other proposals, in that it also attempts to broaden the international contacts of Taipei which, according to its foreign minister Lien Chan, would work on regional and economic international organizations first.[77] This proposal to upgrade relations to the official level also coincided to a large extent with the major objective of dual recognition, although the latter was more concerned with bilateral relations while the former had much broader implications. Revealed immediately after the decision to send a high-level team to attend the ADB meeting in Beijing, the proposal could be argued as giving the delegation a basis on which to ask for an official governmental presence in the organization, too. But as expected, the acceptance of this "one country, two governments" proposal again depended on Beijing. No doubt both sides of Korea and Germany* operated separately internationally. Nonetheless, in the Chinese case, the PRC is by far much bigger and more populous and influential in international affairs than Taipei. The more informed people in Taiwan also know very well that Korea and Germany are different from China. For one thing, Korea and Germany had been separated since the end of World War II as a result of major power

---

*The following analysis refers to the situation in Germany from the end of World War II until the end of the 1980s.

politics, while China under the KMT had at one time or another represented all of China.[78] In the case of Taipei, it is more a question of
resumption and not of establishment of official ties with other countries.
Likewise, it is a matter of readmission to international organizations in
many instances, unlike the two Koreas and Germanies, whose concerns
are primarily establishing the formal ties with others and admission into
international organizations.

In anticipation of objections from Beijing, and to sweeten the suggestion, the KMT minister of justice, Hsiao Tien-tzang, even ventured
to say that if Beijing reacted favorably to the "one country, two governments" proposal, Taipei could then consider terminating the "Temporary
Provisions Effective During the Period of Communist Rebellion."[79] This
could also be seen as necessary if Beijing were invited to attend international conferences in Taipei sponsored by international organizations.
Not recognizing Beijing as the other government and regarding it as a
rebellious organization could make things difficult, not only for Beijing
and the international organizations but also for Taipei, which would have
to deal with the "rebels," a serious crime punishable by law in Taiwan.
However, Premier Yu later clarified that the "Temporary Provisions"
should not be renounced abruptly and that any change should be dealt
with by the Legislative Yuan and not the Executive Yuan. Hsiao Tien-
tzang also made it clear that his view was not a policy statement but a
personal view on the matter.[80] Whatever, it was clear that Beijing could
not accept the proposal, since it considered this a variation on previous
proposals trying to create two Chinas. In reality, two separate governments have existed all along. While Beijing's "one country, two systems"
concept has, to a certain extent, recognized the existence of two political
entities, it refuses to give Taipei leeway to act independently of Beijing,
especially in foreign affairs. Apparently there is a limit to how much
Beijing will concede to Taipei. It would not accept proposals that put the
reunification issue in storage, nor those which it considers to be creating
two Chinas. It is determined to have a last say in Taiwan affairs. The
KMT government has come closer to the recognition of the reality by
considering a de facto "one country, two governments" arrangement for
its own purposes. As noted, it is concerned with its diplomatic problems
and not really with the reunification issue. With diverse motivations and,
in the final analysis, a quest for power by both the CCP and KMT, the
reunification of China will remain unresolved and the reality is that
China will have two governments for the near future if peace prevails in
the Taiwan Strait.

CONCLUDING OBSERVATIONS

For Beijing, the untested policy option in the 1980s was the use of force in reunifying the country. It has not exercised that last-resort option for fear of disrupting developments on both sides of the Taiwan Strait. Still, the use of force cannot be ruled out if the reunification issue remains unresolved for a long time. For some of the people in Taiwan, the option is independence of the island. In fact, that is the goal of the opposition, the DPP in particular. This is not likely, at least in the near future, in view of political realities in China and the world. As for the KMT government, the "one country, two governments" proposal has been considered and it probably is being followed in principle, in spite of the difficulties involved in doing so.

The failure of both sides to consider the numerous proposals on reunification so far is, in varying degrees, a demonstration of a lack of compromising spirit. Beijing's use of force is still possible if no compromise can be reached after a prolonged period. As for Taiwan independence, it could become more popular if the uncompromising opposition gains influence in Taiwan. It could also be considered as a future option if there is no usefulness in compromising with the other side. Taipei's push for a de facto "one country, two governments" approach to international affairs betrays its uncompromising attitude, in the sense that it has vowed to act separately in diplomacy while clinging symbolically to the one-China principle. However, the approach has a sense of realism, since it acknowledges the division of China. The problem is that it does not conicide with China's master plan of "one country, two systems." As a result, it is clear that confidence-building measures, more pragmatism, and the evolution of a compromising spirit will be necessary if both sides ever are to genuinely consider reunification.

NOTES

1. *Liaowang Zhoukan* (Outlook Weekly, overseas edition), 15 August 1988, p. 21.

2. Ibid., 26 December 1988, p. 8.

3. For the latest figures on the military strength of the PRC and Taiwan, see, for example, Far Eastern Economic Review, *Asia Yearbook 1989* (Hong Kong: Far Eastern Economic Review, 1989) pp. 104–105, 232.

4. *Baixing Semi-Monthly* (Hong Kong), 1 June 1985, p. 6.

5. *Free China Journal* (FCJ), 19 December 1988, p. 5.

6. Ibid.

7. Guo-cang Huan, "Taiwan: A View From Beijing," *Foreign Affairs*, Summer 1985, p. 1068.

8. *Far Eastern Economic Review*, 31 March 1988, p. 22.

9. Ibid., 31 March 1988, pp. 22–23.

10. Ibid.

11. Yu-ming Shaw, "Taiwan: A View From Taipei," *Foreign Affairs*, Summer 1985, p. 1056.

12. *Liaowang Zhoukan* (overseas edition), 18 April 1988, p. 25.

13. Paraphrased from an article in Chinese in Ibid., 27 June 1988, p. 8.

14. Paraphrased from an article in Chinese in Ibid., 12 September 1988, p. 4.

15. For a similar interpretation, see *The Nineties*, October 1988, p. 43.

16. This was confirmed in the author's discussions with "the more informed" in various academic, government, and party organizations in Beijing in October 1988.

17. *The Nineties*, September 1988, p. 7, and October 1988, p. 38.

18. Ibid., October 1988, pp. 42–43.

19. *United Daily News* (Taipei), 13 April 1988.

20. *Liaowang Zhoukan* (overseas edition), 18 April 1988, p. 25.

21. See, for example, Chen Qimao, "The Taiwan Issue and Sino-U.S. Relations, A PRC View," *Asian Survey*, November 1987, p. 1162–64.

22. For a legal argument of the Chinese case from the point of view of an academic in Taipei, see, for example, David S. Chou, "The International Status of the Republic of China," *Issues and Studies*, May 1984, pp. 15–18. For a PRC view on this, see, for example, *Liaowang Zhoukan* (overseas edition), 18 July 1988, p. 21.

23. For the legal arguments, see, Chou, "International Status," p. 17.

24. *Liaowang Zhoukan* (overseas edition), 18 July 1988, pp. 21–22.

25. Lu Keng, ed., *Zhongguo Tongyi Wenti Lunzhan* (Debates on Problems of the Reunification of China) (Hong Kong: Baixing Wenhua Shiye Pte. Ltd., 1988), p. 399.

26. See Trong R. Chai, "The Future of Taiwan," *Asian Survey*, December 1986, pp. 1314–15.

27. Ibid.

28. Ibid., pp. 1315–16.

29. Ibid., pp. 1319–23.

30. *Free China Review*, January 1988, p. 58.

31. *Far Eastern Economic Review*, 28 April 1988, p. 16.

32. *The Nineties*, December 1988, p. 35.

33. *Taiwan Studies*, no. 2 (1988), pp. 11–12.

34. *Far Eastern Economic Review*, 18 December 1986, p. 13.

35. *The Nineties*, January 1987, p. 49.

36. Ibid., December 1988, p. 35.

37. For a fuller analysis, see, for example, John F. Cooper, "The Taiwan Independence Movement Factor," in Frederick Tse-shyang Chen, ed., *China Policy And National Security* (New York: Transnational Publishers, 1984), pp. 80–91.

38. See *Taiwan Studies*, no. 2 (1988), pp. 3–7.

39. *FCJ*, 6 February 1989.

40. *The Nineties*, December 1988, pp. 37–38.

41. *FCJ*, 17 October 1988 and 19 December 1988.

42. For details, see Lee Lai To, "Taiwan and Southeast Asia: Realpolitik Par Excellence?," *Contemporary Southeast Asia*, December 1985, pp. 209–20.

43. *Central Daily News* (Taipei), 20 September 1980.

44. *United Daily* (Taipei), 8 April 1989.

45. *Central Daily News*, 8 April 1989.

46. Ibid., 9 April 1989.

47. *China Times* (Taipei), 9 April 1989.

48. For Beijing's refutation of these other proposals, see, for example, two articles written by Li Jiaquan, deputy director and research fellow of the Taiwan Research Institute of the Chinese Academy of Social Sciences in *Beijing Review*, 3 February 1986, pp. 18–26 and 28 March–3 April 1988, pp. 19–23.

49. See, for example, Winston Yang's article in *The Nineties*, January 1985, pp. 66–67, and February 1987, p. 11.

50. *China Times*, 20 April 1988.

51. For details, see Shen Chun-shan's articles in *China Times*, 23 January 1984 and 1 September 1987. See also his discussion with Byron Weng in Hong Kong, as reported in *The Nineties*, May 1985, pp. 41–51.

52. *China Times*, 1 September 1987.

53. Ibid., 23 January 1984.

54. Ibid.

55. Ibid., 1 September 1987.

56. Ibid., 10 May 1987.

57. Ibid.

58. Ibid.

59. Ibid.

60. *The Nineties*, May 1988, p. 54.

61. *China Times*, 25 March 1988.

62. Ibid.

63. See Li Jiaquan's general survey and criticisms of these proposals in *Beijing Review*. See also the debates between Chen Dengcai with Winston Yang and Kao Yinmao in *Liaowang Zhoukan* (overseas edition), 16 November 1987, pp. 6–8; 23 November 1987, pp. 5–6; 27 June 1988, pp. 6–8; and 4 July 1988, pp. 22–23; *The Nineties*, February 1988, pp. 71–73, and November 1988, pp. 86–89. For criticisms of the "one country, two administrations" proposal, see, for example, *Taiwan Yanjiu Jikan* (Taiwan Research Quarterly), no. 3 (1988), pp. 1–7, 16; *Liaowang Zhoukan* (overseas edition), 7 December 1987, p. 21 and 1 August 1988, pp. 21–22. For criticisms on the dual-recognition proposal, see, for example, *Liaowang Zhoukan* (overseas edition), 23 May 1988, pp. 6–7 and *Taisheng* (Voices of Taiwan, Beijing), no. 8 (1988), pp. 12–14.

64. *Taiwan Yanjiu Jikan*, no. 3 (1988), p. 5.

65. *Liaowang Zhoukan* (overseas edition), 1 August 1988, pp. 21–22, and 7 December 1987, p. 21.

66. See, for example, Ibid., 8 August 1988, pp. 5–6 and *Taisheng*, nos. 5 and 6 (1988), pp. 16–18. The so-called B-type of independence refers to the creation of an independent political entity and personality for Taiwan under the one-China principle. It is different from the so-called A-type of independence, which advocates the independence of Taiwan by the people on the island and the rejection of both the KMT and CCP. For the differences between the two types of independence, see *Taisheng*, nos. 5 and 6 (1988), pp. 16–18.

67. *Liaowang Zhoukan* (overseas edition), 20 February 1989, pp. 7–8.

68. Ibid., p. 8.

69. *The Nineties*, April 1989, p. 68.

70. Ibid.

71. *FCJ*, 13 March 1989.

72. Ibid.

73. Ibid.

74. Ibid.

75. Far Eastern Economic Review, *Asia Yearbook 1989* (Hong Kong: Far Eastern Economic Review, 1989), p. 234.

76. *United Daily News*, 9 April 1989.

77. *Central Daily News*, 9 April 1989.

78. See, for example, Shen Chun-shan's article in *China Times*, 23 January 1984.

79. *Central Daily News*, 15 April 1989.

80. *United Daily News*, 19 April 1989.

5

Interactions and Trends in the Taiwan Strait

Presently, there is no indication that there will be official dialogue between Beijing and Taipei on reunification. Officially, Taipei still claims to adhere to the "three-no" policy—no negotiation, no contact, and no compromise— with Beijing. However, Taipei is much more relaxed in sanctioning indirect contacts at the people-to-people level. Such interactions could be classified essentially in three major categories: (1) the visitation program; (2) the cultural program, which includes interactions between academics, cultural or entertainment personalities, and athletes; and (3) trade and investment. For practical purposes, it is more useful for both sides to concentrate on these relatively nonpolitical measures, laying the foundation for further interactions at a higher level. In view of the vast differences in political and socioeconomic terms, these matters are less sensitive and not so difficult to deal with. If properly handled, they could enhance understanding of each other's problems and increase the confidence in each other. In that connection, tension will be further reduced in the Taiwan Strait, making it easier to have a dialogue. Thus, it is useful to analyze to what extent and in what way Taipei and Beijing have been benefiting from these contacts. What will be the impact of these exchanges on the thinking of the leaders of both sides? How will the exchanges be helpful, if at all, to the reunification process?

THE VISITATION PROGRAM

Of all the contacts between the two sides of the Taiwan Strait, the visitation program was an acid test monitored closely by the KMT government to see if the program should be continued and broadened. As noted earlier, out of its own concerns, the KMT preferred to take a gradual, unidirectional and indirect approach in allowing the people of Taiwan to visit the mainland. Certain categories of people, such as those in the military, people holding public office or in the civil service, and KMT officials and cadres, were not allowed to do so. Since the initial six-month observation of the visitation program did not suggest any threats to the security of Taiwan, the KMT decided to allow more categories of people to visit the mainland. This opened up to the possibility of going to the mainland more than once a year for those whose parents, spouses, or children were seriously sick or had died, as revealed in February 1989. Also, in April 1989, the ban on Taipei school staff visits to the mainland was lifted.[1] In concert with its political offensive, the KMT apparently was also politically motivated in this first stage of its changed policy toward the mainland. The hoped-for political results could include, first, improvement of its image at home and abroad, as a reasonable and liberal government doing its part to release frustrations and tensions among its people. Second, through its visitors to the mainland, Taipei would have opportunities to demonstrate the achievements of the KMT. Taipei knew very well that there is a wide gap in standard of living. The visits could only highlight those differences. Third, and related to the second point, it is also possible that Taipei hoped that the CCP could gain a more realistic understanding of the progress in Taiwan over the years, as the mainland receives more and more compatriots from the other side. Finally, as noted in Chapter 2, Taipei wanted to tone down the yearning for independence in Taiwan, and perhaps at the same time demonstrate to the mainland that at least it is not going independent, though also not necessarily working for reunification. Though the KMT has been watching the visitation program closely, it is obvious that the effects are not clear immediately. As a result, assessment of the program after a year is probably more telling than earlier intermittent reports. According to the Taiwan Red Cross, more than 240,000 people registered to go to the mainland from November 2, 1987, the first day of the registration, to the end of October 1988[2]—about 1.25 percent of the population. The percentage is probably higher if people using other channels are also included. Not everyone registering with the Red Cross was approved, however. According to statistics released by the Ministry of Interior in Taipei, of 246,743 applicants, 243,450 were approved for the one-year period, an approval rate of 98.7 percent.[3] It should also be noted that not everyone approved eventually went to the mainland during the period. For the one-year period, 209,036, or 84.7 percent of the

Table 5.1
A Statistical Analysis of Visitors from Taiwan to the Mainland (November 2, 1987, to March 25, 1989)

```
(A) Total Number of Applicants:                    375,141

(B) Total Number of Applicants Approved:    368,207 (98.2%)

(C) Total Number of Approved Applicants

    Who Have Already Gone to the Mainland:

                      244,289 (65.1% of the applicants)

(D) Total Number of Approved Applicants

    Who Have Returned:    232,008 (61.8% of the applicants)

(E) Major Provinces Visited:

              Fujian       47,463 (12.7% of the applicants)

           Guangdong       34,805 (9.3% of the applicants)

            Shandong       32,995 (8.8% of the applicants)

(F) Major Provincial Origins of the Visitors:

              Fujian       41,658 (11.1% of the applicants)

            Shandong       39,554 (10.5% of the applicants)

           Guangdong       36,907 (9.8% of the applicants)

(G) Major Occupations of the Visitors:

             Jobless      300,926 (80.2% of the applicants)

            Business       38,654 (10.3% of the applicants)

(H) Educational Level of the Visitors :

    Primary School and Below  169,661 (45.2% of the applicants)

            Secondary School  151,718 (40.4% of the applicants)
```

Source: Extracted from figures provided by Mainland Visits Service, the Red Cross Society, Taipei, April 1989.

applicants, actually took the trip; among them, 183,793, or 74.5 percent of the applicants, had already returned.[4] An even more revealing breakdown of updated statistics made available by the Taiwan Red Cross is given in Table 5.1.

It is interesting to note that while the aggregate approval rate remained more or less constant (98 percent), the aggregate percentage for people who eventually took the trip dropped from 84.7 percent in October 1988 to 65.1 percent by late March 1989. It is unclear if there was a cooling off of the "China fever" or if people in Taiwan were reluctant to visit the mainland because of the winter. The return rate also had dropped from 74.5 percent to 61.8 percent. This may not be significant, since some might take their time in coming back to Taiwan and others might find it difficult to stay long in China. It is interesting to note that the majority of people who went were jobless (80 percent of the applicants), probably retired people, including a considerable number of old soldiers who followed the KMT from the mainland to Taiwan. The educational level of the visitors was also fairly low, with nearly 86 percent of the applicants having secondary school education or less. As expected, these people visited mostly close relatives such as parents, children, brothers, and sisters. Very few, however, visited their spouses, since it was highly possible that some of the spouses on the mainland may have remarried and their partners in Taiwan may have done likewise.[5] The urge to go to China does not seem to have been felt by the more active, productive, and educated of Taiwanese society. Even among those who had gone to the mainland, it was known from the one-year assessment by the Ministry of Interior that only 36.22 percent would like to go back again, 57.9 percent were undecided, and 5.55 percent would not want to visit their relatives again.[6] As shown in Table 5.2, the same source indicated that only 15.08 percent were used to the rougher life, while the majority found it either difficult to get used to or very inconvenient to live on the mainland.[7]

From Table 2, it seems that other than visiting relatives, the visitors of Taiwan were keen in sightseeing. In the eyes of the KMT, however, whether the intention was to visit relatives or to sightsee or both, the visitors could be easy prey for the united front mapped out by the CCP. Although a majority found life difficult to adjust to and were undecided on whether to return, the KMT was probably cautioned by the fact that 15.08 percent of the respondents were accustomed to the life there and 36.22 percent of the sample would like to go back. Since a majority of them were received or visited by people who were not relatives or friends, or whose identity could not be determined, it gave rise to the suspicion that Beijing could be working on these compatriots from Taiwan. Besides, they all had to spend money on their visit. According to a Taipei estimate, on average, the visitors spent about N.T. $104,000 and 15 to 21 days on the mainland.[8] The various amounts spent by the visitors as disclosed by the Ministry of the Interior in the one-year survey are given in Table 5.3.

Table 5.2
A Survey of Visitors to the Mainland from Taiwan (November 2, 1987, to October 28, 1988)

From a sample of 5,170 questionnaires:

(A) Types of Lodging while on the Mainland:
1. Homes of Relatives	76.49%
2. Hotels with Modern toilets	12.41%
3. Ordinary Hotels	4.02%
4. Others	7.05%

(B) Were You Used to the Life on the Mainland during Your Stay?
1. Used to the Life There	15.08%
2. Not Used to the Life There	45.20%
3. Very Inconvenient	38.23%
4. Others	1.47%

(C) Were You Satisfied with the Service of the Red Cross Society?
1. Satisfied	65.57%
2. On the Whole O.K.	22.95%
3. Needed Improvement	8.78%
4. Others	2.68%

(D) Do You Want to Go to the Mainland to Visit Your Relatives Again?
1. Yes	36.22%
2. No	5.55%
3. Undecided	57.09%
4. Others	1.12%

(E) Were You Received or Visited by People Who Were not Your Relatives and Friends?
1. Yes	42.30%
2. No	44.68%
3. Could Not Determine the Identity of These People	10.75%
4. Others	2.25%

(F) Have You Heard about Other Activities Conducted by Your Fellow Visitors From the Same Area?
1. Sightseeing	52.57%
2. Business	2.47%
3. Activities in Art and Literature	0.77%
4. Others	44.17%

Notes: 1. The "Others" categories denote that the respondents either did not answer the questions or failed to confine their answers to the limits of the questions. 2. If the respondents gave more than one answer, only the first answer would be tabulated.

Source: *China Times*, November 1, 1988.

As admitted by Ma Yin-jeou, executive secretary of the Task Force on Mainland Affairs and chairman of Research Development and Evaluation Commission of the Executive Yuan, these trips did help visitors from Taiwan realize the superiority of Taipei's system. The sanctioning of these visits also

Table 5.3
Amounts Spent by Visitors to the Mainland from Taiwan (November 2, 1987, to October 28, 1988)

Amount in N.T. Dollars	Percent
About $50,000.00	18.74
$60,000.00 to $100,000.00	43.34
About $150,000.00	23.48
Above $150,000.00	13.44

Source: Compiled from a report in *China Times*, November 1, 1988.

improved Taipei's image internationally.[9] However, he also noted that the drawbacks of such visits were, first, that they led to the emergence of what he called a voluntary "China fever," and, second, contributed to a lowering of Taipei's preparedness against its enemies (Beijing).[10]

To what extent will these visits affect the KMT and the reunification of China? While it is still too early to draw any concrete conclusions, it is interesting to note that an intermittent report suggested that 59.9 percent of those who had been to China and 51.4 percent of those who had not did not believe Beijing was sincere in wanting peaceful negotiations with Taiwan; less than 5 percent from both categories believed that Beijing was sincere.[11] And it seems that seeing the differences in life-style and economic system had been more useful in making the people in Taiwan reject the communist regime than their anticommunist education in Taiwan. Although samples of the project suggested that about 70 percent of those who had been to the mainland, a much higher percentage than the report from the Ministry of Interior cited earlier, would like to go to the mainland again and most of them had high praise for the sceneries there, the majority received a negative impression of the socioeconomic situation on the mainland. As a result, the visits deepened their identification with and sense of loyalty to Taiwan, although Ma, as noted earlier, suggested that there was a lowering of preparedness against communism. It seems that while the people of Taiwan welcomed the contact between the two sides, and a majority might not reject the idea of the reunification openly, they would not like to see reunification under the communists. In fact, there were indications in the research showing that those who had been to the mainland were less optimistic about the possibility of reunification.

Since one of the major purposes of lifting the ban on family visits was to dilute the yearning for independence, this objective had by and large been achieved, as demonstrated by the data in the report, shown in Table 5.4.

It is obvious that people who had been to the mainland were much less sympathetic toward the self-determination of Taiwan. They also tended to believe more that the CCP might use force, should Taiwan seek independence. On the whole, the statistics reinforced the arguments that mainland visits would enhance a sense of belonging to Taiwan and, by implication, the contributions and success of the KMT government in Taiwan to a certain extent. If that was the case, the visits did not imply that the two sides are moving toward reunification. But in view of increasing contacts, including indirect economic interactions as analyzed later, and noting the "China fever" referred to by Ma, Taiwan would have to sacrifice the benefits and profits involved should it decide for a political split with the mainland. From this angle, it could help stop the move toward Taiwan independence.

Beijing no doubt welcomed such visitors from Taiwan; but its request for reciprocal visits to Taiwan was treated with much caution. Taipei has accepted only a trickle of such requests. Notably, it has increased the visitation slightly since November 1988 by allowing mainland people to come to Taiwan to attend funerals of parents, spouses, and children or to visit family members who are seriously sick, primarily out of humanitarian reasons, as noted before.[12] Taipei apparently was reluctant to let in Taiwanese staying on the mainland, for fear that they would be used by the CCP for united-front purposes. It further decreed that no members of the CCP would be allowed to come to Taiwan.[13] After much hesitation, and urging from public and sympathetic officials, on March 31, 1989, the KMT government accepted applications to resettle on the island from KMT soldiers of Taiwanese origin who had been stranded on the mainland.[14] Again, the number was small. And according to estimates from the Ministry of Defense in Taipei, the number of such soldiers would be slightly more than 1,400, with only about 800 still living. In fact, the approved number was only 455 as of March 1989.[15] According to the KMT government, such people who had been members of the CCP or its front organizations, should renounce their membership upon arrival in Taiwan.[16] It seems that the KMT has retreated from its total rejection of CCP members, now allowing others to come to the island if they renounce communism or follow guidelines laid down by Taipei.[17]

Table 5.4
A Survey of Views on the Future of Taiwan (in percent)

	Those who were for the self-determination of Taiwan	Those who were against the self-determination of Taiwan	Those who agreed that the CCP could attack or blockade Taiwan if the Independence of Taiwan was put into practice	Those who believed that CCP would use nonmilitary means to interfere forcefully or nondrastic measures to tackle "the independence of Taiwan"
Those who had been to the mainland	7.7	63.8	51.2	8.6
Those who had not been to the mainland (mainlanders)	33.3	48.0	37.3	About 28.0
Those who had not been to the mainland (Taiwanese)	38.9	25.5	22.2	About 28.0

Source: Compiled from data reported in *China Times*, January 20, 1989.

Finally, in opening its door to people from the mainland, Taipei decided to invite outstanding mainland personalities, overseas mainland scholars, and students starting in December 1988.[18] As expected, the number involved would be small; a first batch of five graduate students from the mainland studying in the United States were invited to visit Taiwan in late December 1988. Quite obviously, these visits would be used to promote the "Taipei experience" in development, the professed second stage of Taipei's policy toward the mainland since the 13th KMT Congress. Taipei probably thought that, in view of the poor remuneration for intellectuals on the mainland but the usefulness of these people as opinion makers, it would be wise to invest in some of them for political purposes. In fact, James Soong Chu-yu, then a deputy secretary-general of the KMT, admitted that inviting influential mainland personalities to Taipei might be more useful than recruiting secret agents to attack communism.[19]

CULTURAL EXCHANGES

Contacts between the two sides have been going on in third-country conferences or on other occasions for quite a while. However, as far as Taipei's official sanctions are concerned, contacts in unofficial and nonpolitical international organizations received a green light only slightly after the establishment of diplomatic ties between China and the United States in 1979, when Beijing began to accept and consider Taiwan's membership in these international organizations.[20] The most crucial negotiations were no doubt concerning the International Olympic Committee. The decision was that Taipei would use the committee flag of its National Olympic Committee, and not its national flag.[21] Its name would be "Chinese Taipei," not ROC. Although there were some reservations about continuing to use "Chinese Taipei" because of its political ambiguity, this "Olympic formula," as it turned out, became the model followed for most, if not all, of Taipei's athletic delegations in international sports competitions, a relatively nonpolitical function. In accepting "Chinese Taipei," however, Taiwan is always insisting on parity with Beijing. Also, it insists that the change in its name should not affect its internal affairs. Furthermore, Taipei initially would sanction participation of its teams only in meetings sponsored by international organizations in third countries other than the PRC. As detailed later on, Taipei did not authorize and lay down the conditions for its "people's organizations" to take part in international competitions held on the mainland until December 1988.

As for another category of unofficial and nonpolitical organizations—namely, scientific and academic—Taipei followed more or less the same principle. As a rule, the Taiwan delegation would accept and Beijing would condone any name indicating that the group is from Taipei. An example would be Taipei's admission as the "Chinese Association of Political Science (Taipei)" into the International Political Science Association in April 1989.[22] To be on parity with Beijing, Taipei delegates may want to change the sentence "there is only one China and Taiwan is part of China" to "both mainland China and Taiwan are parts of China" in documents concerning Taipei's and Beijing's participation in some international academic and scientific bodies. A good example was Beijing's participation in an international organization for physicists, when such a change was made in the related documents of the organization.[23]

Since Taiwan was a member of more than 700 international organizations and that, on the average, it had to take part in more than 1,000 international meetings a year by late 1988,[24] it was obvious that some of these meetings would be held on the mainland, forcing Taipei to decide if it should be absent. After some hesitation, a breakthrough took place when the KMT government finally decided to allow a delegation from Taiwan to attend the annual meeting of the International Council of Scientific Unions (ICSU) in China in September 1988. Because of its "three-no" policy, it was not possible for the Academia Sinica, a member of ICSU but an intellectual body under the direct auspices of Taipei's Presidential Office, to attend. In principle, it was emphasized that civil servants and public office holders could not attend meetings on the mainland, although in practice this rule may not have been applied strictly.[25] So a newly created "people's organization," as noted in Chapter 2, was dispatched to the mainland to maintain Taipei's presence in the union. It soon became clear that other "people's organizations," as members of nongovernmental international organizations, would be allowed to attend similar international meetings on the mainland, à la the "ICSU model."[26] Official sanctioning of these meetings was finally declared by the Executive Yuan in December 1988, and it applied to all international academic, cultural, or athletic activities held on the mainland. The announcement highlighted the following points:

1. People's organizations that are members of nongovernmental international organizations may apply to take part in conferences and activities of these organizations held on the mainland.

2. For nongovernmental international organizations in which Taipei is not yet a member, application to join the conferences and activities on the mainland must be considered individually.

3. People's organizations or individuals may take part in such activities and conferences held in third areas but not those solely initiated or sponsored by the mainland.

4. People's organizations or individuals are not allowed to work with the mainland to sponsor or help in the organization of conferences or similar activities.[27]

From the above, it was apparent that the security-conscious KMT still moved very cautiously to relax its interactions with the mainland. Not only did these rules apply solely to what it defined as nongovernmental international organizations, but those functions sponsored by academic, cultural, and athletic organizations of mainland China were out of bounds, be they held in the PRC or in third countries. Moreover, no organization in Taipei was allowed to cosponsor or help in the organization of conferences or similar activities with an organization on the mainland, whether the meeting was in the PRC or in a third country. Nonetheless, the promulgation of these rules was no doubt an important step forward in the interaction of people from both sides of the Taiwan Strait.

One major remaining complication seems to be the name used on the mainland by Taipei's nongovernmental organizations. The general principle was that, while following the instructions from the international organizations as far as its name, flag, or other privileges were concerned, Taipei must not at any time accept an unfavorable arrangement by Beijing.[28] And as far as Taipei's name for its sports teams was concerned, Minister of Education Mao Kao-wen made it very clear: while accepting "Chinese Taipei" in English, he would insist on having the Chinese name "Chung-hua Tai-pei" (Zhonghua Taibei), and not "Chung-kuo Tai-pei" (Zhongguo Taibei).[29] The proper name in Chinese actually was not resolved when Taipei accepted to its name change to "Chinese Taipei" by the International Olympic Committee. Since Chinese was not used by the committee, the issue did not crop up then. However, with the signing of the Sino-British Declaration on the transfer of Hong Kong to the PRC in 1984, it was clear that Hong Kong would be a local government of Beijing, with Hong Kong designated as "Hong Kong, China" in its international activities after 1997.[30] As a result, if the Chinese translation of "Chinese Taipei" was "Chung-kuo Tai-pei" (Zhongguo Taibei), the implication, at least to the KMT, was obvious. To avoid being denigrated to a local government, Taipei insisted that its Chinese name should be "Chung-hua Tai-pei" (Zhonghua Taibei), a less political term related to culture. The trouble was that Beijing seemed to prefer "Zhongguo Taibei" (Chung-kuo Tai-pei)—and to be sure, this was consistent with its policy of reunifying Hong Kong, Macao, and Taiwan with China. The issue did not have to be solved if the international meetings were held in most third areas, where Chinese was not used. However, when functions were held on the mainland or, for that matter, in Hong Kong, Singapore, or even Korea and Japan, the issue would have to be faced squarely, since Chinese would be used by the host country. As a result, there were a series of negotiations on the Chinese name of Taipei's sports teams to the mainland, accomplished through intermediaries to avoid official contact. Finally, Beijing agreed to the use of "Zhonghua Taibei" (Chung-hua Tai-pei), possibly to build good-will in basically nongovernmental interactions.[31] At about the same time, Taipei also disclosed that if it accepted the requests of international organizations to have their conferences in Taiwan, it would follow the instructions of these international organizations on whether people on the mainland, including officials, could attend the functions.[32] In that regard, Premier Yu also stated that Taipei would attend the nongovernmental and *governmental* international conferences organized by international organizations on the mainland.[33] This move was no doubt part of Taipei's desire to make a comeback in international affairs, as noted earlier. But whether this was some sort of quid pro quo between Taipei and Beijing, each making some kind of concession, or a mere coincidence remains unclear. At the time of Premier Yu's statement, it was already known that Taipei would send its finance minister to the ADB annual meeting in Beijing. Since the ADB meeting was no longer of a nongovernmental nature, it showed vividly that Taipei was ready to take up the challenges of attending more official international conferences. As noted before, Taipei's participation in the ADB was meant to be an acid test for its desire to rejoin more official international organizations and also to present its new "one country, two governments" proposal. How Taipei would eventually deal with the name given to it by the ADB—namely, "Taipei, China"—remains to be seen. But certainly the fact that Taipei would take part in the meeting, knowing very well that it would not be possible for Beijing to sanction parity in the name, shows that it was prepared to put up with the arrangement even though it was not willing to accept it. Taipei's rationale probably would be that such names in international organizations do not change a region's existence as a separate political entity. And similar to the way President Lee Teng-hui had put it after his Singapore trip, Taipei may not be satisfied with the name, but it would not let it block its work toward reactivation of its role in international affairs. If this is the case, pragmatism seems to have prevailed. And for Taipei, peaceful competition and coexistence in international organizations, official and unofficial, seem to be more desirable in the future.

It is obvious that Taipei is gradually moving up in its level of contacts with Beijing, from nongovernmental to governmental meetings of international organizations on the mainland and elsewhere. While it has, in principle, rejected attending such meetings sponsored or co-sponsored by mainland organizations, Taipei may relax such restrictions in the future if Beijing makes conciliatory gestures. In fact, it has been argued that it may be worth Taipei's while to allow its scholars in the liberal arts and social sciences to attend conferences of that nature organized by the mainland so that they can make known their views and so that mainland scholars cannot monopolize the interpretation of various issues, especially those in modern Chinese history and social and cultural developments of China.[34]

Finally, Taipei has also relaxed its control on the circulation of publications from the mainland. While illegal publications and circulation of mainland materials have been going on for some years, especially after the lifting of the martial law and the start of visits to the mainland, the policy of the KMT was to restrict the use and circulation of these materials to a small number of institutions under close supervision. Importation of mainland publications was, as a rule, not allowed and no individual was supposed to possess any.[35] Likewise, Beijing could not obtain Taiwan's publications directly from Taipei, although it could get them through third parties like Hong Kong.[36] Apparently, after the lifting of martial law, the KMT relaxed its ban on importing mainland publications that did not promote communism.[37] As expected, publications could not be imported directly from China, and had to be reprinted in Taiwan using traditional and not the simplified characters. After the lifting of the ban on travel to China, Shaw Yu-ming, director-general of the Government Information Office, also announced that it was permissible to bring in publications from the mainland for personal use, provided these materials did not contradict the national interests of Taiwan and propagate communism.[38] He also suggested that when reprinting publications from the mainland, Taipei publishers should obtain authorization from the authors.[39]

Bans on the importation from the mainland of audiovisual materials such as movies, television, and video programs was also relaxed. The official sanction came in July 1988, when the Executive Yuan adopted some key points on the control of publications, movies, and television programs from the mainland. The key points stressed that the materials should not promote communism and proper authorization should be obtained from the authors whenever possible.[40] In relaxing the ban on these materials, the KMT did not disguise its political motivation. As disclosed by Shaw Yu-ming, the KMT government wanted to work on the intellectuals first to get their support.[41] Moreover, the KMT government had in mind to export its cultural products to the mainland in the future, in what it called the cultural offensive, the third stage in Taipei's policy toward the mainland.[42] In this regard, the KMT wanted to use its publications, movies, and other matters to influence people on the mainland.[43] It also wanted to stage exhibitions and shows by performing troupes and the like on the mainland.[44] Since Taipei's news coverage of the mainland was based mainly on secondary sources, journalists, movie and television workers, and others had been demanding to go to the mainland for professional reasons, and the KMT seemed to be quite willing to consider giving them permission to do so in this third stage. This was especially true because some journalists had already been defying the ban. Slightly before the ADB meeting in Beijing, a belated sanctioning of the mass-media professionals, including journalists, to go to the mainland on assignment was announced as part of the KMT's cultural offensive.[45] As expected, reporting of mainland news, whether in writing or by some other means, must pass through a third area; direct transmission was still not allowed. Also, the KMT government emphasized that it would allow mass-media people from Taiwan to go to the mainland, and not the other way around.[46]

It would seem that, as far as its cultural offensive was concerned, the KMT was following its overall policy toward the mainland in having a gradual, indirect, unidirectional and security-conscious approach. For a start, it emphasized selected activities at the people-to-people level and considered reciprocating these rights to the mainland slowly and selectively.

ECONOMIC RELATIONS

Ever since initiating its "peaceful" offensive against Taiwan, and its suggestion of "three exchanges" across the Taiwan Strait, Beijing has been keen to promote economic cooperation. To Beijing, the economic strength of Taipei could be tapped for its own development. It is possible that, for political purposes, Beijing may want to use trade and investment to lure Taipei into the arms of the mainland. This is precisely what Taipei is afraid of. It is always on guard against such moves by Beijing, including the possibility of economic measures to weaken Taipei's position on reunification. However, in view of the growing protectionism in the West; the appreciation of the Taiwan dollar; the increase in the cost of production in Taiwan, especially labor; Taipei's dependence on foreign trade; and, last but not least, the moves by others to break into the China market, there has been a lot of pressure from the business community in Taiwan for the KMT government to sanction and broaden economic ties with the mainland.

With China's emphasis on the Four Modernizations, it would be timely to explore the possibilities of advancing into the China market, in view of its open-door policy since 1978. The economic reforms in China have led to a change inter alia, in its attitude toward foreign trade and investment in Beijing's attempt to use its resources, especially labor and land, in a better way. In 1980, Beijing set up special economic zones in Shenzhen, Zhuhai, Shantou, and Xiamen. Subsequently more cities and coastal areas were opened to the outside world to encourage foreign investments and promote trade. As part of its reforms, Beijing also relinquished some power at the central level, implementated the responsibility system (whereby enterprises are responsible for their profits and losses) and import and export approvals to the local level, as well as relaxed loan and foreign exchange restrictions. Although there were ups and downs in its reforms, especially industrial and urban reforms, it is clear that Beijing is fairly consistent in emphasizing foreign trade and foreign investments in China's modernizations. In fact, the 13th CCP Congress, in October 1987, highlighted the need to join the world economy through the use of foreign capital, technology, and raw materials so as to develop labor-intensive export industries in coastal areas. Zhao Ziyang also talked about an "international cycle" policy in November 1987, an effort to plug China into the international economic circuit. As such, more provinces were opened to develop trade and Guangdong was called upon to be a model for the rest of China. In keeping with China's call to emulate the Taiwan or Hong Kong experiences, and perhaps even compete with these newly industrialized economies, Hainan was made a province, à la Taiwan or Hong Kong.

It would seem that there were obvious reasons for Beijing to cooperate economically with Taipei. If not for political reasons, the two areas have a large potential for trade, since they are close geographically. In addition, the similarity in race and language may help economic interaction. More important, there is room for trade expansion because of developmental differences. As noted in an article published by the Chung-hua Institution for Economic Research in Taipei, the industrial structure of both sides would, under normal circumstances, encourage Beijing to buy large quantities of light industrial materials and consumer goods produced by the so-called sunset industries in Taiwan. It would also be logical for Taipei to secure some of its raw materials from the mainland.[47] It should be noted, however, that while geographic proximity can reduce the cost of transportation, it can be argued that the reduction is not that significant.[48] Also, although Taiwan's businesses might have linguistic advantages and even kinship ties with the mainland, they are not familiar with its political, economic, and social system. The bureaucratic hurdles and unfamiliarity of the China market makes it advisable to conduct trade through a third party, probably Hong Kong.[49] Besides, if there were any trade disputes, arbitration would require the assistance of a third party, owing to Taipei's "three-no" policy.[50] Finally, there is a certain amount of competition in foreign trade of both sides of the Taiwan Strait. The same study by the Chung-hua Institution for Economic Research, in fact, noted that competition was especially keen in certain manufactured goods.[51]

In spite of these factors, it was obvious that many businesses in Taipei could not resist the temptation of jumping on the China-trade bandwagon. As analyzed later on, while there had been ups and downs in Taiwan's China trade, it was obvious that such trade was expanding and that eventually Taipei would need to lay down certain principles to govern the conduct of such interaction. This was done in July 1985, when Taipei announced the three basic principles for Taiwan's China trade: (1) there should be no direct trade with the mainland; (2) manufacturers should have no contact with official mainland Chinese organs or personnel; and (3) no steps would be taken to interfere with indirect trade between the two sides.[52] The KMT government, in recognizing the realities of the economic interaction, underscored its "three-no" policy and the necessity of conducting trade via a third party. Taipei's emphasis on indirect trade might be a result of the fact that the security-conscious KMT government did not want to be overly dependent on the China market, since this could increase the danger of the CCP's using trade as a weapon. Also, and as noted before, Taipei was in the process of upgrading its technological industries; a diversion to China for the production of labor-intensive goods—or what is called sunset industries—would slow down this process and decrease Taiwan's competitiveness with other newly industrializing economies. Likewise, Shaw Yu-ming, spokesman for the KMT government, claimed that it would be easier for Taiwan's businesses to make money elsewhere.[53] Certainly Taipei desired to branch out into other, more desirable noncommunist markets like Southeast Asia, and to strengthen its economic ties with the developed world. Finally, Shaw suggested that Taipei's trade with the mainland depended very much on politics, implying that it was risky and unpredictable as to whether it was profitable to plunge in directly.[54] Perhaps, deep in the mind of the KMT leadership, it was also considered unwise to give a helping hand to the development program of its archenemy.

To further understand the intricacies of the economic relations between Beijing and Taipei, an examination of the volume and nature of Taipei's China trade would be most useful. The trade is indirect, with the bulk of activity conducted through Hong Kong. As such, the statistics of Taiwan's China trade via Hong Kong, given in Table 5.5, should serve as a fairly accurate indicator of the economic trends in the Taiwan Strait.

Table 5.5
PRC's Trade with Taiwan via Hong Kong (in thousands of U.S. dollars)

Year	PRC's Exports to Taiwan (Taiwan's Imports from the PRC)	PRC's Imports From Taiwan (Taiwan's Exports to the PRC)	Total	Balance
1978	46,480	50	46,730	+46,630
1979	55,830	21,300	77,130	+34,530
1980	78,420	242,050	320,470	-163,630
1981	76,310	390,400	466,710	-314,090
1982	89,960	208,230	298,190	-118,270
1983	96,060	168,710	264,770	-72,650
1984	128,030	426,600	554,630	-298,570
1985	115,900	986,840	1,102,740	-870,940
1986	144,220	813,420	957,640	-669,200
1987	289,000	1,226,000	1,515,000	-937,000
1988	478,000	2,242,000	2,720,000	-1,764,000

Source: Figures from 1978 to 1986 are from Lin Yuh-jiun, "Some Aspects of the Indirect Trade between the ROC and the PRC via Hong Kong," *Economic Papers*, no. 114, Taipei: Chung-hua Institution for Economic Research, January 1988, p. 4. Figures of 1987 and 1988 were given by Chen Li-an, Minister of Economic Affairs to the Legislative Yuan in Taipei, as reported in *Economic Daily News* (Taipei), March 17, 1989.

It can be seen in Table 5.5 that the volume of trade increased noticeably from a mere U.S. $46,730,000 in 1978 to U.S. $466,710,000 in 1981, nearly 10 times as much. PRC's import from Taiwan for the same period was even more remarkable, when it increased from U.S. $50,000 to U.S. $390,400,000, an increase of 7808 times! This could be a result of Beijing's giving special preference for Taiwan trade, as demonstrated by its adoption of "Temporary Stipulations Concerning the Broadening of Trade with Taiwan" in May 1979 and the government's "Supplementary Stipulations on Procuring Products from Taiwan," in June 1980.[55] Products from Taiwan were considered to be domestic trade, and no custom duties were levied initially. Apparently, however, there were reservations about giving preferential treatment to Taiwan products, and such treatment was discontinued. While economic transactions with Taiwan were still considered domestic trade, a so-called adjustment tax was put in place for Taiwan products entering after 1981. Moreover, in the same year, such imports would need the approval of Beijing's Taiwan Affairs Office of the State Council or its branches at local levels. This no doubt contributed termporarily to a lessening of economic traffic, leading to a decrease in the volume of trade and imports from Taiwan in 1982 and 1983, as can be seen from Table 5.5. However, Taiwan imports and trade volume began to pick up again in 1984, probably because China's trade surpluses and increase in foreign exchange reserves, as well as the success of its agricultural reforms, led to further reforms in other areas. Trade reforms included decentralization of power by the Ministry of Foreign Economic Relations and relaxation of control over foreign exchange and imports, an attempt to dampen inflation.[56] The resultant boom in trade, however, created problems, especially when China's export level was not able to match its level of imports. This reversed Beijing's trade surpluses to deficits in 1984 and 1985. Its foreign reserves were also decreased, and foreign debt increased in the same period.[57] Beijing subsequently took various measures to curb imports, thus decreasing trade between the two sides in 1986. That did not continue for long, because Beijing did not also alter its basic principle of encouraging three exchanges, including trade between China and Taiwan. Besides, as noted earlier, the 13th Congress of the CCP reinforced the importance of foreign trade and the need for China to join the world economy. Moreover, products from Taipei were offered at very competitive prices. As a result, the temporary decline was swiftly reversed when imports from Taiwan and the volume of trade jumped up again by leaps and bounds in 1987 and 1988.

For Beijing, trade with Taiwan has not been significant when compared to trade with places like Japan, Hong Kong, the United States, and the European Community. On average, Beijing's trade with Taiwan via Hong Kong occupied 1.28 percent of its total trade and 0.55 percent of its exports and 1.99 percent of its imports from 1978 to 1988, as deduced from Tables 5.6 and 5.8. Moreover, except for 1978 and 1979, trade has always been in Taipei's favor. For political purposes, it was clear that the PRC would

Table 5.6
The Foreign Trade of the PRC (in hundreds of millions of U.S. dollars)

Year	Total Exports and Imports	Total Exports	Total Imports	Balance
1978	206.4	97.5	108.9	-11.4
1979	293.3	136.6	156.7	-20.1
1980	378.2	182.7	195.5	-12.8
1981	440.2	220.1	220.1	0
1982	416.0	223.2	192.8	+30.4
1983	436.2	222.3	213.9	+8.4
1984	535.5	261.4	274.1	-12.7
1985	696.0	273.5	422.5	-149.0
1986	738.5	309.4	429.1	-119.7
1987	826.5	394.4	432.1	-37.7

Source: Guojia Tongjiju, ed. *Zhongguo Tongji Nianjian (Statistical Yearbook of China) 1988*, Beijing: Zhongguo Tongji Chubanshe, 1988, p. 721. Statistics from 1978 to 1980 were from the Ministry of Foreign Economic Relations and Trade, while those from 1981 onwards were from China's Customs Office.

Table 5.7
The Foreign Trade of Taiwan (in millions of U.S. dollars)

Year	Total Exports and Imports	Total Exports	Total Imports	Balance
1978	23,714	12,687	11,027	+1,660
1979	30,877	16,103	14,774	+1,329
1980	39,544	19,811	19,733	+78
1981	43,811	22,611	21,200	+1,411
1982	41,092	22,204	18,888	+3,316
1983	45,410	25,123	20,287	+4,836
1984	52,415	30,456	21,959	+8,497
1985	50,825	30,723	20,102	+10,621
1986	63,954	39,789	24,165	+15,624
1987	88,044	53,538	34,506	+19,032

Source: *Taiwan Statistical Data Book 1988*, Taipei: Council for Economic Planning and Development, Taiwan, 1988, p. 208.

Table 5.8
Trade Between the PRC and Taiwan via Hong Kong (in percent)

YEAR	PRC			TAIWAN		
	Exports to Taiwan (percentage of total exports)	Imports from Taiwan (percentage of total imports)	Total Trade with Taiwan (percentage of total trade)	Exports to the PRC (percentage of total exports)	Imports from the PRC (percentage of total imports)	Total Trade with the PRC (percentage of total trade)
1978	0.48	Negligible	0.23	Negligible	0.4	0.2
1979	0.41	0.14	0.26	0.13	0.38	0.25
1980	0.43	1.24	0.85	1.22	0.4	0.81
1981	0.37	2.00	1.16	1.73	0.36	1.07
1982	0.41	1.19	0.76	0.94	0.48	0.73
1983	0.43	0.91	0.65	0.67	0.47	0.58
1984	0.52	1.68	1.11	1.40	0.58	1.06
1985	0.45	2.87	1.83	3.21	0.58	2.17
1986	0.53	2.46	1.59	2.04	0.6	1.5
1987	0.83	3.67	2.22	2.29	0.84	1.72
1988	1.19	5.70	3.42	3.7	0.9	2.4

Source: (i) The percentages of PRC's trade are calculated on the basis of the following figures: Figures of Beijing's exports to and imports from Taiwan for 1978–88 are from Table 5.5. Figures of the PRC's total exports, imports, and trade are from the ones given by the Ministry of Foreign Economic Relations and Trade (MOFERT) for the years 1979–88, as reported in *Beijing Review*, March 6–12, 1989, p. 23. The figures for 1978 are from *Zhongguo Tongji Nianjian 1988* (Statistical Yearbook of China, 1988), Beijing: Zhongguo Tonji Publishing House, 1988, p. 721. The source for the 1978 figures is also from MOFERT. It should be noted that *Zhongguo Tonji Nianjian 1988* used figures from MOFERT only until 1980. After 1981, it used the figures from China's Customs Office. As a whole, the figures on China's overall imports, exports, and trade from the Customs Office were *slightly higher* than that from MOFERT for 1981–88, making the percentage for the PRC's trade with Taiwan *slightly* lower. To be consistent, figures from the MOFERT are used for the period 1978–88. (ii) The percentages of Taiwan's trade are based on the following figures: Figures of Taiwan's export and imports from the PRC are from Table 5.5. Figures of Taiwan's overall exports, imports, and trade are from *Taiwan Statistical Data Book 1988*, Taipei: Council for Economic Planning and Development, ROC, 1988, p. 208, for the period 1978–87, as shown in Table 7.1. Percentages for 1988 are given by Minister of Economic Affairs, Chen Li-an, as reported in *Economic Daily News*, March 17, 1989.

like to keep the momentum going. However, it seems that Beijing could not do much on its own to accelerate exports to Taiwan, which really determined the pace of the China trade, at least with regard to goods from the PRC to Taiwan. As for Beijing's imports from Taipei, there was no doubt that its volume was developing. But because of uneven success in economic reforms; concern with the balance of payments; and, last but not least, its changing policy toward Taiwan trade, Beijing's policy on imports from Taiwan fluctuated in this period, making it quite risky for Taiwan to do business with China, especially for Taiwan businesses new to the China market. Also, although China might set aside a figure for "political purchases," its buying of Taiwanese products, notably light industrial materials and consumer products, was based more on the competitive prices offered by Taiwan.[58] For example, a study by the Chung-hua Institution for Economic Research in Taipei revealed that China set aside H.K. $550 million for "political purchases" of Taiwanese products in 1984; but the figure eventually accounted for only 16 percent of its imports from Taiwan for that year. Apparently, the rest reflected Taiwan's competitive prices and the usefulness of the goods.[59] Probably as a result of these more realistic calculations, there was much room for expansion of trade, as evidenced by the big increases in 1987 and 1988, shown in Table 5.8. On top of its aim to use bilateral trade to accelerate reunification, Beijing wanted to borrow Taiwan's developmental experiences to modernize its own economy. In trading with the other side, Beijing also hoped to attract Taipei's technology and capital, as analyzed later on, to assist in its own industrialization and to alleviate its foreign-exchange shortages.

As far as Taipei was concerned, it preferred to opt for indirerct trade with mainland China, as noted before. While it would be technically difficult to stop the export of Taiwan products across the Taiwan Strait via third areas even if it wanted to, Taipei evidently has been largely in control of imports from the mainland. Apparently, it adopted a cautious approach again, as the volume of imports from China was deliberately kept low by means of economic policies. On the whole, the volume of imports from the mainland had only increased marginally from 1978 to 1986. The portion of these imports averaged a low 0.54 percent of Taipei's total imports from 1978 to 1988. The KMT had officially sanctioned only a trickle of China's products, which it found difficult to replace as announced by the Executive Yuan in 1977. These included mainly Chinese herbal medicine and selected raw materials difficult to substitute.[60] However, with a need for cheaper raw materials, Taipei announced in August 1987 the lifting of the ban on selected items of agro-industrial raw materials from the mainland. This no doubt contributed to the more than 100 percent increase, from U.S. $144 milllion in 1986 to U.S. $289 million in 1987, in Taiwan's imports from the mainland, as shown in Table 5.5 Further relaxation was announced in 1988, when more agro-industrial raw materials were allowed to be imported indirectly.[61] This increased Taipei's imports from the mainland from U.S. $289 million in 1987 to U.S. $478 million in 1988, an increase of more than 65 percent.

Although the KMT would like to tone down efforts to break into the China market, it succumbed to domestic pressures and economic realities to a certain extent. Like it or not, other countries were moving into China. Even South Korea, which had diplomatic relations with Taipei, had done better than Taiwan in trade with China since 1986.[62] As noted before, there was a need to look for other markets, including China, in an attempt to diversify, to react to protectionism in the West, to deal with the rise in the Taiwan dollar, to meet higher costs of production at home, and to eliminate difficiencies in certain raw materials. Moreover, the China trade had been in Taipei's favor since 1980, culminating in slightly more than U.S. $5 billion in surpluses from 1980 to 1988.

As expected, Taipei was concerned with Beijing's political motivations for trade. Thus, it is useful to look at the impact of such trade, especially Taiwan's exports to China, on its economy. From the information available, it can be seen that the increase in local production brought about by Taiwan's indirect trade with the mainland via Hong Kong accounted for about 0.22 percent of Taiwan's GDP for 1978 to 1980, 0.46 percent for 1981 to 1983, and 0.95 percent for 1984 to 1986. In other words, the impact was insignificant.[63] Similarly, exports via Hong Kong accounted for only 0.13 percent of Taiwan's total domestic employment for 1978 to 1980, 0.42 percent for 1982 to 1983, and 1.06 percent for 1984 to 1986. The impact on employment was inconsequential.[64] Since the years 1987 and 1988 witnessed a fairly big increase in exports, the impact on the GDP and employment probably will be higher. Moreover, because of Taipei's heavy dependence on the U.S. market, which accounted for 44.5 percent and 38.8 percent of its exports in 1987 and 1988, respectively, a small percentage increase in its exports to other areas, including the PRC, might indicate the ascendance of a significant trade partner for Taiwan.[65] In fact, Shaw Yu-ming ventured to suggest that the economy would be hard hit if Taiwan had more than 5 percent of direct trade with the mainland, should the latter stop economic interaction.[66] Whatever the case, trade with the mainland does offer certain advantages for Taiwan. Not only can mainland China supply cheap agro-industrial raw materials and a ready market for Taiwan products, it can also help Taiwan upgrade its industry if the opportunity is skillfully exploited. The China market may allow some of Taiwan's so-called sunset industries to prolong their life if such industrialists move their businesses to the PRC. Even though this may hamper Taipei's shift to more high technological and service-oriented industries, the new lease on life for the sunset industries could prevent bankruptcy of small- and medium-size enterprises that would be hard hit by the KMT government's move to phase out labor-intensive industries. More important, if Taipei could promote sales of more advanced goods like telecommunication products, automatic data-processing equipment, and other high-tech items, it would expedite its own industrial development. Finally, it was noted that if the technological gap between the mainland and Taiwan were widened, the China trade would be more of a complementary nature, thus making it costly for China to boycott Taiwanese products.[67]

With the growth in indirect trade between the PRC and Taiwan, it was quite natural that investment and technological cooperation were born. This is especially true at a time when the PRC opted for an open-door policy with its special economic zones and coastal areas. Foreign capital, including that from Taiwan, was needed for China's industrialization. To alleviate its foreign-exchange shortage and debt problems, Beijing also found investment from abroad extremely helpful. Taiwan investors were particularly welcome, not only for reunification purposes but also for their knowledge of the labor-intensive manufacturing most relevant to China's present stage of development. For Taiwan investors hard hit by the rise in the Taiwan dollar and the cost of labor, mainland China was a new option. They were attracted by the special treatment offered by Beijing. Notably, as early as May 1983, the State Council promulgated "Methods on Preferential Treatment of Taiwan Compatriots Investing in the Special Economic Zones." Not only would Taiwan investors have all preferential treatment enjoyed by other foreign capitals in the four special economic zones and on Hainan island, but they would find additional special treatment on the mainland.[68] As more and more economic interaction developed, it became difficult for Taipei to stop the flow of capital to the mainland. President Lee Teng-hui, in fact, reluctantly disclosed that there was a need to consider selectively relaxing Taiwan's restrictions on investment and trade.[69] However, Lee underscored the point that this was on the condition that such investments on the mainland would not adversely affect Taiwan, that these industries could not survive in Taiwan anyway and that the KMT government had not come up with a method to help and guide them.[70] Apparently, Beijing was keen to attract more investment from Taiwan. When compared with trade, investment from the island involved not only the flow of needed foreign funds for development but the transfer of technological and managerial know-how as well. If properly handled, investment from Taiwan could be binding, useful in attracting Taiwanese compatriots to have a stake in the development of the mainland. Naturally, this would help the reunification process, too. As a result, it was not surprising that more areas were opened to Taiwan investors. And in July 1988, the State Council promulgated more stipulations on encouraging investment on the mainland.[71] These stipulations gave Taiwan investors preferential treatment in all provinces, autonomous regions, and municipalities directly under Beijing and the special economic zones, but also the special islands and areas for land development, such as Hainan province, Fujian, Guangdong, Zhejiang, and other coastal areas.[72] The stipulations also aimed to provide legal protection of the rights and privileges of Taiwan investors. In view of the growing number of disputes related to investment and trade, Article 20 of the July 1988 stipulations provided for these disputes to be resolved by consultation or mediation. If not, they could be arbitrated by the relevant authorities in China or Hong Kong.[73] Since legal contacts between the two sides were absent, and most trade and investments with China had to be conducted through Hong Kong, Taiwan businesses actually found it more convenient and less risky politically to have their cases arbitrated in Hong Kong rather than in China. For that purpose, agreements were reached by the end of 1988 to establish a China Commercial Affairs Coordination Committee in Hong Kong by the China Council for the Promotion of International Trade, the Taiwan Trade Mark and Patent Society, and Taiwan Trade Society of Hong Kong to mediate and solve, inter alia, business disputes.[74] All parties involved in this agreement claimed to be people's organizations and not representatives of the government, be it Beijing, Taipei, or Hong Kong.

The efforts to woo Taiwan investors paid off to a certain extent. It was known that Taiwan investment had increased since 1983, and the investments were mostly in light industries such as the production of shoes, umbrellas, and toys; prawn and eel breeding; electronics; and hotels.[75] Beijing was eager to make known to the world that such investments were forthcoming, and fairly detailed reports of Taiwan investments in places like Xiamen, Shenzhen, Beijing, Shanghai, Fujian, and Zhejiang were available.[76] According to Beijing, as of late 1988, several hundred small- and medium-sized enterprises from Taiwan had already invested on the mainland. Large enterprises in Taiwan had also sent inspection delegations to tour China, prospecting for business. The investments from Taiwan could range from hundreds of thousands of U.S. dollars to U.S. $1 million.[77] And for the year 1988, according to China, nearly 300 projects were funded by Taiwan investors who had committed more than U.S. $200 million, three times the number of projects and amounts of previous years.[78] It is unknown if these figures are accurate, since such investments are often undertaken through joint ventures with foreign companies based in Hong Kong or via other investment methods. Nonetheless, it is clear that China is paying much more attention to Taiwan's investments or, for that matter, trade. In fact, to better deal with the booming trade and investment from Taiwan, an "Economic and Trade Relations with Taiwan Bureau" was set up by the Ministry of Foreign Economic Relations and Trade in late 1988 or early 1989. The United Front Work Department of the CCP also set up a fifth bureau on the economic united front at about the same time.[79] This no doubt highlighted the increasing importance of economic ties with Taipei and the opportunities that they could offer China. In fact, Yuan Mu, spokesperson for the State Council, did not disguise the fact that preferential treatment for Taiwan businesses were based on the premise of promoting "the peaceful reunification of the motherland according to the principle of 'one country, two systems.' "[80] This will no doubt make the Taipei authorities extra careful in relaxing trade and investment with China and in promoting the "Taiwan experience" to the mainland. Thus Taipei has to caution its prospective businesses interested in the China trade against the economic and political risks involved, notably the changing situation on the mainland. Besides, it has to realize that, in Taiwan's political offensive to promote the "Taiwan experience," the CCP could make use of it for its own political purposes. It also could be very critical of the Taiwan model.[81] While acknowledging that the lessons of Taiwan's developmental model could be useful, Beijing probably also knows very well that the experiences cannot be repeated in toto, since Taiwan emerged as an economic power under special circumstances. As argued by an article in *Liaowang Zhoukan*, Taiwan's success was caused by five major factors—namely, a sound infrastructure laid down by the Japanese in the colonial days; assets and equpiment brought over from the mainland by the KMT government; talent transferred from the mainland to Taiwan by the KMT; economic and military aid from the United States, and the cold war and hot wars, notably the Korean and Vietnam Wars, which stimulated growth in Taiwan.[82] Whether we accept all these arguments or not, there is some truth in them. China could not and should not copy Taiwan, except for selected areas. Besides, Beijing is aware of the political and economic ills that Taiwan has felt in its development over the years.[83] It is also aware of Taipei's political objectives in trying to counteract the "peaceful" offensive of the CCP, moving toward a flexible diplomacy and consolidating its power at home by promoting the Taiwan model.[84] In spite of these reservations and apprehensions, Beijing will continue to encourage economic interaction because of the possible political and economic benefits that come from welcoming Taiwan trade and investment, as noted earlier.

Finally, it should be mentioned that the blossoming of economic ties between the two sides of the Taiwan Strait has given rise to the idea of some sort of Pan-Chinese Economic Community or Circle. The idea was to follow the example of the European Community, to form a similar organization for Taiwan, mainland China, Hong Kong, Macao, and even Singapore to promote economic cooperation.[85] Since reunification was unlikely to take place in the near future, the suggestion was for the separation of politics from economics and the concentration on the latter as a step toward eventual reunification. On paper, there may be economic reasons for such a move, especially among the PRC, Taiwan, and Hong Kong. However, it is too idealistic, and in fact is impractical politically. It is unrealistic, to say the least, to think that Singapore would be part of this circle. Yes, 76 percent of Singapore's population is Chinese and it would like to have closer economic ties with Hong Kong, Taiwan, and China, but it would be unwise for Singapore to ignore the feelings of its minorities and its neighboring countries, Malaysia and Indonesia. At a time when Singapore is emphasizing its Singaporean identity, a multiracial society, and is making an effort to promote its friendship with neighboring states, or for that matter, states of the Association of Southeast Asian Nations (ASEAN), it would be counterproductive to join such an economic circle, which probably would create misgivings at home and misunderstandings in the region. Likewise, suggestions to include the economic forces of the Chinese in Southeast Asia in the circle would probably strain the relationships of these Chinese with their own governments. This is especially true in countries where the Chinese problem is still a sensitive issue.[86] Moreover, that may create diplomatic and political problems for Beijing and possibly Taipei, since China's relations with the so-called overseas Chinese is always an explosive issue in Sino-Southeast Asian relations. Even for the suggestion of forming an economic system among Taiwan, Hong Kong, and the PRC,[87] it would be unrealistic to think politics could be put aside to further economic cooperation. The argument that emphasizes the bondage of a common language, blood ties, and economic complementarity as factors favoring the economic union may be just an ideal to promote, an expression of the wishes for a better and stronger China. At a time when it is fashionable to talk of various forms of economic cooperation in the Asian Pacific region, the idea of a Chinese economic circle for Taiwan, Hong Kong, the PRC, and possibly other Chinese abroad could be seen to promote the economic interests of all Chinese. Still, such an organization would probably create suspicions not only in the areas involved but among others in the region who are not members of this proposed "club." More important, the political basis and political will to do it are absent. In the final analysis, establishment of such an economic union depends a lot on the economic cooperation between Beijing and Taipei, especially after 1997 when Hong Kong is part of China. However, unlike the European Community, which consists of countries with free enterprise, the ideologically opposed KMT government in Taiwan and the CCP government on the mainland would be strange bedfellows. More important, the refusal of Taipei to have any official, direct, and bilateral contact with Beijing, and its natural suspicion that Beijing could use this circle for its united front against Taipei, would make it politically unfeasible.[88] Beijing might also be apprehensive of Taipei's possible use of the proposed scheme to highlight problems on the mainland for political purposes. As a result, policy-makers on both sides may find this scheme too academic and impractical to warrant serious efforts, at least for the time being.[89]

The unfeasibility and immaturity of the proposal, however, does not stop the triangular economic relationship from growing. Perhaps it would be best to let it develop and take shape naturally for a while. Any plans to formalize and broaden the relationship at this time would serve at best as an academic ideal. It might also cause alarm or antagonize others unnecessarily.

CONCLUDING OBSERVATIONS

It can be seen from our analysis that increased traffic between the two sides of the Taiwan Strait via third areas has in many ways made Taipei's "three-no" policy less meaningful. The proscribed areas have been narrowed and the major forbidden areas remain mainly direct trade and bilateral talks at the official level. However, all signs indicate that there will be closer economic interaction. More important, the ADB meeting in May 1989 in Beijing attended by Finance Minister Shirley Kuo had, to a certain extent, moved Taiwan a significant step toward official contact. However, reunification is by no means imminent. Essentially, what Taipei is interested in is to make a comeback in the international community, not reunification. Its relaxation of bans on travel and trade and other cultural exchanges was by and large forced onto it by demands at home and, to a certain extent, from abroad. It often lagged behind the sentiments of the Taiwan people, and policy changes toward the mainland were often a retroactive recognition of the realities. Moreover, Taipei remained determined to penalize those who were obvious offenders of the rules and regulations laid down in its mainland policy. In the mean time, it has made use of these interactions to launch what it calls a political offensive against the mainland and to consolidate its power at home. In view of the increasing interaction, it is natural that certain legal problems regarding marriages, citizenship, hereditary rights, legal or illegal migration, would have to be dealt with. As a result, temporary laws regulating relations between the two sides were under consideration beginning in early 1989.[90]

For the three major types of interaction between the two sides, Taipei has more decisive influence on the scope and outcome. With its more advanced state of development and higher standard of living, the traffic, mainly from Taipei to the mainland, not only did not endanger Taipei's own security but probably improved its image among the mainland populace. A comparison of the two sides would probably be in Taipei's favor, and this has led to, among other things, illegal migration to Taiwan.[91]

Beijing has less bargaining power and has so far failed to tempt or pressure the KMT government to talk about reunification. It has to be satisfied to work primarily on the Taiwan people who come to the mainland for a visit. And these people are mostly from the lower strata of Taiwan, so the patience and hard work put in by Beijing may not pay off that much. In the short term, it seems that Taipei is gaining more than Beijing, but whether the long-term results of the interaction will be favorable to reunification are still uncertain. Economic ties between the two sides are probably the major area that could bring both some unambiguous benefits. Although not banking on the mainland economically, Taipei had reluctantly admitted that it could derive certain advantages from the China market, in view of Taiwan's own economic problems. Beijing may also feel that it is worth emphasizing this, not only for political reasons but borrow economic strength from the outside, including Taiwan. One is also reminded of the Japanese example, as analyzed in Chapter 3, in that Beijing could contemplate using Taiwan businesses trading or investing on the mainland to lobby for the formation of one China. That again is a long and arduous process, especially since Taipei is on guard all the time. For the time being, like it or not, Beijing has to wait patiently for the reunification of China.

NOTES

1. *China Times*, 22 February 1989, and *Central Daily News*, 18 April 1989. For a chronology of events of the visitation program, see *China Mainland Studies* (Taipei), August 1988, pp. 92–98 and September 1988, pp. 99–104.

2. *United Daily News*, 31 October 1988.

3. *China Times*, 1 November 1988.

4. Ibid.

5. According to the statistics from the Red Cross Society in Taipei, only 2.1 percent of the applicants visited their spouses.

6. *China Times*, 1 November 1988.

7. Ibid.

8. *United Daily News*, 18 February 1989.

9. *Independence Morning Post*, 18 February 1989.

10. Ibid.

11. *China Times*, 20 January 1989. The research was conducted by four academics based on responses from a sampling of ordinary people, those who had been to the mainland and responsible persons from various people's organizations in Taiwan. The research techniques used were telephone interviews of 1,028 people in Taiwan, 437 questionnaires filled out by those who had been to the mainland, in-depth interviews, and analysis of related documents, policies, and other materials. Unless otherwise stated, the data of the following analysis are based on this report.

12. *China Times*, 22 November 1988.

13. *United Daily News*, 9 November 1988.

14. *United Daily News*, 16 March 1989.

15. Ibid.

16. Ibid.

17. *United Daily News*, 4 December 1988.

18. *Central Daily News*, 2 December 1988.

19. *United Daily News*, 1 February 1989.

20. *The Nineties*, May 1985, p. 42. This was disclosed by Shen Chun-shan, then a professor and later Minister Without Portfolio of the Executive Yuan in Taipei.

21. Ibid., p. 43.

22. *Central Daily News*, 13 April 1989.

23. *The Nineties*, May 1985, p. 44.

24. *United Daily News*, 22 October 1988.

25. Ibid., 19 August 1988 and 13 September 1988.

26. Ibid., 21 September 1988.

27. Paraphrased from a report in *Central Daily News*, 2 December 1988.

28. *United Daily News*, 2 December 1988.

29. Ibid.

30. See *Beijing Review*, 1 October 1984, Documents, p. iv.

31. *China Times*, 8 April 1989.

32. *China Times*, 8 April 1989.

33. *Central Daily News*, 8 April 1989.

34. *United Daily News*, editorial of 13 September 1988.

35. Ibid., 26 June 1987.

36. Ibid., 28 August 1988.

37. *Sunday Times* (Singapore), 26 July 1987.
38. *Central Daily News*, 25 March 1988.
39. Ibid.
40. For details of these key points, see *Central Daily News*, 29 July 1988.
41. Ibid., 3 August 1988.
42. Ibid.
43. Ibid.
44. *United Daily News*, 1 November 1988.
45. *Central Daily News*, 18 April 1989.
46. For details of the announcement, see ibid.
47. *Economic Outlook Quarterly* (Taipei), 10 January 1986, p. 44.
48. *China Times*, 7 January 1988.
49. Ibid.
50. Ibid., 8 January 1988.
51. *Economic Outlook Quarterly*, 10 January 1986, p. 45.
52. Ibid., p. 43.
53. *United Daily News*, 18 June 1988.
54. Ibid.
55. *Central Daily News*, 12 September 1988, and *Economic Outlook Quarterly*, 10 January 1986, p. 47.
56. For details, see Lin Yuh-jiun, "Some Aspects of the Indirect Trade Between the ROC and the PRC via Hong Kong," *Economic Papers*, no. 114 (Taipei: Chung-hua Institution for Economic Research, 1988), p. 6.
57. For details, see ibid.
58. See, for example, *Economic Outlook Quarterly*, 10 January 1986, pp. 47–48.
59. Ibid., p. 48.
60. Ibid., p. 46.
61. *Independence Morning Post*, 21 June 1988.
62. *China Times*, 24 February 1989.
63. Lin Yuh-jiun, "Mainland Trade Assessments," *Free China Review*, April 1989, p. 30. This article was based on her paper published by Chung-hua Institution for Economic Research as *Economic Papers*, no. 114, in 1988, in "Some Aspects of Indirect Trade."
64. Ibid.
65. *Economic Daily News*, 31 December 1988. See also the analysis of Chao Kang, a research fellow of Chung-hua Institution for Economic Research at the time in *China Times*, 7 January 1988.
66. *United Daily News*, 18 June 1988.
67. *Economic Outlook Quarterly*, 10 January 1986, p. 52.
68. For details, see, for example, *Liaowang Zhoukan* (Outlook Weekly, overseas edition), 8 February 1988, pp. 9–10.
69. *Economic Daily News*, 24 April 1988.
70. Ibid.
71. For details, see, for example, *Economic Daily News*, 7 July 1988.
72. Ibid.
73. Ibid.
74. *Beijing Review*, 3–9 April 1989, p. 26.
75. Ibid., p. 25.

76. For the details of these investments, see, for example, a series of reports in *Liaowang Zhoukan* (Outlook Weekly, overseas edition), 22 August 1988, pp. 8–12.

77. *Beijing Review*, 3–9 April 1989, p. 25.

78. *Liaowang Zhoukan* (Outlook Weekly, overseas edition), 26 December 1988, p. 13. The translation of this Chinese article in *Liaowang Zhoukan* to English in *Beijing Review* put it as nearly 400 projects with a total investment topping U.S. $600 million. See *Beijing Review*, 3–9 April 1989, p. 26.

79. *Ching-nien Jih-pao* (Taipei), 1 January 1989.

80. *Beijing Review*, 18–24 July 1989, p. 5.

81. See, for example, *Liaowang Zhoukan* (Outlook Weekly, overseas edition), 27 March 1989, pp. 4–6.

82. Ibid., p. 5.

83. See, for example, ibid.

84. Ibid., p. 6.

85. For details, see, for example, the proposal by Professor Cheng Chu-yuan in *China Times*, 6 June 1988.

86. The suggestion to include the Chinese in Southeast Asia could be seen, for example, in Cheng Chu-yuan's commentary in *China Times*, 4 February 1989.

87. See, for example, *Ming Pao* (Hong Kong), 10 October 1988.

88. See, for example, the editorial in *Central Daily News*, 5 February 1989.

89. It was reported that Deng Xiaoping was not receptive to the idea in January 1989, although it was not sure if he was totally against it since Chinese officials and scholars still talked about it. See, for example, *China Times*, 9 March 1989, and *Independence Morning Post*, 6 March 1989.

90. For a summary of the draft of such laws, see *United Daily News*, 19 February 1989.

91. *The Nineties*, February 1989, p. 60.

6
Conclusion

By the end of the 1980s, both sides of the Taiwan Strait developed more specific organs and policies to deal with one another. Indirect interaction between the two sides has become commonplace, an improvement when compared to earlier periods. However, it was clear that reunification was by no means near. Beijing, in mapping out a strategy based on the "one country, two systems" proposal, was not willing to accept Taipei on equal terms. And yet "the middle kingdom," the PRC, still hopes for the return of the "prodigal son," Taiwan, to the fold. Taipei was not interested in making peace, or for that matter, in making war, with the other side. It also had no desire for reunification or independence, leading some observers to call this a strategy of "four nos": no war, no peace, no reunification, and no independence. The impasse produced two de facto governments and, to a large extent, a de facto confederal state in which both parts claim to have only one China. The political glue that binds them seemed to be the rather intangible, albeit important, emphasis on nationalism, patriotism, and a sense of history.

In the mean time, disconcerting developments may keep the two further apart. After forty years of separation, ties have been weakened. The better economic performance of Taipei has widened the gap in standard of living. Localization of the KMT government and restructuring of the political institutions in Taiwan have driven the KMT to pay more attention to its domestic affairs. The rise of the opposition in Taiwan also has complicated the reunification issue, especially when some from the opposition openly ask for the independence of Taiwan. The KMT has no doubt eased restrictions on indirect contact with the mainland, and toned down its anachronistic slogan of "recovering" the mainland under the "three principles of the people." However, direct contact remains prohibited. More important, the KMT has refused to hold official bilateral talks with the other side. It has rejected the "one country, two systems" proposal—even those who are more inclined to work for reunification in Taiwan find the proposal unpalatable. As a whole, Taipei is keen to promote its political offensive and cultural offensive and to promote the "Taiwan experience" to the mainland.

Apparently, Beijing has not considered Taipei's "offensives" a threat. It probably believes that there are more advantages than disadvantages to receiving and exploiting these measures from Taipei. Quite obviously, Taiwan enjoys a higher standard of living, and this will reflect negatively on the PRC. However, Beijing may believe that the contacts sanctioned by Taipei could be exploited for its united front and could promote a better and more realistic understanding of each other's problems. The CCP probably is confident enough that it has established itself domestically and internationally, and that Taipei would not be a major threat to the mainland. From its perspective, it would be ideal if Taiwan, together with Hong Kong and Macao, are incorporated into China. The resources of these areas certainly could be tapped to upgrade development on the mainland. While it is difficult for the mainland to catch up with Taipei, it would not be difficult for certain parts of China, especially the big cities and the special economic zones, to narrow the gap. China's economic reforms in what it has called "socialism with Chinese characteristics" may also make it easier in time for Taiwan to consider closer ties. As a result, there has emerged a new emphasis in China's "peaceful" offensive against Taipei to build up socioeconomic ties, and thus to speed the movement toward reunification. Quite naturally, Beijing would also use the Hong Kong example to lure Taipei into accepting its master plan. It seems that Taipei, with Beijing's concurrence, would continue its presence in the Hong Kong Special Administrative Region after 1997, in order to promote its political and socioeconomic interests.[1]

Presently and in the near future, Taipei would be very much occupied with its domestic issues. In that way, it would make sure that there will be no disruption of its development plans from Beijing's manipulations of interaction in the Taiwan Strait or creation of tension. Taipei is, of course, interested in rejoining the international community for its own development. President Lee's visit to Singapore and Finance Minister Shirley Kuo's attendance at the ADB meeting in Beijing denote the rise of pragmatism in Taipei's diplomacy. As the world's 13th largest trade entity, and with foreign reserves of over U.S. $70 billion, it could well use economic diplomacy for its own purposes. In fact, by early 1989 Taiwan had already established commercial ties with about 140 nations and operated 62 trade or representative offices in 41 of these places under various names like the Sun Yat-sen Cultural Centre in Belgium or the Far East Trade Centre in Greece.[2] It also intended to move into more official economic organizations. For a start, its interest in the ADB was maintained by attendance at meetings in 1988 and 1989 and probably future annual meetings, although Taipei was not satisfied with its changed name. Taipei has indicated that it would like to join the General Agreement on Tariffs and Trade (GATT) and possibly the Organization for Economic Cooperation and Development (OECD).[3]

Taipei's recent diplomatic moves are in some ways similar to those of Germany and Korea. After Chancellor Willy Brandt's renunciation of the Hallstein Doctrine, two states in one nation were recognized in West Germany's ostpolitik. East Germany also responded by asking the other side to accept two separate and equal states in Germany. The sense of realism led finally to the signing of a treaty in 1972, ending the use of force toward each other and marking the beginning of cooperation based on humanitarian and political grounds. In terms of international relations, and this is the part which may inspire Taiwan, both Germanys had a seat in the United Nations and did not claim to have the exclusive right to represent Germany or to exclude one another in bilateral official relations with third countries. In the case of Korea, there have been intermittent talks between the two sides for humanitarian, economic, and trade reasons. Officially, the two sides meet not only in the Military Armistice Commission but also at parliamentary talks. It is also proposed that the North-South dialogues be elevated to a higher level.[4] What is relevant to Taipei is perhaps the fact that, despite North Korea's rejection of the South's proposal to adopt "cross recognition" by the major powers, both Koreas have not excluded each other in their official bilateral relations with third countries or membership in some U.N. organizations.

Even with these examples, it has been noted that the situations are not exactly the same. Unlike the noncommunist portions of Germany and Korea, Taipei dwarfs immensely when compared to its counterpart—in terms of land, population, political clout in world affairs, and other aspects. It knows that as a David, it has to try much harder to contend with Goliath in its drive to carve a niche for itself in world affairs. Besides, in the German and Korean cases, the involvement and understanding of the major powers have contributed to dialogues between the two sides. In the Chinese case, the relationship is basically between Taipei and Beijing, although the former still receives help from the United States. However, Taipei knows that Washington has to be realistic and take into account Beijing's objections to closer Taipei-Washington relations. Washington—or for that matter, many other states—does not want to get involved in the delicate issue of reunification. In fact, for many states, especially those in the Asian Pacific region, it is preferable to leave the issue to the Chinese, as long as peace is kept and no armed conflict disrupts the strategic balance and economic development in the region.

It should be noted that Beijing had diplomatic ties with East as well as West Germany in the 1980s. Although Beijing has formal ties with North Korea, and supports the latter's call for reunification of Korea on a confederal basis, China–South Korean relations seem to have moved a lot closer in recent years, especially in the economic arena. However, when considering China's reunification, Beijing apparently follows its own Hallstein Doctrine and refuses to grant equal status to its counterpart in world affairs, let alone accepts a confederal arrangement.[5] Beijing, however, does seem to be willing to give Taipei breathing space in world affairs, provided the latter accepts its status in official organizations as a local government of China. Beijing's emphasis on a unitary government and as the center of government is not likely to change in the near future, although it would allow Taipei to be called "Chinese Taipei," or Zhonghua Taibei in nonofficial organizations.

Since the KMT government has to face elections and is challenged by opposition parties, its margin to change policy, including policy toward the mainland, depends to a certain extent on the sentiment of the electorate. It is also based on its assessment of whether the changes will benefit the KMT in Taiwan and the anticipated reactions of the mainland. It is obvious that Taipei is, and will be in the short term, interested in keeping PRC-Taiwan bilateral contacts at low levels, since that seems to be working well for the KMT. Any bilateral contacts at higher levels would be uncalled for, since Taipei's elite thinks that its bargaining power will be duly reduced. Official and direct contacts, especially in conferences sponsored by international organizations, seem inevitable. The encounter of Finance Minister Shirley Kuo at the ADB meeting with Chinese representatives in Beijing set a precedent that probably will be repeated in similar fashion elsewhere. As the KMT becomes more confident and pragmatic, bilateral meetings or dialogues between the two sides might eventually be accepted and some kind of representation in each other's territory will be necessary.

This, however, does not mean that the two sides will be ready to reunify. Taipei sees the benefit in adhering to its one-China policy so as not to excite the other side. However, it would like to postpone talks on reunification to give itself more time and leeway to develop and make the Taipei government more representative of the people. Beijing will continue to offer the "one country, two systems" proposal for reunification. It has every intention of proving that the concept will work in Hong Kong and Macao. Whether it has the knowledge and cooperation of the local people to accomplish it is another thing. Beijing's trouble is that it does not have much to offer Taipei, especially in political terms. The CCP is anxious to have reunification, but finds it difficult or even counterproductive to push the idea too hard on an economic upstart. While it will continue to mouth the sentiments of the homesick KMT old guard and stress the blood ties to promote reunification, this strategy will be ineffective as the older generation leaves the scene and the new generation in Taiwan may not feel that attached to the mainland. Beijing's problem is confounded by the uncertainties of China after Deng Xiaoping. Since the policy toward Taiwan was mapped out mainly by Deng Xiaoping, it is unknown whether Deng's policy will be maintained when he leaves the political scene. But if pragmatism can prevail in post-Deng China, Beijing will emphasize more confidence-building measures to lay the groundwork for eventual official talks on reunification. More practical and mutually beneficial proposals, such as the promotion of a realistic understanding of each other and more trade, would be encouraged. All of these efforts will take time to bear fruit, however. While the Chinese, especially those on the mainland, may want to have one China, and some may console themselves by saying philosophically that *fen jiu bi he* (unity must come after a long separation), the road to reunification will be long and tortuous.

NOTES

1. *Sing-tao Jih-pao* (Hong Kong), 15 March 1989.

2. *Far Eastern Economic Review*, 2 February 1989, p. 29.

3. For an argument in support of Taipei's entry into the GATT and OECD, see, Andrew B. Brick, "The case for Taipei's Membership in International Economic Organizations," *Backgrounder*, no. 82 Asian Studies Center (Washington, D.C.: the Heritage Foundation. 1988).

4. *Far Eastern Economic Review*, 2 March 1989, pp. 21–22.

5. For China's reasons for accepting the Korean confederal arrangement and rejecting the same for China, see, for example, *Ming Pao* (Hong Kong), 10 October 1988.

Postscript

With the death of Hu Yaobang in mid-April 1989, China became engulfed in what turned out to be a major movement against the communist regime. The movement began with a small number of students gathered at Tiananmen Square to place wreaths in Hu's honor. Hu's supporters apparently also wanted to right the wrongs against the seemingly liberal ex-general secretary. As the demonstrations grew and spread to other parts of China, when students were joined by other segments of the population, the demands were broadened into a pro-democracy movement. The participants defied bans to demonstrate, staged hunger strikes, and became more and more defiant as the movement gained momentum. The response from the CCP under Deng Xiaoping was not clear at the very beginning. However, by late April if not earlier, it was obvious that Chinese leaders considered the situation very serious, as reflected in an editorial of April 26 in the *People's Daily*. The editorial called for a firm stand against the "turmoil" and described the situation as a grave political struggle facing the whole party and the Chinese people.[1] This stern warning went unheeded. As internal party debates on how to handle the pro-democracy movement began to be resolved in favor of the hardliners, tougher actions were taken against the demonstrators. First, martial law was declared in Beijing on May 20, after the failure of some half-hearted efforts to have a dialogue with student leaders. Second, and more important, troops from all over the country were moved close to Beijing to take action against the students and others, culminating in the violent suppression of the movement in Beijing on June 3–4, 1989. Ordered to suppress the students and their supporters by force, if necessary, PLA troops fired into demonstrators who attempted to block the work of the army, killing hundreds or more. While the full story of the episode remains to be told, and is beyond the scope of this study, suffice it to say that the Tiananmen Square incident did irreparable damage to China's national development and its international relations. More related to this study, the incident undid much of the hard work that the CCP had put in to reunify Taiwan or, for that matter, Hong Kong, with the mainland. Reactions from Taiwan and Hong Kong seemed to indicate that the reunification process would be a very difficult one.

THE CREDIBILITY OF CHINA'S REUNIFICATION POLICY AT STAKE

To the people of Hong Kong and Taiwan, the use of force in the June 3–4 Tiananmen Square incident, and the subsequent arrests of the "counterrevolutionaries," showed vividly the extent to which the hardliners would tolerate freedom and autonomy in special administrative regions. Hong Kong residents joined by leftists in the colony had earlier given material support and staged unprecedented massive demonstrations in support of the pro-democracy movement. They witnessed with anguish and horror, through their own media or in person, the clampdown on the students. Obviously, their budding desire to move toward a more representative government for Hong Kong after 1997 was shattered, and whatever illusions that some might have for communist rule in Hong Kong evaporated. As a result, the "one country, two systems" proposal—the basic law and all their promises—seemed all the more empty and meaningless. Confidence in the future of Hong Kong and in the CCP was further eroded, suggesting that the continuous outflow of Hong Kong talent might increase.

On the other hand, Beijing under Deng Xiaoping did not seem particularly pleased with the Hong Kong people, since the latter were seen to be interfering in the internal affairs of the mainland and the media were considered critical of the regime. Thus Ji Pengfei, director of the Hong Kong and Macao Affairs Office under the State Council, reaffirmed Beijing's policy toward Hong Kong and Macao. He underscored the point that some Hong Kong and Macao people had added fuel to the flames of turmoil while on the mainland. Ji's advice was that "Hong Kong and Macao should not interfere in or attempt to change the socialist system in the mainland either, not speaking of allowing some people to use Hong

Kong and Macao as a base for subversion of the central government."[2] Likewise, Jiang Zemin, who replaced Zhao Ziyang as the general secretary of the CCP, emphasized that "the well water does not interfere with the river water," meaning that capitalism in Hong Kong and socialism on the mainland should not bother each other.[3] Subsequently reports in China reiterated Jiang's point and particularly warned the All Hong Kong Alliance in Support of the Patriotic Movement in China, a pressure group formed during the Chinese student demonstrations in May and June 1989.[4] Nonetheless, Beijing emphasized that China's policy toward Hong Kong and Macao which had been formulated in line with the "one country, two systems" proposal, would remain unchanged. In view of the disruptions, the period of soliciting opinons to the Basic Law (draft) for Hong Kong would be extended to the end of October 1989.[5] Even with the resignation and/or expulsion of a few Hong Kong members of the Basic Law Drafting Committee and the Consultative Committee, the naturally cool response to the solicitation of opinions to the Basic Law (draft) from Hong Kong residents and the various disruptions of work in China as a result of the clampdown, it seems that Beijing was bent on adopting the Basic Law by the NPC in the spring of 1990.

In the meantime, China did not seem to be very happy with the British in the Sino-British Joint Liaison Group and the Hong Kong government. The Joint Liaison Group, a diplomatic body set up under the Sino-British Joint Declaration of 1984 to liaise and consult on implementation of the accord, was scheduled to have its 13th round of talks in London in July 1989, but it was called off by the British government because of the clampdown. By the time when it was resumed, it seemed that Britain was prepared to adopt a stronger posture by putting the blame on Beijing for Hong Kong's crisis in confidence. It was prepared to introduce a relatively quicker pace of democracy for the colony before 1997 and to ask for more safeguards on the maintenance of public order in the Basic Law. In fact, Barrie Wiggham, the Hong Kong Government's secretary for general duties, asked Beijing to delay the promulgation of the Basic Law and not to station the PLA in Hong Kong after 1997.[6] While the British moves might have been aimed at diverting attention from the demand for the right of abode for more than 3 million British passport holders in the colony, and it remains to be seen how much London is going to pursue a "tougher" line toward Beijing, China certainly was irked by the British. It accused London of interfering in the drafting of the Basic Law and contravening the 1984 Sino-British Joint Declaration. It was most adamant in insisting that it had every right to station troops in Hong Kong, as made known by

Deng Xiaoping in 1984.[7] While the massive demonstrations in Hong Kong
during May and June in support of the pro-democracy movement might
have indicated a political awakening of the Hong Kong people, China did
not want any drastic changes in Hong Kong's political structure. It would
probably look with great skepticism on the need to introduce a bill of
rights, as proposed by the Hong Kong government to restore confidence
in Hong Kong's future.[8] It was also perturbed that Britain under Margaret
Thatcher wanted to "internationalize" the Hong Kong issue in forums such
as the meeting of the Group of Seven in Paris in July 1989, the United
Nations General Assembly meeting in September 1989, and the Common-
wealth Heads of Government meeting in Kuala Lumpur in October 1989.[9]
From all indications and the three-day meeting of the Sino-British Liaison
Group meeting in late September, it was clear that Beijing would not make
concessions and maintained that it had the right to move troops into Hong
Kong "for purposes of defense" according to the Sino-British Joint Declaration. It was also resolute in telling the British to mind their own
business about Hong Kong after 1997. As for the possibility of foreigners
using Hong Kong as a base for anti-Beijing activities and Hong Kong's
interference in mainland affairs, it was known that the standing committee
of the NPC might propose articles in the Basic Law that would bar Hong
Kong residents from taking part in anti-PRC activities and severely curb
press freedom in the Hong Kong Special Administrative Region.[10]

China's displeasure with Britain with regard to Hong Kong seemed
unabated when it lashed out at London's decision to relocate its naval base
in Hong Kong from the edge of the colony's central business hub to an
outlying island. To Beijing, this was a related development regarding the
stationing of Chinese troops in the future, and the move could be an attempt
by the British to prevent China from setting up a naval presence in Hong
Kong's financial district. Moreover, China, according to Xu Jiatun, then
head of the Xinhua News Agency in Hong Kong, considered that this issue
could be settled by the Sino-British Joint Liaison Group and should not
be announced unilaterally by the British.[11] Apparently, China was also
piqued by Hong Kong's decision to allow a Chinese dissident swimmer
to go to the United States instead of repatriating him to China. This led to
Beijing's warning that the incident would ruin cooperation between China
and Hong Kong and adversely affect the normal contacts between the two
people. Subsequently, it refused to accept the return of illegal Chinese
immigrants from the British colony, at least for a little while, probably to
unnerve the Hong Kong government and to show that Beijing's long arm
can reach across the border and make life unsettling in Hong Kong, should

the latter breach its limits of tolerance.[12] To further control and inhibit Hong Kong's reportage on mainland affairs, Beijing announced that journalists from the colony would have to apply to the local branch of the Xinhua News Agency 15 days prior to any assignment on the mainland.[13] It also put pressure on the All Hong Kong Alliance in Support of the Patriotic Movement in China to disband.

As 1989 drew to a close, it was learned that London was finalizing a package to offer full British nationality to 50,000 "key" people and their families in order to meet the needs of the residents of Hong Kong and to calm the crisis in confidence. Again, this package will surely produce further conflicts between the British and Chinese governments, since the latter looked at the move with great suspicion and could claim that it might contravene the 1984 Sino-British Joint Declaration on the future of Hong Kong.[14]

In spite of all the sound and fury from China, it would seem, however, that Beijing is keen on repairing its image in the colony before the takeover in 1997. Although people's confidence in the future of Hong Kong was in tatters immediately after the June crackdown, Beijing seems determined to sell the "one country, two systems" concept, undoubtedly with much more difficulty this time around. While there was no way that Beijing could stop people from emigrating and buying an "insurance policy" to move out of Hong Kong, Beijing would try hard to win back some support from the colony, probably by sweetening its policy toward Hong Kong. This may not be just for Hong Kong but also for Taipei, since Beijing wants to repair its "peaceful" intention in reunifying the country. The experiment in Hong Kong has to be attractive enough to lure Taipei to talk on improvements in PRC-Taiwan relations and, it is hoped, on the question of reunification of China at a later stage. As it was, some businesses and individuals in Hong Kong were already maintaining a careful public posture that did not come across as antagonistic to Beijing. It remains to be seen, however, if Beijing can succeed in an uphill battle to win over the skeptical hearts and minds of Hong Kong to preserve stability and economic prosperity before 1997 and beyond.

TAIPEI'S POLITICAL OFFENSIVE

Ever since the KMT government revealed its interest in considering the "one country, two governments" proposal, Taipei has been interested primarily in consolidating its gains on the island and carving a niche for itself in the international community. The death of Hu Yaobang and the subsequent student agitations did not arouse much attention from the KMT leadership. On the whole, Taipei's response was low-key and cautious. Thus the Central Standing Committee of the KMT, meeting on April 26, 1989, generated only verbal endorsement of the pro-democracy movement, considering it important for spreading the "Taiwan experience" to the mainland.[15] The media in Taipei no doubt reported the events; some newspapers gave considerable coverage to the turmoil on the mainland, indicating that there was still some empathy between the people of Taiwan and those on the mainland. However, Shirley Kuo's trip to Beijing to attend the ADB meeting, at least as far as the media in Taipei were concerned, overshadowed the student protests. To Taipei, Kuo's trip was much more important, a bold testing of the waters for de facto recognition of two separate political entities in China and the "one country, two governments" proposal. Since the CCP government wants to dwarf the KMT government into a local government of China as far as the ADB goes, it was not surprising that Taipei again protested the designation of "Taipei, China" for its delegation at the meeting. Only this time, Taipei officially protested the name.[16] Nonetheless, by and large it followed international protocol in attending the meeting. The Taipei delegation met Beijing officials primarily in functions hosted by the ADB, but it tried to avoid meeting in occasions arranged separately by the host country, China.[17] The excitement about Shirley Kuo's trip in Taiwan, and the general acceptance of the usefulness of such close encounters with Beijing and other countries in official occasions, was a boost to the KMT government's strategy for a comeback in the international community. As the euphoria surrounding the ADB meeting began to subside and the situation in China began to get worse for the students, it seems that relatively more attention was paid to the tension on the mainland. This was especially true when the events in China attracted worldwide support, particularly from the West and in Hong Kong, where there were massive demonstrations in support of the students. Still, the KMT's response was very conservative; it was not really prepared to take concrete action. After declaration of martial law in Beijing, the spokesperson for the KMT government issued "A Statement by the Government of the Republic of China on the Movement for Freedom and Democracy in Mainland China" on May 21, 1989, declaring Taipei's steadfast support for the pro-democracy movement and condemning the Chinese communists.[18] It was also known that President Lee Teng-Hui and KMT Secretary-General Lee Huan had called for meetings examining the situation and deliberating a proper response.[19] It seems that, at that time, the KMT was still holding a wait-and-see position, in spite of all the polemics that Taipei would join hands with mainland compatriots to fight the communists and act as the "rear guard." However, the general public and the nonruling elite of the KMT, notably the ordinary KMT members of the Legislative Yuan, were more forthcoming in demanding the government take action against the communists.[20] In fact, an unprecedented massive demonstration in support of the pro-democracy movement, similar to those earlier in Hong Kong and elsewhere, took place in Taipei on May 31, 1989.[21]

The KMT's cautious posture before the June 3–4 incident, according to Shaw Yu-ming, director-general of the Government Information Office, was attributed to Taipei's not wanting to give the Chinese communists an excuse for suppressing the movement.[22] While there may be some truth in this, it should be noted that the KMT probably had other concerns as well. For one thing, Taipei had its own share of problems from university students. It probably did not want to be seen encouraging student agitation on the mainland nor contradicting itself by supporting students on other sides while putting the lid on democracy at home. In fact, at the time of the pro-democracy movement on the mainland, some students at Taiwan National University clashed with university authorities about the election of the student union president and "self-determination" of the students.[23] More than 800 academics from 22 institutes of higher learning also petitioned the Legislative Yuan for academic freedom and campus democracy in the drafting of legislation for the universities.[24] For another, the KMT was caught up in the problems created by the resignation of Premier Yu in May. These problems were not really settled until late May, when it was known that Lee Huan would succeed the premier and that James Soong would take over Lee Huan's job in the KMT as the new secretary-general.[25] The personnel changes in the government as well as the party certainly would have required considerable KMT energy and attention to paving the way for a smooth transition. Most important, the KMT government's priority lay more in the development of Taiwan and the security of the island. Its concern with the mainland and related policy toward the mainland were secondary and had to be subsumed under Taipei's primary concern with development and security on the island.[26] This was made abundantly clear by President Lee Teng-hui in the first day of the second plenary session of the 13th Central Committee of the KMT, June 3, 1989. While self-congratulating the KMT's claim that the demands of democracy and freedom on the mainland were the inevitable result of Taipei's gradual and relaxed policy and reiterating the KMT's support of the pro-democracy movement, President Lee admitted unequivocally that there was no way for the KMT government to exercise its rule on the mainland for the time being and that it would be best for Taipei to be courageous enough to admit this fact and map out practical and pragmatic policies based on effective rule in its own area of influence.[27] In terms of foreign affairs, there was de facto recognition that Taiwan could not represent the whole of China, although Lee talked about one China and that it must be unified eventually. Nonetheless, the KMT's emphasis on self-concern and self-preservation did not prevent it from watching the situation closely. In fact, officials of the KMT were summoned by President Lee to an emergency meeting on the morning of June 4, 1989, after news of the June 3–4 crackdown. An emergency press conference was held at 11:30 A.M. the same morning to allow President Lee to make known Taipei's stand.[28] On top of his condemnation of the Chinese communists in their use of force and indicating his support of the pro-democracy movement, President Lee also urged in the press statement that the people of Taiwan "remain alert to the Chinese Communists' inclination towards the use of violence and military force, and to be prepared, on the eve of the collapse of the Chinese Communists, for any action that they might risk taking."[29] Accordingly, the armed forces in Taiwan were put on alert, indicating Taipei's security consciousness and its emphasis on self-preservation. Apparently, Lee felt compelled to make other concrete responses toward the events in China. These were made known by James Soong to the participants of the KMT meeting on June 4, 1989.[30] They were also made known officially by the government on June 7, 1989, when it spelled out its response in the "Measures to Support the Mainland China Democracy Movement."[31] Other than condemning the CCP and alerting its own armed forces, Taipei declared that it would ask the Red Cross to transmit aid to the Chinese on the mainland. It called upon like-minded nations to stop all transfers of military equipment and technology to Beijing. It also urged the world media to broadcast the truth of what was happening on the other side of the Taiwan Strait.[32] The new premier, Lee Huan, also made it clear that there would be no contraction of the relaxed visitation program, although he asked the businesses of Taiwan to exercise more caution in trading with the mainland.[33] The emphasis was still very much on the export of the "Taiwan experience" and the use of political rather than military offensives against its rival.[34] In concert with this emphasis, Taipei launched a propaganda blitz against Beijing by breaking the latter's blackout on news concerning the Tiananmen incident. It volunteered to provide aid to mainland students and scholars abroad who had their passports or stipends revoked. It also declared that it would invite pro-democracy participants to visit Taiwan and organize conferences to discuss the developments on the mainland.[35] More administrative measures adopted in principle by the Ministries of Education, Foreign Affairs, the Interior and the Government Information Office were announced on June 16. These included the proposal from the Ministry of Education to give financial aid to mainland students and scholars involved in the pro-democracy movement abroad; the proposal from the Ministry of Foreign Affairs to give three-year or six-year passports for identification purposes to mainland students or scholars who wanted to forsake their Beijing passports; the proposal from the Ministry of the Interior to invite pro-democracy participants by people's associations to visit Taiwan; and the measures adopted in launching a propaganda campaign against the main-land.[36] On top of these, the most dramatic measure adopted by the KMT government to exploit the situation on the mainland was the approval by the Task Force on Mainland Affairs of a policy governing indirect mail and telephone calls across the Taiwan Strait. While claiming to adhere closely to the "three-no" policy, the new policy brought forward for early implementation allowed people of Taiwan to call those on the mainland if they were connected through Hong Kong or other places starting June 10. Since the connections in Hong Kong, Japan, and the United States were automatic, there was de facto direct telephone communication and sub-sequently other types of telecommunications as a result. Likewise, simpli-fied procedures were adopted to send mail from Taiwan to the mainland. All such mail would not have to be handled by the Red Cross. Instead, Taiwan would send it to the mainland via Hong Kong. Again, there was de facto direct mail service shortly after the June Tiananmen Square incident.[37] In concert with these moves, other sectors in Taiwan were encouraged to join the efforts to break the news blackout imposed by Beijing. For example, the *United Daily News* dispatched a million copies of newspapers, attached to weather balloons, across the Taiwan Strait. Taiwan ships were asked to distribute news scrapbooks and transport newspapers or even radios to mainland sailors or residents they might meet on the high seas or elsewhere.[38] These efforts were aided by the govern-ment's Broadcasting Corporation of China effort to expand the number of its shortwave channels and broadcast time to provide more information.[39] To demonstrate its sorrow and respect for those who had been killed, Taipei's governmental institutions and others lowered their flags to half-mast on June 14, 1989.[40]

Taipei's somewhat belated reaction to the developments on the main-land denoted its recognition of the realities of politics in China. It realized it could not really replace the Chinese communists on the mainland, at least for the time being, as emphasized by Lee Huan before the turmoil. Even with the chaos produced by the pro-democracy movement, Taipei did not make any attempt to overthrow the communist regime, although it did try to use the episode to project itself favorably, not only on the mainland and at home but to Chinese abroad and to the international community. In view of its emphasis on self-preservation and its priority on development at home, Taiwan found the Tiananmen Square incident very useful in cooling down the "China fever" and diluting whatever illusions that some in Taiwan might have about the CCP and its policy on reunification. The concern of the people of Taiwan for their compatriots on the mainland also made the opposition's claim that the Taiwanese were not Chinese less credible. It should be noted, however, that although the reactions of the people on Taiwan revealed that they could not totally separate themselves from the mainland, and that emotionally they were still linked to the people on the other side, the limited and cautious reactions of the KMT revealed that pragmatism was still in command and that Taipei would prefer to steer the island into a safe haven for its people in a secluded place off the Chinese coast. While rhetorically reiterating its interest in one China, it was much more occupied with "coercing" Beijing and persuading the international community to recognize a separate Taipei. As a result, the Tiananmen Square incident was exploited by Taipei at a time when many countries, especially those in the West, were abhorred by the mainland's use of force against unarmed citizens. The events allowed Taipei to show its successful developmental experiences and to be worthy of membership in the international community. With its skillful use of economic diplomacy, its "elastic" posture in establishing ties with other countries, and its more favorable international environment, Taipei was able to woo smaller states into having official ties with it. It began to score some success when countries like Grenada, Liberia, and Belize, at the risk of antagonizing Beijing, felt it "profitable" enough to upgrade their relations with the KMT government to the official level in the latter half of 1989.[41] While these smaller states clearly had adopted a two-China policy in having official ties with both Beijing and Taipei, and that soon proved unacceptable to Beijing, as analyzed later, the KMT government turned over a new leaf in its diplomacy. It showed clearly that it would accept diplomatic ties with other countries even if the latter had formal ties with Beijing. In addition, Lee Huan indicated clearly that the emphasis of Taipei's diplomacy in the future would not be just to have economic relations with countries but to upgrade its relations to the official level.[42]

The initial jubilation in Taipei when Grenada and Taiwan established diplomatic ties on July 20, 1989, gave the impression that the KMT government was keen to test the use of dual recognition in international affairs. To prevent Beijing's pointing an accusing finger at Taipei for creating two Chinas, however, it denied its acceptance of this formula and it attributed this to Grenada and other third parties. As far as the KMT government was concerned, so the argument went, it had never recognized the diplomatic documents signed between the "rebels" in China and Grenada, since Beijing and Taipei had never really accepted each other officially. According to Taipei, the question of two Chinas and dual recognition did not arise.[43] However, others conceded that the move with regard to Grenada was dual recognition under the one-China principle, in the sense that the practice was applicable only to foreign affairs. This was considered to be an exigent measure to deal with the separateness of the two sides of the Taiwan Strait in the transitional period before the eventual reunification of China.[44] Still others noted that the move would invariably give rise to suspicions of revived interest by the KMT in the "one country, two governments" proposal, which was considered earlier by the Executive Yuan under Premier Yu although denied as government policy later by President Lee.[45] Whatever the case, it was clear that the KMT government would continue the pragmatic line laid down by President Lee, as first revealed by his trip to Singapore in early 1989. Other visits, including those conducted by high-level officials of Taipei's Ministry of Foreign Affairs in their "private capacity" to places in Southeast Asia, Europe, and other countries in 1989, underscored the renewed activist posture to rescue Taiwan's sad state of affairs in foreign relations and upgrade its relations with other countries to a semi-official or even official level, if possible.[46] Taipei even considered expanding its economic relations with socialist countries like Albania, the Soviet Union, North Korea, the Indochinese states, and Cuba. Earlier, Taiwan had sanctioned direct trade with seven of the Eastern European states. By August 1989, it was known that Taipei was considering upgrading its indirect trade with the Soviet Union, North Korea, and Albania by having "three exchanges" in transportation, communication, and foreign exchange and taking other measures to facilitate economic intercourse between Taiwan and these socialist countries.[47] Direct trade with the Indochinese states and Cuba was also in Taipei's cards.[48] On top of this, officials from Eastern Europe might be allowed to come to Taiwan, depending on the merits of each case.[49] And in concert with this move, some Soviets had already been to Taipei to take part in international meetings. These included two Soviet observer delegates who attended an economic meeting for Pacific Basin countries in Taipei in May 1989.[50]

Taipei's pragmatism also had its impact on its policy toward Hong Kong and Macao. On the one hand, the Tiananmen Square incident reinforced the KMT's belief that China's smiling diplomacy was a farce, a bait to lure it to the conference table to discuss reunification of China, and that Beijing would not hesitate to use force to achieve its objective. Beijing's intolerance of the people of Hong Kong in supporting the pro-democratic elements on the mainland, and the liberal sector of Hong Kong's move to ask for more genuine measures to guarantee Hong Kong's autonomy, reinforced Taipei's cynicism and criticism about the "one country, two systems" proposal. On the other hand, the decision of the KMT to stay in Hong Kong even after 1997 did not seem to have changed. The principle laid down by the KMT, as revealed by Deputy Prime Minister Shih Chi-yang in March 1989, was to use Hong Kong, or for that matter, Macao, as a stepping stone to spread ideas on democracy and freedom to the mainland, thus refuting the "one country, two systems" proposal and preventing Beijing from downgrading Taipei to a local government. The KMT also proclaimed that it would support Hong Kong in safeguarding its prosperity and its moves toward democracy and freedom.[51] From the announcements made by the KMT in mid-June and early August 1989, it seems that these principles were not altered. The KMT also revealed that it had worked out its short-term, medium-term, and long-term policies toward Hong Kong and Macao, and had classified those policies as part of its policy toward the mainland.[52] The use of force to crush the dissidents in Beijing did not seem to have influenced the KMT to stay in Hong Kong after 1997. The contacts between Taipei and Hong Kong might be direct contacts between the two sides of the Taiwan Strait when Hong Kong became part of China after 1997, although the KMT government could argue that it still had no direct dealings with the authorities in Beijing. In the meantime, Taipei had worked out contingency measures to help the people of Hong Kong and Macao in the aftermath of the Tiananmen Square incident. It announced that Taipei would consider giving refuge to former pro-Beijing elements who could be persecuted by the CCP as a result of their support to the pro-democracy movement during their sojourn in Hong Kong and Macao.[53] It would also consider giving Taipei's passports to these people.[54] It further claimed that it would simplify the immigration procedure for residents in Hong Kong and Macao to move to Taiwan and would help these people to migrate to third countries if they wanted to.[55] In its declared objective to fight for freedom and more political rights for the people of Hong Kong and Macao, the KMT government even wanted to ask the CCP to guarantee: (1) the promise of not changing the system in Hong Kong for 50 years and letting Hong Kongers run Hong Kong after 1997; (2) acceptance of suggestions from the people of Hong Kong in amending the Basic Law; and (3) noninterference in the policies of the Hong Kong government through the Sino-British Joint Liaison Group and abstinence from sending communists to administer Hong Kong.[56]

From these moves, it seemed that Taipei was quite prepared to accept Beijing's professed arrangement for Hong Kong and Macao to a certain extent. It was pragmatic enough to realize that Hong Kong could still be useful as a launching pad for promoting its "Taiwan experience." By having continuous contact with Hong Kong, Taipei probably would keep alive the communication channels with the mainland. This could not only serve its economic interests but, more important, be a barometer for the actions and reactions of Beijing toward the KMT government when the latter changes its domestic as well as foreign affairs. Since Taipei's ambitions to take over Hong Kong as a financial center and absorb the talent from Hong Kong may not work out in view of the probability that Hong Kong will stay an important international economic entity after 1997, and the reluctance of Hong Kong residents to immigrate to Taiwan for one reason or another, the KMT is realistic enough to accept these and prepare to meet with officials of the Hong Kong Special Administrative Region after 1997. In fact, the ADB meeting in Beijing in May 1989 indicated clearly that KMT officials were prepared to meet CCP officials in Beijing, not to say Hong Kong. One possible worry of some in Taipei is that Hong Kong's refugee problem might be shifted to Taiwan when the colony is returned to China. With the spreading of Taiwan's success story on the mainland, the attraction for mainlanders to move to Taiwan would be enhanced and the KMT's refugee problem could thus be compounded. This prompted Taipei to be very strict in admitting illegal immigrants and levying heavy fines for those who dared to employ these people from the mainland.[57]

BEIJING'S "PRINCIPLED" POLICY TOWARD TAIPEI

After the death of Hu Yaobang, the most significant and immediate development in PRC-Taiwan relations was no doubt the ADB meeting in early May 1989. Beijing did not use the occasion to embarrass the delegates from Taipei. In fact, it tried to accommodate the sensitivities of the Taiwan delegation in its immigration procedure, accommodations, and other details.[58] Apparently, China wanted to treat Taipei's presence at the ADB meeting in a low-key fashion. Its primary concern was to see that Taipei would not be able to make use of the occasion to produce two Chinas, and as a result its stand on having a one-China policy and the naming of Taipei as "Taipei, China" was upheld at the insistence of Beijing. The meeting itself did not produce any "hiccups" in Beijing-Taipei relations, since China displayed "brotherly love" toward Taiwan. Special emphasis was placed on treating the Taiwan delegation as kin from the other side of the Taiwan Strait. Chinese leadership might have been embarrassed or perturbed by on-going student pro-democracy actions, which by then had spread in the Chinese capital and to other parts of China. But the ADB meeting was not disturbed that much, especially when compared with the Sino-Soviet summit in mid-May 1989. Problems in PRC-Taiwan relations arose only after the ADB meeting, when China was engulfed in domestic turmoil. There were many journalists from Taiwan present for the ADB meeting; the KMT had earlier sanctioned reporters, film-makers and television and radio personnel to visit the mainland in order to pursue what Taipei called its "cultural offensive" against the mainland. A large number of these who came for the ADB meeting stayed on to cover the pro-democracy movement. Problems began to arise when the PRC propaganda apparatus alleged that undercover agents of the KMT were fanning the flames of dissent on the mainland.[59] To "prove" its case, in late June 1989 Beijing announced the arrests of a number of KMT agents working on the mainland.[60] Although the KMT admitted that it had agents on the mainland, it denied their involvement in the pro-democracy movement.[61] And, of course, it would be naïve to think that the KMT agents could have exerted so much influence. But Beijing apparently would like to divert the attention of its people to these agents and shift the blame to the other side of the Taiwan Strait. This probably reinforced Taipei's belief that it would be better to take precautionary measures, including military preparedness, in case Beijing wanted to take drastic measures as a desperate move to shift the attention of the people on the mainland. Some people from Taiwan could have been involved in the turmoil to a certain extent—notably, one Taiwanese journalist was caught meeting with a prominent dissident on Beijing's wanted list. A reporter from Taiwan's *Independence Morning Post* was detained for having contacts with a dissident, then subsequently released after some interrogation by security officials. However, he and a colleague from the same newspaper were asked to leave the mainland after their admission of "guilt."[62] Subsequently, Beijing seemed to be more careful in allowing reporters from

Taiwan to come to the mainland. After the *Independence Morning Post* incident, it required Taiwan reporters to obtain permission for their assignments from either the New China News Agency in Hong Kong or other diplomatic missions of China.[63] Nonetheless, it was obvious that Beijing did not want to strain PRC-Taiwan relations. After all, it still had its interest in promoting the reunification of China. In fact, as early as June 26, Tang Shubei, Beijing's deputy director of the Taiwan Affairs Office of the State Council, issued the first statement after the Tiananmen Square incident regarding the unchanged policy toward Taiwan. Although he had misgivings about Taipei's alleged actions, he reiterated Beijing's basic policy for the solution of Taiwan—namely, "peaceful reunification and one country, two systems" for the two sides of the Taiwan Strait.[64] Subsequent CCP leaders such as the newly elected general secretary Jiang Zemin, Li Xiannian, and Wu Xueqian restated Beijing's "peaceful" strategy in reunifying the country.[65] On top of this, China announced as early as June 20 that there would be no changes in Beijing's trade and investment policies toward compatriots from Taiwan.[66] This was reiterated subsequently.[67] To be more specific, Tang Shubei from the State Council's Taiwan Affairs Office had some rather detailed suggestions on how China would bridge the gap. Notably, he suggested on June 27 that exchanges be on a direct, mutual and equal basis.[68] And on September 15, 1989, he suggested that the CCP and KMT negotiate directly about the concrete problems that had cropped up as a result of the exchanges. These could include the smuggling of people, especially young girls and rare animals, from the mainland to Taiwan.[69] While Beijing might be very critical of Taipei because of the alleged interference by so-called Taipei spies and journalists, by and large it was following its former policy of a "peaceful offensive" against Taiwan. After the Tiananmen Square incident, Beijing was keen to preserve law and order on the mainland. It would like to maintain peace and stability in the Taiwan Strait so that it could tackle its many developmental problems at home. Based on previous experiences in dealing with the people of Taiwan, Beijing still valued these relationships not only for the four modernizations but for the reunification of China.

Beijing probably was quite relieved that contact at least at the unofficial level was not adversely affected. Except for a short period after the Tiananmen Square incident, the people of Taiwan were quick to resume their practical contacts with the other side. Not only did athletic teams attend functions on the mainland starting in August 1989, but quite a number of people's organizations went to China for a visit.[70] Some residents also seemed keen to tour the mainland, considering it was a good time to go in view of decreased tourism.[71] Contact with the mainland was facilitated by the de facto direct telecommunication links starting in early June 1989. Likewise, trade did not seem to be affected except for a short period after the June crackdown. From the studies by the Chung Hwa Institute for Economic Research in Taipei, it can be seen that businesses from Taiwan were prompt to return to the mainland to make a quick profit.[72] They were cashing in on Beijing's problems stemming from Western economic sanctions against China after the June incident. The major attraction for Taiwan businesses remained the cheap labor and plant sites on the mainland. On top of these, there were the special privileges like tax holidays and managerial autonomy, dished out to investors from Taiwan by Chinese officials eager to attract money to the mainland. Beijing's only concern probably was the fact that trade was always in Taipei's favor. And for the first seven months of 1989, Beijing's deficit in such trade through Hong Kong was H.K. $10.648 billion, as shown in Table 7.1.

Table 7.1
PRC's Trade with Taiwan via Hong Kong (January–July 1989) (in billions of Hong Kong dollars)

Trade Across the Strait	Value	Percentage Change from 1988
PRC Imports from Taiwan	13.313	61
PRC Exports to Taiwan	2.665	30
PRC Deficit	10.648	71

Source: Chung Hwa Institute for Economic Research, as reported in *Far Eastern Economic Review*, November 16, 1989, p. 69.

Although it has been argued that the actual balance could be in Beijing's favor if one takes into account the value involved in the smuggling traffic, tourism, and personal remittances from Taipei to the mainland, the deficits from the "official" statistics obviously were a concern of the PRC resulting in a subsequent move by Beijing to require the Taiwanese to channel all their trade through 68 designated state-run companies.[73]

Finally, Beijing did not condone Taipei's strategy to upgrade relations with the outside world. It has always criticized Taiwan's elastic diplomacy as an attempt to create two Chinas, or one China, one Taiwan. It has also considered such a strategy as a move by Taipei to delay reunification of China.[74] As noted in previous chapters, Beijing adhered closely to a unitary government, even under the "one country, two systems" proposal. It claims to be the only legal government representing China, and that Taiwan is part of China although it does not object to the unofficial ties Taipei has in its economic, trade, and cultural exchanges with other countries. However, when Taipei began to opt for development of official or even semi-official ties with other countries that had already established diplomatic ties with the PRC, Beijing clearly had doubts about Taipei's professed objective of having one China. The critical test came when Taipei managed to attract Grenada to establish formal ties in July 1989, even though the latter had diplomatic ties with the PRC since 1985. Beijing's decision was to suspend diplomatic relations with Grenada in early August 1989, thus thwarting what it considered Taipei's attempt to pursue an elastic diplomacy, "to bring about 'dual recognition' or to create 'two Chinas' or 'one China, one Taiwan.' "[75] Probably, Beijing calculated that it could afford to break its link with a small country and that, chances are, Taipei might succeed in tempting only small countries which could use the economic help from Taiwan. For larger countries, especially those which had vital strategic and economic interests in common with China, Beijing's hope was that they might not be tempted to follow Grenada's example and could exert their influence on the China policy of others. More important, it was a matter of principle that China severed its relations with Grenada. If it swallowed its pride and accepted dual recognition, it would open a Pandora's box of diplomatic embarrassment for Beijing, giving Taipei more breathing space in international affairs. Quite obviously, that would set a precedent that could also hamper or at least slow down the process of reunification. As a result, it was not surprising that Beijing likewise severed its formal ties with Liberia and Belize in October 1989, when the latter countries resumed diplomatic ties with Taipei.[76]

CONCLUDING OBSERVATIONS

As a result of the Tiananmen Square incident in June 1989, the CCP faced probably the most severe test of its rule at home and abroad. On the domestic front, not only did it have to meet on-going development problems of its economy but also deal with the perennial challenge of unifying its leadership and people, whose views had been polarized by the pro-democracy movement. No doubt Ziang Zemin, who replaced Zhao

Ziyang as general secretary of the CCP, had been designated by Deng
Xiaoping as the core of the third-generation leaders. However, it was quite
obvious that the junior status of Jiang Zemin, the rising influence of the
military under Yang Shangkun, the conservatism and unknown ambitions
of Premier Li Peng and others in the Politburo, and most important, the
aging of Deng Xiaoping point to future problems in political succession.
Whether the CCP can calm the storm engendered by the Tiananmen Square
incident and regain the confidence of the people, especially the intellectuals and students, is also a litmus test for the party to reassert its authority
and leadership. On the foreign front, the crushing of the student-led
protests and demands by Beijing generated a barrage of condemnations
from the West. Americans were most abhorred by what they considered to
be a brutal crackdown on the pro-democracy movement. Colored by its
own value system based on a pluralist democracy and egged on by vivid
and dramatized reports, the United States, together with other industrialized nations, took action, notably imposing economic sanctions against
China. While it is not the intention here to deliberate on actions taken by
the United States, suffice it to say that despite the Bush administration's
interest in preserving long-term strategic relations between Washington
and Beijing, the actions taken by the United States and other industrialized
nations will adversely affect not only China's Four Modernizations but its
international relations, at least for a while. In view of the hard-line policy
adopted by the CCP, it would be politically unwise and morally wrong for
Washington to "persuade" Taipei to have a dialogue with the other side.
As made known by Richard Solomon, assistant secretary of state for East
Asia and the Pacific for the Bush administration, in Senate hearings after
the Tiananmen Square incident, the United States reaffirmed its adherence
to the six-point guarantee to Taiwan made by the Reagan administration
on the eve of the announcement of the second Shanghai communiqué of
1982.[77] As noted in Chapter 3, as far as reunification of China is concerned,
the United States would not be a mediator and it would not exert pressure
on Taipei to enter into negotiations with the CCP.

International pressure was not confined to that from the industrialized
nations. Developments in Eastern Europe in the second half of 1989 also
put the hard-liners in Beijing on the defensive. At a time when most Eastern
European countries were moving down the road toward political and
economic reform and were questioning the authority of the communists
and the effectiveness of a centrally planned and state-owned economy,
without any sign of interference from the Soviet Union under reform-
minded Gorbachev, Beijing seemed to be the odd man out in pursuing

retrogressive measures. Demolition of the Berlin Wall and the influx of large numbers of East Germans into West Germany demonstrated vividly not only the problems of a socialist state but the irrepressible desire of people to seek freedom and a better life in a more liberal environment. It also brightened prospects for the reunification of Germany, in which communism would not be as influential as before. These developments in Eastern Europe must have produced a lot of soul searching among the Chinese leadership. However, it is doubtful that they will change much the thinking of the present CCP leadership. From all indications, Beijing might feel it all the more important to defend what it has done and insist on having tight control over the mainland.

In spite of these domestic and international problems, Beijing did not change its policy much toward Taipei. Beijing watched with concern the limited success Taipei had in establishing official ties with small states and upgrading its relations with others in one way or another. It was also very critical of talk on the independence of Taiwan, advocated notably by a faction of the Democratic Progressive Party, the New Country Alliance, in the election campaign at the end of 1989.[78] The seeming unwillingness or inability of the KMT government to deal with such supposedly seditious acts right away was probably another cause of concern for Beijing, leading the latter to suspect the KMT government of complicity.[79] The trouble was that there was not much that Beijing could do about it other than mobilize its propaganda apparatus to attack the developments and reiterate that it would react strongly—that is, it would use force should Taiwan go independent.[80] More important, the results of the December 2, 1989, election produced the worst losses in 40 years for the KMT: it lost several key county executive posts and received 58 percent of the total vote, down from 70 percent in 1986.[81] Although the KMT still captured a majority of the votes, and many opposition candidates who did not support the independence option were also elected, the New Country Alliance won 20 of their 32 contests for the Legislature Yuan and other local offices.[82] As a result, after the election Beijing expressed doubts about whether the KMT could block the independence movement and suspicions concerning the KMT's "conniving attitude" toward such activities.[83] At a time when Taipei was also pursuing a de facto separatist policy at least in terms of its foreign relations, Beijing could not but be worried that Taiwan was heading for a separate, if not independent, identity by design or through changes in the political contour of the island.

Other than warning the KMT of such movement toward independence, Beijing probably would use Hong Kong as an example of successful implementation of the "one country, two systems" proposal and would indicate to Taipei its determination to permit a certain amount of autonomy to special administrative regions. The trouble is, of course, that there is a limit to how far Beijing could go. By mid-December 1989, it was already known that the Beijing-dominated drafting committee of Hong Kong's Basic Law had declared that only about one-third of the legislature would be returned by direct elections by 1997.[84] Quite obviously, the committee also reiterated Beijing's right to station troops in Hong Kong and that an antisubversion clause would be inserted in the Basic Law.* With these moves, Beijing would find it difficult to calm the fears of the Hong Kong people and lessen the skepticism toward Beijing's sincerity in granting autonomy to special administrative regions. Nonetheless, Beijing is most likely to be able to have its views prevail in future arrangements for Hong Kong, despite protests from some in Hong Kong and the desire of London to quicken the democratic process in the colony. This is especially true in areas where it feels that it is exercising its right as a sovereign state to protect its own security and interests. Nevertheless, it has to be sensitive to the aspirations and needs of Hong Kong people who will stay after 1997. A prosperous and stable Hong Kong will continue to be useful to Beijing as a window to the outside world and as a source of energy or example for China's Four Modernizations and reunification.

As for Taipei, developments after the Tiananmen Square incident reinforce the impression that its top priority remains the prosperity, stability, and security of the island and not the reunification of China. While the crackdown on the mainland may have sparked the concern of people on Taiwan with the fate of their compatriots on the other side, the situation could be a two-edged sword, in the sense that they might also see the benefits of the two sides remaining separate, especially when emotional concerns give way to pragmatic calculations. It might become evident that it would be difficult for them to accept the communist regime in Beijing, and better to dissociate from the other side, at least for the time being. The policies of the KMT government also have taken the more realistic approach, as noted in its elastic diplomacy and its reaction to the mainland demonstrations. For its policy toward the mainland, the KMT government is prepared to be flexible and accommodate the demands of its people in PRC-Taiwan relations while promoting the "Taiwan experience" on the mainland. It is careful enough to preserve its own security by not antago-

---

*An anti-subversion clause was added to Article 23 of the final draft of the Basic Law adopted in April 1990. See *Beijing Review*, 30 April–6 May 1990, Documents, p. 5.

nizing the other side too much. To a certain extent, the KMT government seems prepared to legalize the separateness of the two sides, as demonstrated in its adoption of the draft of the Temporary Stipulations on People's Relations between the Taiwan Area and Mainland Area by the Mainland Task Force of the Executive Yuan in October 1989. If this is accepted by other branches of the KMT government, Taipei would recognize the laws on the mainland to a certain extent, in order to solve the problems related to duties and responsibilities of the people on both sides in areas like immigration, residency, employment, marriage, investment and trade, hereditary rights, communications and telecommunications, and legal matters in the 54 stipulations.[85] These stipulations also allow members of the CCP to come to Taiwan provided they state that membership clearly in their applications. However, in spite of all the pressure from the business community in Taiwan to have direct trade and investment with the mainland, the stipulations do not sanction such activities, although indirect economic relations remain unrestricted. From this, it is apparent that while Taipei is interested in launching a political and cultural offensive against the mainland through people-to-people contact, it is still reluctant to sanction direct investment and trade, not to say technical cooperation, for fear of strengthening its nemesis.[86] It has only sanctioned indirect trade and investment through a third country or area, since these transactions cannot effectively be prevented, either administratively or technically.

After its relatively poor performance in the December 1989 elections, as noted earlier, the KMT may find it all the more difficult to crush the demands for an open and democratic government. This will open expression of the desire to have a separate if not independent Taiwan, especially from the opposition. While reiterating its one-China policy and the territorial integrity of one China, out of its belief, or perhaps more important, its fear of retribution from Beijing, the KMT government may be tempted to opt for a separate way for its own good, politically and economically. Whether it will eventually garner enough courage to go independent under more favorable circumstances, or accept a nebulous political link with the mainland under the one-China principle remains to be seen.

NOTES

1. *People's Daily*, 26 April 1989.
2. *Beijing Review*, 3–9, July 1989, p. 6.
3. *Straits Times* (Singapore), 13 July 1989. See also *Liaowang Zhoukan* (overseas edition), 24 July 1989, p. 24.

4. See particularly *People's Daily*, 21 July 1989, and *Liaowang Zhoukan* (overseas edition), 21 August 1989, pp. 3–4.

5. *Liaowang Zhoukan* (overseas edition), 24 July 1989, p. 24.

6. *Far Eastern Economic Review*, 31 August 1989, p. 17.

7. *Straits Times*, 2 September 1989 and 10 October 1989.

8. *Far Eastern Economic Review*, 26 October 1989, p. 19.

9. *Far Eastern Economic Review*, 2 November 1989, p. 11. See also *Beijing Review*, 6–12 November 1989, p. 5.

10. *Straits Times*, 16 October 1989.

11. Ibid.

12. *Far Eastern Economic Review*, 19 October 1989, p. 20, and 2 November 1989, pp. 10–11.

13. *Straits Times*, 6 November 1989.

14. For details, see *Far Eastern Economic Review*, 28 December 1989, pp. 10–11.

15. *China Times* (Taipei), 27 April 1989.

16. *China Times*, 6 May 1989.

17. *China Times*, 5 May 1989.

18. For the full text of the statement, see *Free China Review*, August 1989, p. 19.

19. *China Times*, 23 May 1989.

20. Ibid. See also the editorial of the *China Times* on 22 May 1989.

21. See, for example, the report in *The Nineties*, July 1989, pp. 42, 102.

22. *China Times*, 2 August 1989.

23. *China Times*, 28 May 1989.

24. *China Times*, 3 June 1989.

25. *China Times*, 20 May 1989 and 31 May 1989.

26. See, for example, the speech by Shaw Yu-ming to the American Enterprise Institute as reprinted in *Free China Review*, October 1989, p. 41.

27. *China Times*, 4 June 1989.

28. *Free China Review*, August 1989, p. 22.

29. For the full text of Lee Teng-hui's press statement, see Ibid., p. 18.

30. *China Times*, 5 June 1989.

31. *Free China Review*, October 1989, p. 41.

32. For the details of these measures, see, *China Times*, 5 June 1989.

33. Ibid.

34. See the remark by Lee Huan in the Legislature Yuan on 16 June 1989, as reported in *China Times*, 17 June 1989.

35. *The Nineties*, July 1989, p. 42. See also *Free China Review*, October 1989, p. 41.

36. For details, see *The Nineties*, July 1989, p. 42.

37. For the details of these measures, see *China Times*, 8 June and 9 June 1989.

38. *Free China Review*, August 1989, p. 22.

39. Ibid.

40. *China Times*, 14 June 1989.

41. See the reports in *China Times*, 21 July 1989 and *United Daily News*, 3, 4, 13, and 14 October 1989.

42. *China Times*, 29 July 1989.

43. *China Times*, 22 July 1989.

44. See, for example, *China Times*, 21 July 1989.

45. See, for example, *China Times*, 22 July 1989. For President Lee's denial of the acceptance of the "one country, two governments" proposal as Taipei's policy, see *China Times*, 9 May 1989.

46. For an analysis of the trips made by Taipei's foreign minister Lien Chan, see *China Times*, 18 July 1989.

47. *China Times*, 15 August 1989.

48. Ibid.

49. *China Times*, 14 August 1989.

50. *China Times*, 14 and 15 May 1989.

51. *The Nineties*, September 1989, p. 58.

52. Ibid.

53. *China Times*, 14 June 1989.

54. *China Times*, 15 June 1989.

55. *China Times*, 21 June 1989.

56. Ibid.

57. See, for example, *China Times*, 20 June 1989.

58. For details, see the report in *Liaowang Zhoukan* (overseas edition), 15 May 1989, p. 6. See also the reports in *China Times*, 30 April, and 1, 4, 5, 6, and 7 May 1989.

59. For a summary of these activities allegedly conducted by the KMT agents, see, for example, *Liaowang Zhoukan* (overseas edition), 7 August 1989, pp. 4–6.

60. See, for example, *China Times*, 23 June 1989.

61. Ibid.

62. See the reports in *China Times*, 11 and 12 July 1989. See also *The Nineties*, August 1989, pp. 76–80.

63. *The Nineties*, August 1989, p. 80. See also *China Times*, 15 July 1989.

64. *Beijing Review*, 10–16 July 1989, p. 8. See also *China Times*, 28 July 1989.

65. See, for example, the chronology of these statements in *China Times*, 16 September 1989.

66. *China Times*, 21 June 1989.

67. See, for example, *Liaowang Zhoukan* (overseas edition), 10 July 1989, p. 5–6.

68. *China Times*, 28 June 1989.

69. *China Times*, 16 September 1989.

70. *The Nineties*, November 1989, p. 30.

71. Ibid.

72. *Far Eastern Economic Review*, 16 November 1989, pp. 68–69.

73. Ibid., p. 69.

74. See, for example, *Beijing Review*, 2–8 January 1989, pp. 6–7; 9–15 January 1989, pp. 4–5; and 3–9 April 1989, p. 4.

75. *Beijing Review*, 14–20 August 1989, p. 7. See also *Liaowang Zhoukan* (overseas edition), 21 August 1989, p. 20.

76. See *Beijing Review*, 23–29 October 1989, pp. 5–6 and 13–19 November 1989, pp. 11–12.

77. *China Times*, 14 June 1989.

78. See, for example, the reports in *China Times*, 8, 9, 23, and 26 November 1989.

79. *China Times*, 9 November 1989.

80. *China Times*, 26 November 1989.

81. *Straits Times*, 7 December 1989.

82. *Straits Times*, 11 December 1989.

83. Ibid.

84. *Straits Times*, 16 December 1989.

85. For details of the 54 stipulations, see *China Times*, 10 October 1989.

86. See, for example, Shaw Yu-ming's speech to the American Enterprise Institute in Washington, D.C., in August 1989, as reprinted in *Free China Review*, October 1989, p. 43.

Selected Bibliography

The following bibliography is a guide to the more important sources from China, Taiwan, and Hong Kong, and to some essential secondary sources.

PRIMARY SOURCES

Books and Pamphlets

Bao Hengxin, ed., *Taiwan Zhishi Cidain* (A Dictionary of Knowledge on Taiwan). Fuzhou: Fujian Renmin Chubanshe, 1988.

Basic Law of the Hong Kong Special Administrative Region of the People's Republic of China (Draft). Hong Kong: The Drafting Committee for the Basic Law, 1989.

Committee on Foreign Affairs, *China-Taiwan: United States Policy, Hearing Before the Committee on Foreign Affairs, House of Representatives, Ninety-Seventh Congress*. Washington, D.C.: U.S. Government Printing Office, 1982.

Constitution of the People's Republic of China. Beijing: Foreign Languages Press, 1983.

Deng Xiaoping, *Jianshe You Zhongguo Tese De Shehui Zhuyi* (Building Socialism with Special Chinese Characteristics), revised ed. Hong Kong: Joint Publishing, 1987.

———, *Jianshe You Zhongguo Tese De Shehui Zhuyi* (Building Socialism with Special Chinese Characteristics). Hong Kong: Joint Publishing, 1985.

———, *Selected Works of Deng Xiaoping, 1975–1982*. Beijing: Foreign Languages Press, 1984.

Draft Basic Law of the Hong Kong Special Administrative Region of the People's Republic of China (for Solicitation of Opinions). Hong Kong: The Drafting Committee for the Basic Law, 1988.

Institute of Taiwan Studies, Chinese Academy of Social Sciences, ed., *Taiwan Yanjiu Wenji* (A Collection of Papers on Taiwan Studies). Beijing: Shishi Chubanshe, 1988.

Institute of Taiwan Studies, Xiamen University, ed., *Jinri Taiwan Yibai Wen* (One Hundred
       Questions and Answers on Present Day Taiwan). Fuzhou: Fujian Renmin
       Chubanshe, 1988.
Li Jiaquan and Lin Yingxian, eds., *Taiwan Jingji Shi Zenyang Fazhan Qilai De* (The
       Development of the Taiwan Economy). Beijing: Renmin Ribao Chubanshe, 1989.
Li Xi, Wang Shumin, and Hu Zheng, eds., *Taiwan Tongbao Tanqin Luyou Falu Shouce*
       (A Legal Handbook on Family Visits and Sightseeing for Taiwan Compatriots).
       Beijing: Falu Chubanshe, 1987.
Mao Jiaqi, ed., *Taiwan Sanshi Nian 1949–1979* (Thirty Years of Taiwan, 1949–1979).
       Henan: Henan Renmin Chubanshe, 1988.
Tai Baolin, *Taiwan Sheshui Mianmian Guan* (Different Aspects of Taiwan Society).
       Henan: Henan Renmin Chubanshe, 1989.
Zhao Chunyi, ed., *Yiquo Liangzhi Gailun* (A General Treatise of One Country, Two
       Systems). Jilin: Jilin Daxue Chubanshe, 1988.
Zhao Guoliang, Lin Xifan, Wang Yizhu, Ge Ning, eds., *Shehui Zhuyi Chuji Jieduan Lilun
       Ziliao Xuanbian* (Selected Materials on the Theory of the Primary Stage of
       Socialism). Beijing: Zhongguo Renmin Daxue Chubanshe, 1987.
Zhongyang Sheyhui Zhuyi Xueyuan Tongyi Zhanxian Lilun Jiaoyan Shi, ed., *Yige
       Guojia Liangzhong Zhidu* (One Country, Two Systems). Beijing: Shumu
       Wenxian Chubanshe, 1987.

Journals, Periodicals, and Newspapers

Beijing Review (Beijing)
Central Daily News (Taipei)
Central Monthly (Taipei)
China Directory (Tokyo)
China Times (Taipei)
Contemporary International Studies (Beijing)
Dagong Bao (Hong Kong)
Economic Daily News (Taipei)
Free China Journal (Taipei)
Free China Review (Taipei)
Guangming Ribao (Beijing)
Hong Kong Times (Hong Kong)
Independence Evening Post (Taipei)
Independence Morning Post (Taipei)
International Studies (Beijing)
Liberty Times (Taipei)
Ming Pao (Hong Kong)
Outlook Weekly (Beijing, domestic edition)
Outlook Weekly (Beijing, overseas edition)
People's Daily (Beijing)
Red Flag (Beijing)
Sing-tao Jih-pao (Hong Kong)
South China Morning Post (Hong Kong)
Straits Times (Singapore)

Survey of International Affairs (Shanghai)
Taisheng (Beijing)
Taiwan Research Quarterly (Xiamen)
Taiwan Studies (Beijing)
United Daily News (Taipei)
Wenhui Bao (Hong Kong)
Youth Daily (Taipei)

SECONDARY SOURCES

Books and Pamphlets

Barnett, A. Doak, *U.S. Arms Sales: The China-Taiwan Tangle*. Washington, D.C.: Brookings Institution, 1982.

Chen, Frederick Tse-shyang, ed., *China Policy and National Security*. New York: Transnational Publishers, 1984.

Cheng, Joseph Y. S., *Hong Kong in Transition*. Hong Kong: Oxford University Press, 1986.

Chiu, Hungdah, ed., *China and the Taiwan Issue*. New York: Praeger, 1979.

————, ed., *Normalizing Relations With the People's Republic of China: Problems, Analysis and Documents*, Reprints Series in Contemporary Asian Studies, Vol. 14, No. 2. (1978) School of Law, University of Maryland.

————, and Robert Downen, eds., *Multi-system Nations and International Law: The International Status of Germany, Korea and China*, Reprints Series in Contemporary Asian Studies, Vol. 45, No. 8. (1981) School of Law, University of Maryland.

————, Y. C. Jao, and Yuan-li Wu, eds., *The Future of Hong Kong: Toward 1997 and Beyond*. New York: Quorum Books, 1987.

Clough, Ralph N., *Island China*. Cambridge, Mass.: Harvard University Press, 1978.

Gold, Thomas B., *State and Society in the Taiwan Miracle*. New York: M. E. Sharpe, 1986.

Harding, Harry, *China's Second Revolution: Reform After Mao*. Washington, D.C.: Brookings Institution, 1987.

Hinton, Harold, *Communist China in World Politics*. Boston: Houghton Mifflin, 1966.

Hsiung, James, et al., eds., *The Taiwan Experience 1950–1980*. New York: American Association for Chinese Studies, 1981.

Kissinger, Henry, *White House Years*. Boston: Little, Brown, 1979.

Kuo, Shirley W. Y., *Taiwan Economy in Transition*. Boulder, Colo.: Westview Press, 1983.

————, Gustav Ramis, and John C. H. Fei, *The Taiwan Success Story*. Boulder, Colo.: Westview Press, 1981.

Lasater, Martin L., *The Taiwan Issue in Sino-American Strategic Relations*. Boulder, Colo.: Westview Press, 1984.

————, *U.S. Policy Toward China's Reunification*. Washington, D.C.: Heritage Foundation, 1988.

————, *Policy in Evolution: The U.S. Role in China's Reunification*. Boulder, Colo.: Westview Press, 1989.

Li Da, ed., *Taiwan Yu Santung* (Taiwan and the Three Exchanges). Hong Kong: Wide Angle Press, 1987.

———, ed., *Yiguo Liangzhi Yu Taiwan* (The One Country, Two Systems and Taiwan). Hong Kong: Wide Angle Press, 1987.

———, ed., *Meitai Guanxi Yu Zhongguo Tongyi* (U.S.–Taiwan Relations and the Reunification of China). Hong Kong: Wide Angle Press, 1987.

———, ed., *Kaifang Taiwan* (The Opening of Taiwan). Hong Kong: Wide Angle Press, 1988.

———, ed., *Lee Teng-hui Yu Taiwan* (Lee Teng-hui and Taiwan). Hong Kong: Wide Angle Press, 1988.

Li, Victor H., ed., *The Future of Taiwan*. New York: M. E. Sharpe, 1980.

Lu Keng, ed., *Zhongguo Tongyi Wenti Lunzhan* (Debates on Problems of the Reunification of China). Hong Kong: Baixing Wenhua Shiye Pte., 1988.

Mendel, Jr., Douglas, *The Politics of Formosan Nationalism*. Berkeley, Calif.: University of California Press, 1970.

Ming-min, Peng, *A Taste of Freedom: Memoirs of a Formosan Independence Leader*. New York: Holt, Rinehart and Winston, 1972.

Sanford, Dan C., *The Future Association of Taiwan with the People's Republic of China*. Berkeley, Calif.: Center for Chinese Studies, Institute of East Asian Studies, 1981.

Scalapino, Robert, Seizaburo Sato, Jusuf Wandandi, and Sung-joo Han, eds., *Asian Security Issues: Regional and Global*. Berkeley, Calif.: Institute of East Asian Studies, 1988.

Shaw Yu-ming. *The Prospects for ROC-US Relations Under the Reagan Administration*. Taipei: Asia and World Institute, 1983.

Solomon, Richard H., *The China Factor: Sino-American Relations and the Global Scene*. Englewood Cliffs, N.J.: Prentice-Hall, 1981.

Tien, Hung-mao, *The Great Transition: Political and Social Change in the Republic of China*. Stanford: Hoover Institution Press, 1989.

Wang, Yu San, ed., *The China Question: Essays on Current Relations between Mainland China and Taiwan*. New York: Praeger, 1985.

Whiting, Allen, *China Crosses the Yalu: The Decision to Enter the Korean War*. New York: Macmillan, 1960.

———, *China Eyes Japan*. Berkeley and Los Angeles: University of California Press, 1989.

Wolff, Lester L., and David L. Simon, eds., *Legislative History of the Taiwan Relations Act*. New York: American Association for Chinese Studies, 1982.

Journals and Periodicals

Asian Survey (Berkeley)
Asia Yearbook (Hong Kong)
Baixing Semi-Monthly (Hong Kong)
Cheng Ming (Hong Kong)
China Mainland Studies (Taipei)
China News Analysis (Hong Kong)
China Quarterly, The (London)

Contemporary Southeast Asia (Singapore)
Economic Outlook Quarterly (Taipei)
Economic Papers (Taipei, Chung-hua Institution for Economic Research)
Economist, The (London)
Far Eastern Economic Review (Hong Kong)
Foreign Affairs (Baltimore)
Foreign Policy (New York)
Issues and Studies (Taipei)
Journal of Asian Studies (Ann Arbor)
Ming Pao Monthly (Hong Kong)
Nineties, The (Hong Kong)
Pacific Affairs (Vancouver)
Pacific Review, The (London)
Problems of Communism (Washington, D.C.)
Seventies, The (Hong Kong)
Studies on Chinese Communism (Taipei)
Tide Monthly (Hong Kong)
Yearbook on Chinese Communism (Taipei)
World Politics (Princeton, N.J.)

Index

ABOUT THE AUTHOR

LAI TO LEE is a Senior Lecturer in political science at the National University of Singapore. The author of *The Structure of the Trade Union System in China 1949–1966* and *Trade Unions in China: 1949 to the Present,* he is also the editor or co-editor of four books on China, Southeast Asia, and the Asia-Pacific region.